Transforming Socialist Economies

March 30, 2005

To Marty –

With warm regards,

Dan Erikson

Transforming Socialist Economies

Lessons for Cuba and Beyond

Edited by

Shahid Javed Burki
EMP Financial Advisors

and

Daniel P. Erikson
Inter-American Dialogue

palgrave
macmillan

First published 2005 by
PALGRAVE MACMILLAN
Houndmills, Basingstoke, Hampshire RG21 6XS and
175 Fifth Avenue, New York, N. Y. 10010
Companies and representatives throughout the world

PALGRAVE MACMILLAN is the global academic imprint of the Palgrave Macmillan division of St. Martin's Press, LLC and of Palgrave Macmillan Ltd. Macmillan® is a registered trademark in the United States, United Kingdom and other countries. Palgrave is a registered trademark in the European Union and other countries.

ISBN 1–4039–3662–5

This book is printed on paper suitable for recycling and made from fully managed and sustained forest sources.

A catalogue record for this book is available from the British Library.

Library of Congress Cataloging-in-Publication Data
Transforming socialist economies : lessons for Cuba and beyond / edited by Shahid Javed Burki and Daniel P. Erikson.
p. cm.
Includes bibliographical references and index.
ISBN 1-4039-3662-5 (cloth)
1. Communist countries–Economic policy. 2. Former communist countries–Economic policy. 3. Former communist countries–Economic conditions. 4. Post-communism–Economic aspects. 5. Cuba–Economic policy. I. Burki, Shahid Javed. II. Erikson, Daniel P.

HC704.T73 2004
330.9171'7–dc22

2004052328

10 9 8 7 6 5 4 3 2 1
14 13 12 11 10 09 08 07 06 05

Printed and bound in Great Britain by
Antony Rowe Ltd, Chippenham and Eastbourne

Contents

List of Figures

List of Tables

List of Maps

Notes on Contributors

Shahid Javed Burki is Chief Executive Officer of EMP Financial Advisors and has been working on development issues for more than four decades. He previously served at the World Bank as Vice President for Latin America and Director for China and Mongolia. A native of Pakistan, Mr Burki has served the Pakistani government in a variety of positions, including Minister of Finance. He has authored or edited nine books on topics of international economics, China, Latin America, and Pakistan. A former Rhodes Scholar, he holds degrees from Harvard and Oxford Universities.

David O. Dapice is Professor of International Economics at Tufts University and senior fellow of the Vietnam Program at Harvard's John F. Kennedy School of Government. He has worked on development topics for more than thirty years and has contributed to several books on Vietnam and other countries in Asia.

Jorge I. Domínguez is Clarence Dillon Professor of International Affairs, and director of the Weatherhead Center for International Affairs at Harvard University. He has authored or edited more than a dozen books on Cuba and Latin America.

Daniel P. Erikson is director of Caribbean Programs at the Inter-American Dialogue, a leading forum for Western Hemisphere affairs based in Washington, DC, where he manages a project on Cuba and the international financial institutions. He has previously worked as a research associate at Harvard Business School and is a former recipient of the Fulbright fellowship in Mexico. Mr. Erikson received his Masters in Public Policy from Harvard's John F. Kennedy School of Government and is a graduate of Brown University.

Chris Hartwell is an international economist on the Iraq and Afghanistan Financial Task Force at the United States Department of the Treasury. He has eight years of economic consulting experience throughout Eastern Europe and Central Asia and has worked for the German government on European Union accession issues.

Zahid Hasnain is economist for the World Bank in Pakistan. He received his PhD in political science from the University of Chicago, and holds degrees from Cornell and Cambridge Universites. His research focuses on the political economy of development.

Svetlana Vtyurina is Advisor to the Executive Director for the Russian Federation at the International Monetary Fund, where she assesses the implementation of IMF programs by member countries in Central and Latin America, Eastern Europe, and other regions. She has experience working in capital markets and financial sector development. She holds an MBA in International Finance from George Washington University.

Acknowledgments

Since the idea for this book was conceived in the fall of 2001, the staff and leadership of the Inter-American Dialogue have played a vital role in the project's success. Dialogue President Peter Hakim supported our desire to extend beyond the starting point of Cuba's economic policy to explore how market-oriented reform unfolded in a range of countries. Claudio Loser, the former director for the Western Hemisphere at the International Monetary Fund and a visiting senior fellow at the Dialogue, read through all of the essays with a sharp eye and insightful comments. Other members of the Dialogue's staff made important contributions during different periods of the project's gestation, including Annie Lord, Rachel Menezes, and our intern Erin Connors. Program assistant Peter Wolf was instrumental in coordinating the first phase of the project, and his successor, Adam Minson, expertly handled the final copyediting process and helped to prepare the manuscript for publication. We thank everyone at the Inter-American Dialogue for their invaluable contributions to this book.

We also gained from the expertise of the Dialogue's Cuba Working Group, who supplied ideas and advice on the volume, and many of the chapters benefited from the comments and feedback provided by colleagues and economists in a variety of venues. Zafer Ecevit, formerly of the World Bank, deserves special mention for taking the time to read through several draft essays. At Emerging Markets Partners, Virginia Baker helped to keep the project moving despite the demanding travel schedule of its co-editors. Our editor Amanda Watkins from Palgrave MacMillan was a pleasure to work with during the publication process, and editorial consultant Nick Brock provided top-notch editorial and logistical assistance.

We wish to thank the authors whose hard work and expertise has contributed so much to this initiative, including David Dapice, Chris Hartwell, Zahid Hasnain, and Svetlana Vtyurina. Each of them went above and beyond the call of duty to contribute first-rate essays to a project that required collaboration and editing over a period of two and a half years. In particular, we would like to thank Harvard University's Jorge Domínguez for his enormously valuable contribution to our efforts to think creatively about Cuba's economic future, and his sage advice on how to produce a book that does justice to its complex and compelling subject. We hope that all future endeavors can be so fruitful.

Shahid Javed Burki and Daniel P. Erikson
Washington, DC

Foreword

Five years ago, in 1999, the Inter-American Dialogue set out to build a policy dialogue involving Cuban economic analysts and decision makers, on the one hand, and a range of current and former national, regional, and international economic policy officials, on the other. This initiative emerged at a time when substantial changes were taking place in the Cuban economy, including limited opening to foreign direct investment, the legalization of some small-scale private activity, and an effort by the Cuban government to diversify its international trading partners.

Our work on Cuba and the international financial institutions led to the creation of a Washington-based working group with the active participation of a dozen senior economists, most of whom had been affiliated with the International Monetary Fund, the World Bank, and the Inter-American Development Bank. The group has been chaired by Shahid Javed Burki, an accomplished economist who knows well the economies of both Latin America and East Asia. Formerly finance minister of Pakistan, Burki has served as the World Bank's Vice President for Latin America and the Caribbean, and earlier directed the Bank's work in China for many years.

Burki thought that Cuban decision makers and international policy makers would both benefit from new analysis of the experience of other transition economies. To better set their own policies and goals, it would be helpful for them to know what has worked elsewhere, what has failed, and why. He provided the intellectual direction for this effort to delve more deeply and systematically into the challenges facing countries engaged in market-oriented reform and to seek the relevant lessons for Cuba. In so doing, he worked closely with Dan Erikson, the head of the Inter-American Dialogue's work on Cuba since 2001. As the co-director of this effort, Erikson has also made an important intellectual contribution to this work through his own chapter, his collaboration on the concluding essay, and his skillful editing and management of the publication process.

I also want to express the Dialogue's appreciation to two colleagues who contributed in invaluable ways to this thought-provoking volume that is so sharply relevant to Cuba's future. In addition to writing a chapter on Cuba and co-authoring the conclusion, Jorge Domínguez of Harvard University helped to develop the ideas behind this book and assisted in guiding the project towards publication. Similarly, Claudio Loser, visiting senior fellow of the Inter-American Dialogue, assumed an informal advisory role that included reading through and providing extensive commentary on all of the draft chapters.

The Inter-American Dialogue's research and publications are designed to improve the quality of public debate and decision on key issues in Western Hemisphere affairs. The Dialogue is both a forum for sustained exchange among leaders and an independent, nonpartisan center for policy analysis on US–Latin American economic and political relations. The Dialogue's one hundred members – from the United States, Canada, Latin America, and the Caribbean – include prominent political, business, labour, academic, media, military, and religious leaders. Our research agenda focuses on four broad themes: democratic governance, inter-American cooperation, economic integration, and social equity. This book, *Transforming Socialist Economies: Lessons for Cuba and Beyond,* is designed to aid Cuban economists and many others to understand the future economic challenges the island faces and usefully show how others have dealt with them in different countries.

The Inter-American Dialogue wishes to express its gratitude to the Swedish International Development and Cooperation Agency (SIDA) and the John D. and Catherine T. MacArthur Foundation for their financial support of this book.

Peter Hakim
President
Inter-American Dialogue

Part I
Introduction

1
Transforming the State in Socialist Economies

Shahid Javed Burki

In the early 1990s, the disintegration of the Soviet Union and the accompanying collapse of communism in Eastern Europe captured the imagination of political observers who believed they were witnessing the final moment in a struggle of competing world orders. In the United States, the highly respected social scientist Francis Fukuyama advanced the view that the triumph of western capitalism over Soviet communism marked 'the end of history'. Indeed, more than a decade later, experience confirms that representative democracy and market economics had earned a definitive, if flawed, victory in that region of the world. Yet a global analysis reveals that the process of economic transition remains controversial, deeply divisive, and, above all, incomplete.

In 2004, approximately 1.4 billion people in Asia – representing more than one fifth of the world's population – continue to live under the communist regimes of China, Vietnam, and North Korea. Another 400 million people live in the countries of Eastern Europe and the former Soviet bloc that have experienced radically divergent fortunes in the transition from socialism, ranging from the relative affluence of the Czech Republic and Poland to the persistent penury of the Central Asian Republics. On the periphery of the United States, Cuba is still the socialist exception in a hemisphere otherwise characterized by the acceptance of free-market economics. In short, history did not end. If anything, the fundamental differences in how societies are organized and economies are managed have far more staying power than was predicted a decade ago. This volume reviews the diverse paths taken by socialist countries and offers a revealing study of the advantages and challenges inherent in various strategies of economic reform.

A new global context

The economic dimension of the transition from socialism has played out in unique ways and with vastly differing results in dozens of countries across the globe. However, while the process of 'market liberalization' is often discussed in the global or abstract sense, the reality is that the systems and economies involved have unique cultures and traditions that have shaped the trajectory of their reform. What works in Russia may work less well in China, and the model that has benefited Vietnam will not necessarily take root in Cuba. At the same time, it is important to recognize that all countries that undertake market reform face certain common challenges, and a comparative analysis can illuminate how reform strategies work in a variety of different settings. With this perspective in mind, we sought to review the transition processes of Russia, Eastern Europe, the Central Asian Republics, China, and Vietnam, and to reflect on their relevance for Cuba, a communist country on the verge of more wide-ranging economic transformation. While the lessons gleaned from this study are relevant to all transition countries, special consideration is given to what the historical experience portends for Cuba's future.

Of course, the international context for economic transition from socialism is far different today than when the first wave unfolded in the early 1990s. The transition process no longer fits into the checks and balances of the Cold War that dominated world affairs for nearly half a century. Indeed, the subject has largely been eclipsed by the conflicts of the new global order, represented by the events of September 11, 2001 and their aftermath. Today, the world is struggling with a version of the 'clash of civilizations' predicted by the celebrated social scientist Samuel Huntington – a conflict between western liberalism and Islam. In fact, the fall of the Soviet Union and the entry of Russia, its successor state, did little to prevent these conflicts and may have even aggravated them by unleashing new forces. In the past three years, wars have been fought in Afghanistan and Iraq, led by the United States with the acquiescence – and various degrees of participation – of the countries of the former Soviet bloc.

Further, the shift away from the Cold War has facilitated the efforts of East Asia's two most significant socialist countries to integrate into the global economy. China's close cooperation with the western powers of the United States and Europe has been rewarded with full entry into the World Trade Organization, and Chinese presence is now felt in all areas of international affairs. Since the 1980s, Vietnam has also taken significant steps to dismantle key aspects of central planning while maintaining the political authority of the Communist Party. Vietnam has opened its economy to sizable inflows of foreign direct investment, and has a full and robust relationship with the International Monetary Fund and the World Bank. This trend has only underlined what was already apparent over the last decade – that countries adopting market socialism face few obstacles to integrating into the global economy. If the full-scale transition of Eastern Europe and the Soviet Union represent one model, then the mixed economies of Asia and, potentially, Cuba, represent an alternative path.

The discussion above provides some context for the analysis of transforming the state in socialist economies that comprises the majority of this book. Contrary to the conventional wisdom of the early 1990s, the communist ideology did not disappear from the globe with the fall of the Soviet Union. In China and Vietnam, it has instead become increasingly adaptive, incorporating market mechanisms and moving towards a pragmatic model of market socialism. Even Cuba has opened up to some foreign investment, leaving only the rogue state of North Korea as a country almost entirely isolated from global financial flows. In all of these countries, the communist ideology has survived as a political system, in part because communism has put down deeper indigenous roots than in Eastern Europe, where it was imposed by a foreign power. As a system of economic management, however, the time of communism has clearly passed. In their own way, China and Vietnam have followed the trend set by the former Soviet Union and Eastern Europe of bringing capitalism and market forces into daily economic management. Cuba has followed, although to a far lesser degree. However, these countries have not jettisoned the political system they had adopted decades ago at a time when the communist ideology attracted many adherents. Their example raises important questions about the role government should play during economic transition. Is 'market socialism' or 'shock therapy' a better path to follow in transforming the role of the state?

In retrospect, deep philosophical divisions about the proper role of the state framed the conflict between communism and capitalism that engaged the world for nearly half a century. In pure socialist systems the state was predominant, all-encompassing, and paternalistic – ordering the lives of the citizens according to what the leaders thought was good for the people in whose name they governed. By contrast, in a capitalist system, the state plays a supportive role, creating an environment and prescribing the bounds within which the private sector is expected to operate. The underlying system of laissez faire is placed within well-defined boundaries in order to promote the public good. Different perceptions of the state's role in society have provided an important subtext for the major conflicts that have dominated world history over the last half-century, and these passions will once again leap to the foreground when one considers the example of Cuba.

Cuba indeed presents an interesting counterpoint to the apparent success of the mixed economies of China and Vietnam and the wrenching growing pains that have afflicted, to a greater or lesser degree, the economies of Eastern Europe and the former Soviet Union. As the lone communist country in the Western Hemisphere, the unrivalled leadership of Fidel Castro and his senior policy advisors has ensured that Cuba has been highly resistant to change. Although severely affected by the loss of Soviet subsidies in the early 1990s, the Cuban system has remained largely intact, resisting the rapid transition to market economics witnessed in Eastern Europe and Russia, and also eschewing the more limited reforms embraced by China and Vietnam. While Cuba instituted some incremental market reforms in the early 1990s, government ownership continues to be the norm, and many reforms have been scaled back considerably. Significant attention has been paid to the prospect of Cuba's rapid transition to a market-oriented democracy in the future, but in reality this outcome is far from preordained. In fact, Cuba is destined to be a future flash point in the debate about how best to transform socialist economies – and we asked our authors to keep a comparison with Cuba in mind as they prepared their analyses about what type of economic governance best suits economic transition. This understanding serves as a starting point for an analysis on transforming socialist economies, with an emphasis on what systems have created the best results for the citizens who live in the areas governed by different state apparatuses.

Economic governance: less is more?

The concept of governance is crucial to economic management in every country, and the term itself has evolved significantly over the past few years. In the 1990s, the disintegration of the Soviet bloc convinced policy makers engaged with guiding the process of development in the developing world to opt for a minimalist state. This approach towards the state's role was encapsulated in a doctrine that took the name of 'The Washington Consensus' for the simple reason that its main exponents were the development and financial institutions operating out of the US capital city: the International Monetary Fund, the World Bank Group, the Inter-American Development Bank, and related advisory think tanks and research organizations.

'The Washington Consensus' policies encouraged developing countries to minimize the role of the state in managing the economy, while opening their economies to trade, foreign investment and other types of financial flows. It suggested that the state's role should be limited to regulatory and supervisory functions, and that it should confine its involvement in the economy to prescribing the boundaries within which the various parts of the private sector were to operate. However, the application of 'The Washington Consensus' to a number of countries – particularly those in East Asia and Latin America in the late 1980s and much of the 1990s – did not produce the anticipated results. It failed to quicken the pace of development in Latin America, and it exposed several countries in East Asia to the volatility that now characterizes the way the global financial system works. Whereas developed countries have the depth to absorb this volatility, that is not the case in even the more advanced developing countries such as Malaysia, South Korea and Thailand. All of these experienced severe financial shocks beginning in the summer of 1997, resulting in the East Asian financial crisis that led to a considerable chastening of the expert opinion that held sway at the time.

The crisis gave rise to a body of fairly influential opinion that maintains that the kind of state withdrawal and opening to the outside world advocated by the practitioners of 'The Washington Consensus' and practiced, at their behest, by a number of developing countries, exposed them to many dangers. Speculative financial flows can – and in fact did – buffet these economies and cause great harm. As a result, it is now considered legitimate to opt for a more activist state which can lay down a number of barriers against the entry of short term capital which was the major cause of the severe financial agony experienced by the countries of East Asia. The minimalist state, once thought to be the economic savior of the developing world, proved to be something of chimera.

It is against this background that we review the delicate work of changing the role of the state that has been undertaken by so many countries around the globe. This has happened or is happening not only in the countries that have been called for a dozen years 'countries in transition'. This work is proceeding in almost all nation-states. It is going on in developed and developing countries; in the nations of Africa, Asia, Europe, Latin America and North America; in the economies that are pre-industrial, industrial and post industrial. And also in those countries that are very poor and those that are very rich. The role of the state and the quality of governance associated with it have become active subjects for discussion around the world.

The concept of governance, so closely associated with the role of the state, has also evolved substantially over the last half-dozen years. This happened as development practitioners, who were working with a range of different types of governments, came to realize that the role of the state needed to be clearly defined if it was to be able to tackle some of the most important problems facing developing countries. According to one interpretation made popular by the 1999 edition of the *Human Development in South Asia Report* – an annual publication – governance is a concept with economic, political, and civic dimensions. While the democratic structures and processes of political and civic governance are important aspects of transition, this book mainly concerns itself with economic governance, and, in particular, the appropriate role of the state in relation to the market. This question drove the advent of 'The Washington Consensus' and continues to reverberate in the debate around the transition from socialism. How should one characterize the quality of economic governance in socialist versus free-market systems? Does a well-governed socialist state have economic advantages over a poorly governed capitalist one? What are the relative advantages and disadvantages when comparing how 'shock therapy' or 'market socialism' affect economic governance in a country in transition?

The reality, of course, is that good governance is absent from most parts of the developing world, including the former socialist countries of Eastern Europe and Central Asia. Therefore, any discussion of transition must cover all the aspects of good governance and not simply the redesign of the economic system. But quality of governance alone is not enough – countries also have to be willing to undertake fundamental reforms if they wish to become competitive in the world economy. Economists began to define the process of transition more than a decade ago. A consensus quickly developed among those who studied this process that it should cover at least the following five areas: liberalization, macroeconomic stabilization, privatization, financial sector reform, and legal and institutional reform.

Liberalization is the process of permitting most prices to be determined in free markets rather than being dictated by the central government, accompanied by trade liberalization that allows the relatively free flow of goods across borders by removing or easing non-tariff barriers and lowering tariffs. *Macroeconomic stabilization* is primarily the process through which inflation is brought under control and lowered over time. This requires discipline in government spending, vigilance over the growth of the money supply, and prudent management of the exchange rate in order to attain sustainable balance of payments. *Privatization and restructuring* involve the transfer of state-owned assets to the private sector, or, if they remain in government control, a restructuring that exposes them to market forces. *Creating financial institutions or transferring them to the private sector* facilitates the privatization of assets in the productive sectors of the economy. These two processes have to go hand in hand. The transformation of the financial sector is important since the new owners will need to tap capital from the banks or from the capital markets for the enterprises they have acquired, rather than accessing financial resources through the state budget. *Legal and institutional reform* involves the redefinition of the role of the state in the economy, establishment of the rule of law, introduction of regulations to govern the working of the enterprises in various sectors; introduction of appropriate competition policies; and introduction of bankruptcy laws. Although speed and sequencing may vary, all five of these reforms are essential to the transition process.

While these were the basic areas of reform, development practitioners who advised the governments of those countries in transition disagreed on the time during which these changes should be made. On the one hand, some experts argued for the 'big bang' approach, otherwise known as 'shock therapy'. This approach argued that gradual reform would introduce new distortions into the economy, creating rent-seeking opportunities that would greatly complicate the process of change. Other practitioners in the area of transition came to the opposite view. They believed that distortions that had materialized over time in the economic and financial systems in communist countries could only be addressed gradually. They advocated patience and pragmatism. Proceeding with haste, they argued, could be extremely disruptive and could frighten policy makers away from pursuing a policy of transition altogether. As the following essays will show, in cases ranging from Central Asia to Eastern Europe to China to Cuba, both approaches have important advantages and disadvantages – and neither provides a quick fix to the woes of a socialist system.

A wealth of experience

How transition actually occurred – the areas it covered and the time over which it was undertaken – is the central theme of the book. But this is more than a purely academic or historical exercise, because the lessons apply to the challenges that many of these countries continue to face today. While many of these experiences have a broad relevance to the study of economic transition, we chose to emphasize the particular relevance for Cuba precisely because that country maintains a commitment to Marxist economics nearly unmatched in the world. Yet the economic and political pressures facing the island are likely to necessitate substantial reform in the near or medium term. For the international economics community, policy makers in the United States and elsewhere, and not least the Cubans themselves, the reform trajectories of the world's major communist countries will have renewed immediacy as solutions are sought for how best to shift away from central planning.

In undertaking this research, we recognize that transition economics and the Cuban economy are fields of study that have been well tilled. But much of the story has yet to be written, and the past decade is filled with mishaps, mistakes and successes which have important lessons for the future. Russia's free-market reforms initially faltered due to the prevailing economic culture, while the Czech Republic's rapid reform far surpassed the sluggish performance of Slovakia, its sister nation. China and Vietnam have created a formula for market socialism that has dramatically improved their economies, but is it too good to last? The Central Asian Republics have gained new strategic relevance since September 11, yet their people have struggled to escape the systemic inefficiencies that characterized their economies during Soviet rule. The Washington-based international financial institutions have undertaken different strategies to accommodate the economic circumstances and political leadership in socialist and post-communist countries, and their approach to Cuba may potentially have a decisive impact on the island's future as well. This book represents an effort to plumb the wealth of experience of transitional economies, and to draw broad conclusions about how best to transform the socialist state.

2

Cuba's Economic Transition: Successes, Deficiencies, and Challenges[1]

Jorge I. Domínguez

Cuba's economic transition began formally on 23 June 1990 when the Political Bureau of the Cuban Communist Party issued the following statement: 'The solid stability of the country, together with intelligent policies, attract the confidence of foreign investors and open the way for cooperation in the form of joint ventures. This does not clash with our socialist system; rather it means speedier use of potential resources.'[2] Days earlier, on Cuba's premier beach, Varadero, President Fidel Castro publicly inaugurated the first hotel built jointly between a foreign investor and a Cuban state enterprise since the Cuban government seized all foreign-owned tourist enterprises in 1960. The foreign partners had the funds, management expertise, and marketing skills that Cuban enterprises lacked, he said. Somewhat hesitantly, he added: 'We do not know how to run a hotel, how to handle tourism and – I don't know if I should use the word or not – how to make the most money from tourism, how to exploit tourism.'[3]

The decision to welcome foreign direct investment casts aside one of the foundation stones of the political economy of Cuban socialism, built on the expropriation of foreign property. The promotion of tourism was another shift. Although some tourism had persisted in the intervening decades, in 1959 and 1960 part of the moral claim of revolutionaries in power was the extirpation of the image that Cuba was the whorehouse of the Caribbean. In the decades that followed, tourism plummeted.

The 1990 economic reform decisions were smart and necessary. They were the prelude to other economic reforms that the Cuban government enacted in the years that followed. They responded to the vast changes already under way in the Soviet Union and the collapse of hitherto communist Eastern Europe; they anticipated the disintegration of the Soviet Union itself 18 months later. They signalled a public change in economic strategy while reaffirming fidelity to the socialist political system and to a set of values associated with it – the public ownership and operation of most of the means of production, centralized planning and decision making, single-party rule, the public provision of education and health care

FLORIDA
(UNITED STATES)
Miami
Key West
N
Nassau
BAHAMAS
Havana
Varadero
Sagua la Grande
Pinar del Rio
Colón
CUBA
Caibarién
Cienfuegos
Sancti-Spiritus
Trinidad
ISLA DE PINOS
Camagüey
TURKS & CAICOS
ISLANDS
Banes
Holguín
Manzanillo
Baracoa
Santiago
de Cuba
Guantánamo
CAYMAN
ISLANDS
HAITI
Port-au-Prince
JAMAICA
Kingston
0
200 Kilometers
0
200 Miles

Map 1 Cuba

free of charge, and the public provision of highly subsidized food, transportation, housing, and pensions, among other objectives.

The economic reform package that Cuba would have in place by the mid-1990s distinguished the path that its government followed from those that had brought down ruling communist parties in Europe at the end of the 1980s. In contrast to the European experiences, the Cuban Communist Party and its leaders succeeded: they remained in power. They reactivated the country's economy after a recession shorter (four years) than in former Soviet Central Asia (six years), and sustained key aspects of social welfare.

However, Cuba's economic reforms of the 1990s need further reforming in order to set Cuba on a sustainable growth path. This chapter focuses on this question in the light of the comparative experience of other communist or post-communist countries. The starting premise is that the initial stages of the Cuban economic transition were successful in many ways. Financial calamity compelled the government to undertake a series of pragmatic reforms to accommodate economic distress. But the policies adopted created new problems and failed to address others. The first wave of economic reforms was insufficient to set the economy on a sustainable growth path within the framework of Cuba's current political system.

The crisis

Cuba's crisis was severe, as Table 2.1 shows. During the second half of the 1980s, the economy had been stagnant. Gross domestic product (GDP) failed to grow while exports and imports weakened. Between 1990 and 1993, trade collapsed. The plunge was sudden and dramatic, and GDP lost nearly 30 per cent of its value over that short period. In 1994, the economy bottomed out, and it grew modestly for the remainder of the decade. In the second half of the 1990s, as Tables 2.1 and 2.2[4] indicate, imports recovered to some extent but exports actually declined. A trade deficit appeared that, though not large by international standards, was problematic because Cuba's access to international capital markets for new funds is basically limited to suppliers' credits. Inflation was negligible in the second half of the 1980s and moderate from 1990 to 1993. There was an inflationary spike between 1993 and 1994, however, with inflation accelerating less rapidly though still fast in 1995 when the GDP price deflator (1985 = 100) reached 157.2. The economy then stabilized, and the GDP price deflator remained basically unchanged through the end of the 1990s.[5]

The catalyst of the crisis was, for the most part, external. The Soviet Union had engaged in several forms of subsidies which amounted to outright grants to the Cuban economy. These included paying several multiples of the prevailing international price for Cuban sugar, subsidizing the price that Cuba paid for Soviet sales of petroleum, and supplying all weapons free of charge to the Cuban armed forces. In addition, the Soviet

Table 2.1 The Cuban economy, 1985–2000*

	Year			
	1990	*1993*	*1994*	*2000*
GDP[a]	99.9	70.4	70.9	81.4
GDP per capita	95	65	66	74
Imports[b]	92.3	25.0	29.3	60.5
Exports[b]	90.4	19.3	23.1	28.2
GDP deflator	103.5	117.0	142.6	157.9[c]

Notes:
*1985 = 100.
a. GDP is gross domestic product in 1981 constant pesos.
b. Imports and exports are in current pesos.
c. Deflator statistic in column for 2000 is actually for 1998.
Source: Computed from Comisión Económica para América Latina y el Caribe, *La economia cubana: Reformas estructurales y desempeño en los noventa* (Mexico: Fondo de Cultura Económica, 2000), Tables A.2 for GDP 1985–95, A.12 for GDP price deflator 1985–98, and A.32 for exports and imports 1985–93. Computed from Oficina Nacional de Estadística, *Anuario estadístico de Cuba, 2000* (Havana, 2000), page 94 for GDP 2000 and page 128 for exports and imports for 1994 and 2000. Population data from Oficina Nacional de Estadística, *Anuario estadístico de Cuba, 2001* (Habana, 2002), Table II-1.

Table 2.2 The Cuban economy's recent performance, 1997–2002*

	1997	*2002*
GDP[a]	89	105
GDP per capita	89	104
Imports[b]	83	86
Exports[b]	109	84

Notes:
*2000 = 100
a. GDP is gross domestic product in 1997 prices.
b. Imports and exports are in current pesos.
Source: Oficina Nacional de Estadísticas, *Anuario estadístico de Cuba, 2002* (Havana, 2003), Tables III–1, III–3, and III–4.

Union provided loans at low interest rates to cover the high bilateral trade deficits that emerged. The Soviets awarded low-interest-bearing loans for major economic development projects, such as the construction of a nickel ore processing plant and a nuclear power plant, among others, as well as many scholarships to train Cubans in the USSR in various professional endeavours. Most of these assistance programmes were ending late in the Soviet period; they all ended with the dissolution of the Soviet Union.[6]

The Cuban economy also suffered from fundamental flaws. Despite these massive Soviet subsidies, Cuba's GDP did not grow at all during the second half of the 1980s. Any economy would have been hurt by large adverse exogenous shocks but Cuba's stagnant and inefficient economy was devastated. A better economic future for Cuba requires an improvement in how the economy functions. Cuba's GDP growth rates have been anaemic since 1985 except for three years (1996, 1999, and 2000). The economy fell in six of the last 18 years and registered growth rates below 3 per cent in seven other of those years (including in 2002 and 2003).[7] GDP per capita trends were poorer still.

Nevertheless, Cuba's social performance was noteworthy in the 1990s, especially when compared to several former communist countries. At the end of the decade, several of Cuba's social indicators remained good by international standards. In 2002, the infant mortality rate per thousand live births was 6.5. Fewer infants died at birth in Havana than in Washington, DC. The number of inhabitants per medical doctor was 168.[8] Over 97 per cent of children ages 6 to 14 were enrolled in school. Retention rates in primary, junior high school, senior high school, and vocational and technical schools exceeded 95 per cent. (The adult illiteracy rate dropped below 4 per cent in the 1981 census.) However, the economic decline affected the population adversely. The intake of calories fell by 27 per cent between 1990 and 1996. It became very difficult to obtain medicines and, for a number of years, food. New diseases appeared and those that had seemed eradicated reappeared. The quality of medical services also deteriorated.[9] In 2002, the working age population (ages 14 to 64) still had a calorific intake 57 per cent below the recommended nutritional standards and a protein intake 68 percent below the pertinent standards.[10] Schools suffered from lack of books, lab equipment, and other pedagogical materials. School cafeterias served less and lower-quality food. The government cut enrollments in higher education by 45 per cent from 1991 to 1995.[11] Twelve per cent of urban Cubans (in 2002, three-quarters of Cubans lived in urban areas)[12] earned less than 100 pesos per month (less than $5 per month at the prevailing legal exchange rate), had no access to dollars, grew no food, and received no food subsidies.[13] They suffered extreme poverty.

In 1996, the Communist Party's top school for cadres published a book for the educated general public to explain what had happened to Cuba's economy and what measures had been adopted to address this crisis. The book's opening says that Cuba's key victory in the 1990s was to have resisted. The political system was sustained and economic recovery policies were enacted.[14] And yet, those are surely insufficient goals.

In 2000, on the eve of the Cuban economy's new slowdown, GDP per capita in constant prices remained still 26 per cent below its 1985 level (Table 2.1). Exports in current prices plummeted between 1997 and 2002; imports contracted sharply after 2000 (Table 2.2). During the world recession in 2001–2, the prices of Cuba's main export products declined but dollar revenues from international tourism also dropped 6 per cent between 2000 and 2002 – the first time this had happened since the start of the economic reforms.[15] To restore and sustain the social safety net and improve the quality of life, to enable the Communist Party to govern and remain politically competitive in Cuba's future, and to serve the public interest irrespective of the governing party, the economy must recover fully and start to grow again.

The repertoire of successful policies in 1990–3

At the January 1990 meeting of the Council for Mutual Economic Assistance (often known by its initials as CMEA or COMECON), the Soviet Union proposed that all trade among member communist countries was to be conducted on the basis of market prices and convertible currencies. The motion was approved. In effect, Cuba was given one year's notice to prepare for an economic shock.

In the period 1990–3, the Cuban government adopted three kinds of policies to address this challenge: elements of economic liberalization to provide avenues for recovery; some institutional reforms to facilitate economic liberalization; and deferral of economic stabilization in order to maintain a basis of political support. All three would accomplish their goals in the short to medium term. There was an obvious short-term trade-off between political and economic stabilization, and the Cuban leadership initially emphasized the former over the latter. The decision to defer economic stabilization ultimately only managed to postpone the moment of reckoning for three years.

Economic liberalization first As noted, the signal that much was about to change in Cuban economic policy was the June 1990 Political Bureau statement welcoming foreign direct investment and, specifically, the development of the tourism sector. Those two economic reforms alone account for much of the Cuban economy's recovery. These economic liberalization measures preceded the adoption of economic stabilization measures.

Institutional reforms second Some institutional reforms were also adopted in advance of economic stabilization measures. The 1991 Fourth Party Congress authorized amending the 1976 Constitution to provide for some private property rights. Article 15 of the 1992 Constitution authorized the executive committee of the Council of Ministers, at its discretion, to grant property rights for various economic activities. Article 15 asserts that all productive property belongs to the state (except for a fraction of agriculture that has always been and remains in private hands). Such property cannot be privatized "except in those unusual cases where the full or partial transfer of some entity to natural or legal persons would advance the country's development and is not adverse to the political, social, and economic foundations of the State, provided the Council of Ministers or its Executive Committee approve in advance." This change was enacted because foreigners wanted some property protection before investing.

Article 15 provides weak constitutional protection for property rights. Nonetheless, it would serve as a cornerstone for the expansion of foreign direct investment in Cuba in the years ahead. However, no privately owned Cuban businesses big enough to hire non-relatives were authorized during the following 13 years.

Economic stabilization deferred Economic stabilization was deliberately deferred in the early 1990s. Instead, the government chose to run a budget deficit to buy political insurance. Fiscal revenues plummeted by 22 per cent while budget expenditures increased 2.5 per cent (both in current prices) from 1990 to 1993. During those critical years, the government cut its expenditures for defence and internal security (by 38 per cent) and administration (by 8 per cent) to make room for an 83 per cent increase in subsidies to cover losses in state enterprises. Subsidies as a percentage of budget expenditures rose from 26 to 42 per cent between 1990 and 1993. Public health expenditures rose 15 per cent, too, as the government struggled to sustain a key sector. The budget deficit reached 10 per cent of GDP in 1990; it ballooned to 33 per cent of GDP in 1993.[16] Economists should tear their vestments at these policies and their results, but they served the party leadership's main goal: buying political time and helping to keep the communist party in power. (In this respect, Cuban policies resemble those also pursued in Bulgaria and Uzbekistan to sustain the legacies of communist parties in power.)[17]

In May 1990, the Communist Party polled the population as one element to design this strategy. Its pollsters found that only 20 per cent believed that the food supply was good, only 10 per cent thought that public transportation was good, and only 10 per cent believed that the housing supply was good. But 77 per cent averred that public health services were good and 83 per cent affirmed the same regarding schools.[18] These findings on the high regard for the health care services and schools are believable because they come from the same poll that uncovered highly critical information. Accordingly, the government invested its resources to sustain its strengths.

Economic stabilization at last In the early 1990s, Cuba's fiscal policies led inevitably to high inflation rates, posing a different threat to political stability. Cuba had experienced rather stable prices up to the end of the 1980s (see Table 2.1) but inflation accelerated after 1990. Monetary liquidity leapt 121 per cent between 1990 and 1993.[19] The inflation spike in 1993–4 galvanized the government into action. During these years, official prices remained fixed for the most part but a vast illegal market developed, in which prices skyrocketed. (The fiscal imbalance and accelerating inflation of the early 1990s also mirrored the experience of Russia and Central Asia as described in other chapters.)

The specific shock that finally compelled the government to change was the disastrous 1993 sugar harvest when output was about half that of the previous year (and the lowest in thirty years). At last the government enacted reforms to stabilize public finances. The fiscal adjustment was dramatic. From 1993 to 1994, revenues jumped by 34 per cent; expenditures fell 3 per cent across nearly all categories of the budget. Subsidies as a fraction of the budget dropped to 28 per cent, roughly returning to the 1990 level. The deficit as a percentage of GDP fell to 7.4 per cent. Monetary liquidity fell by 10 per cent.[20] The exchange rate stabilized. From the respective first semester in 1989 to 1993, the exchange rate rose in the illegal market from 7 to 120 pesos per dollar. In August 1994, it fell abruptly to 80 pesos per dollar, reaching 25 pesos per dollar a year later.[21] Cuba's fiscal balance continued to improve through the remainder of the 1990s. In 2002, the deficit was 3.2 per cent of GDP while subsidies still accounted for a rather high 19 per cent of the budget.[22] (In contrast to Russia or Bulgaria, Cuba did not have financial meltdowns or hyperinflationary episodes in the remainder of the 1990s.)

More economic liberalization In the summer of 1993, the government enacted three other liberalizing economic reforms. First, it authorized Cubans to hold and use hard currencies, including US dollars remitted by the Cuban diaspora, and expanded travel opportunities for Cuban-Americans. Second, it authorized self-employment. A licensed self-employed person could not hire non-relatives, however, thereby limiting the opportunities for small-business development. Third, it transformed most state enterprises in agriculture into semi-private cooperatives – Unidades Básicas de Producción Cooperativa (UBPCs). These new cooperatives could use the land they tilled but ownership remained in state hands. Substantial regulatory burdens, including price controls, also limited the autonomy of UBPCs.[23] In the fall of 1994, the government adopted a fourth pair of liberalizing economic reforms by authorizing private agricultural and handicraft markets. Producers could sell their remaining surplus after they had met their obligations to the state.

The architect of these successful policies of economic adjustment and continuing economic liberalization was the new Finance Minister José Luis Rodríguez, soon promoted to Economy Minister. Vice President Carlos Lage backed him. President Fidel Castro authorized the changes. The three deserve credit for a remarkable feat of economic and political stabilization over a short time. Armed Forces Minister Raúl Castro played a key role advocating the authorization of free agricultural markets to increase food output.

The repertoire of successful policies in 1994–2001

The liberalizing economic reforms adopted in 1993–4 had mixed effects in the years ahead but, on balance, improved economic efficiency and growth.

One standard is their impact on the income of ordinary Cubans. In *current* pesos, the salaries of state employees increased 27 per cent during the years of recovery (1994–2000). But the income of the UBPC semi-private cooperatives increased by only 19 per cent. Sugar cane UBPCs were the most important of these cooperatives, yet they performed least well. In harvest year 1994–5, their first in operation, only 23 per cent of the UBPCs were profitable, a proportion that dropped below 8 per cent in the next two harvests. The government eventually increased prices paid to sugar cane producers so that the proportion of profitable UBPCs reached 63 per cent in 2000.[24]

Although the UBPCs were not particularly good for their members, they were the most efficient units of sugar cane production in Cuba and, in these terms, the UBPC reforms succeeded. The government, perhaps inadvertently, ran an experiment in agricultural organization in the late 1990s when six different kinds of entities operated in Cuban agriculture. In addition to the UBPCs, the Interior Ministry, the Armed Forces, and the Sugar Industry Ministry also ran their own sugar cane farms. Moreover, two kinds of private agricultural cooperatives also grew sugar cane. Agricultural production cooperatives (CPAs) pooled their land and worked it jointly. Credit and service cooperatives (CCS) were formed by private farmers who owned and tilled their own land but joined to obtain credit, purchase equipment, and market their products. Table 2.3 summarizes agricultural output per worker in the six types of organizations, with harvest year 1993–4 set to equal 100.

The late 1990s was a disapointing time for Cuba's sugar-cane agriculture in terms of output, efficiency, and prices, but the evidence in Table 2.3 suggests that efficiency plummeted most sharply in state enterprises run by the Armed Forces, Interior, and Sugar Ministries. All three kinds of cooperatives performed better than the state farms, yet the Cuban government did not grant any greater autonomy to the cooperatives or shift more productive activities from the state to the cooperative sector. The UBPCs, in particular, suffered from sustained and intrusive interference from state agencies.[25] The most likely reason for the failure to deepen these reforms is President Castro's publicly stated aversion to market-oriented policies in agriculture.[26] (In contrast, Shahid Javed Burki reports on the spectacularly successful agricultural reforms in China, which had transferred ownership of land back to the families living and working on farms and deregulated controls over family farms.)

Table 2.3 Cuba: agricultural output per worker across farm types, 1999–2000*

UBPC	*CCS*	*CPA*	*Sugar ministry*	*Interior Ministry*	*Armed Forces*
90	83	83	69	59	48

Notes:
*1993–4=100
Source: Computed from Armando Nova González, 'El cooperativismo en la agricultura cañera en Cuba de 1993 a 2000', *Economía y desarrollo*, no. 129 (June–December 2001), 58.

From 1994 to 2000 income increased fastest for those Cuban private producers who suffered from fewer regulatory burdens. Farmers in private cooperatives saw their income rise by 50 per cent (2.5 times the rate of increase in UBPCs) while farmers who owned and tilled their land witnessed a spectacular increase of 423 per cent derived principally from their ability to sell products in free agricultural markets. The income of private non-agricultural producers jumped by 180 per cent, benefiting from the reform that authorized free handicraft markets and self-employment.[27] Sociological field research in several Cuban localities provides convergent evidence: private farmer cooperatives were typically better and more profitable performers than state farms in comparable lines of production.[28]

The liberalizing economic reforms and associated income effects changed Cuba's occupational profile. At the time of the 1981 census, the state employed 92 per cent of the labour force. By 2002, that proportion had fallen to 77 per cent. Most of the growth in non-state employment occurred among private farmers (including those who tilled on their own or joined in credit and services cooperatives) whose share of the labour force rose from 7 to 11 per cent, and among cooperative members whose proportions rose from 1 to 8 per cent. Employment in joint ventures did not exist in 1981 but represented less than one per cent of the workforce in 2002. Self-employment accounted for 1.6 per cent of all workers in 1981, rising to 3.8 per cent in 2002.[29]

Self-employment reforms have also succeeded, but their impact was limited because the government imposed very high licence fees, taxes, and other regulations. Thus in the late 1990s the proportion of self-employed persons grew more slowly than perhaps expected; it peaked at 4.1 per cent in 1999 but fell slightly thereafter. Taxes that the self-employed paid to the government fell from 206 million pesos in 1997 to 123 million pesos in 2001, though tax evasion may also avoid nearly confiscatory fees and taxes.[30]

The policies that fostered dollar remittances from the Cuban diaspora succeeded, though the exact magnitude of those remittances is difficult to measure. Cuba reports that international transfers amounted to $470 million in 1994 and $813 million in 2002. Most of that sum is remittances (some of it is donations). The United Nations Economic Commission for Latin America and the Caribbean estimates that remittances amounted to $537 million in 1995 and $700 million in 1999. For comparison, the value of sugar exports fell from $760 million in 1994 to $447.4 million in 2002.[31] The liberalization of remittances was, therefore, crucial to Cuba's balance of payments.

The original liberalizing economic reforms adopted in 1990 – foreign direct investment and tourism – were the most successful. Gross revenues from international tourism more than doubled from 1994 to 2000, when they exceeded $1.7 billion, dropping 6 per cent by 2002. However, given the 16 per cent plunge in the value of Cuba's goods exports since 2000, international tourism revenue has become the economy's mainstay. International visitors reached 619,000 in 1994 and 1,744,000 in 2000, then dropping 5 per cent by 2002. Foreign direct investment in the telephone system and the Cuban government's efforts to reach out to parts of the Cuban diaspora – whose members, once called 'worms', had become 'butterflies', officially re-labelled as the 'Cuban community abroad' – doubled international telephone toll traffic from 1994 to 2000, when it reached 5.4 million hours (dropping to 4.8 million hours by 2002).[32]

Foreign direct investment also lifted Cuban mining exports from $201 million worth in 1994 to $599 million in 2000, before dropping to $432 million in 2002 as a result of lower prices. Foreign direct investment in Cuba's petroleum and natural gas reserves yielded impressive results. Cuba produced 274,000 tons of crude petroleum in 1980, 671,000 in 1990 and, with the help of foreign direct investment, 3.6 million tons in 2002. It produced less than 20 million cubic metres of natural gas in 1996, rising to 585 million cubic metres in 2002.[33] During this period, Cuba advanced significantly towards energy self-sufficiency. Credit for the development of these enterprises goes to Basic Industries Minister Marcos Portal.

These results are remarkable because there has been so little foreign direct investment and its flow has been so unstable, as shown in Table 2.4.[34] Note that the enactment of the US Democratic Liberty and Solidarity Act of 1996 (better known as Helms-Burton) had no apparent effect on foreign direct investment in Cuba.[35] Cuba received more such investment in 1997 and 1998 than in 1995 and 1996. The drop in 2001 can best be attributed to the international recession.

More institutional reforms In the mid-1990s, the government adopted two additional institutional reforms. In response in part to lower foreign direct investment in 1995, the government enacted a new law to promote and regulate foreign direct investment beyond the narrow confines set in the 1992 Constitution. Law 77 establishes the terms for investment, provides rights and means to settle disputes including expropriation, and describes the government's discretion in accepting or rejecting investments. As a practical matter, the government emphasizes joint ventures between equal partners instead of permitting the development of wholly owned foreign firms, which Law 77 also permits.

Table 2.4 Cuba: foreign direct investment flows, 1994–2001

	1994	*1995*	*1996*	*1997*	*1998*	*1999*	*2000*	*2001*
FDI (US$ millions)	563	5	82	442	207	178	448	39

Source: *Anuario estadístico de Cuba, 2000,* 128; *Anuario estadístico de Cuba, 2002,* Table VI–1.

Another institutional reform transformed some 'plain' state enterprises into quasi-private state firms. The state remains their only shareholder but managers exercise more personal discretion over decisions. Some quasi-private firms engage in international economic transactions because a parallel institutional change abolished the state's centralized approach to international trade. Decree-Law 187 promotes managerial capacities throughout the economy.[36] This was a daunting task. In 1993, 69 per cent of all state enterprises were unprofitable and in receipt of state subsidies.[37] Some state enterprises in agriculture began to sell their surpluses in the free agricultural markets after they, too, had met their obligations to the Ministry of Agriculture; in 1996, state enterprises already accounted for one-fifth of the value of agricultural sales in these free markets.[38]

The combination of joint ventures with international partners and the new entrepreneurial behaviour of a number of state enterprises generated a new environment of enterprise profitability that began to transform the government's fiscal accounts. Table 2.5 summarizes the fiscal impact of the new economic reforms. Overall official revenues have increased moderately. But Table 2.5 shows a dramatic rise in government revenues from the taxation of enterprise profits (joint ventures and quasi-private state firms); these grew nearly three times faster than total state revenues. It also shows an even faster increase in taxation on the utilization of the labour force in these kinds of enterprises – a growth rate 3.5 times faster than total state revenues. In contrast, contributions declined from state enterprises that have yet to be transformed into semi-private firms. Revenues from taxation of self-employment show the limited fiscal impact of this reform.

In short, the policies of economic and political stabilization and economic liberalization that the Cuban government adopted in the first half of the 1990s succeeded. The economic collapse was averted and recovery commenced. Some fiscal balance was re-established. Sufficient political support for the regime was obtained, although such support was far less substantial than before 1990, and the welfare effects on the population remain severe.

Table 2.5 Cuba: state revenues in 2000–2*

Year	*Total state revenues*	*Taxes on enterprise profits*	*Taxes on labour force use*	*Taxes on self-employed*	*Payments from state enterprises*
2000	122	328	390	71	58
2002	132	360	462	64[a]	74

Source: Computed from *Anuario estadístico de Cuba, 2000,* 105, and *Anuario, 2002,* Table IV–4.
Notes:
a. This statistic refers to 2001.
*1996 = 100.

Nevertheless, the economic recovery has yet to return GDP to the level achieved in the mid-1980s. Although the government no longer faced an economic and political abyss by the mid-1990s, the economic reform process slowed down and the government allowed new problems to fester as a result of inappropriately designed economic liberalization policies.

Problems generated by some of the new economic policies

Some of Cuba's economic problems in the early twenty-first century are the unintended consequences of policies adopted in the 1990s. Cuba will need to reform these reforms in order to generate sustained growth. This section highlights three problems: multiple exchange rates, the formation of oligopolies, and a contradictory approach to foreign direct investment. The first problem stems from partial dollarization, which created severe price distortions and market segmentation. The other two were created by flawed institutional reforms. One problem bears on how the government reorganized the economy to create partial privatization, leading to the formation of oligopolies, while the other stems from Cuba's weak institutional foundation to attract effective and efficient foreign firms. As vividly highlighted in the cases of the Central Asian Republics, partial-reform equilibrium – Cuba's circumstance in these three problematic areas – unfairly empowers insiders to exploit the nation's assets and creates opportunities for the corrupt exercise of arbitrage.

Multiple exchange rates The Cuban economy's partial dollarization, resulting from measures adopted between 1990 and 1993, created a system of multiple exchange rates and led to the formation of structurally semi-independent parallel economies. Partial dollarization occurred in part through the legalization of holding and using dollars remitted by Cuban-Americans, but it owes more to structural economic policies. The government chose to segregate product markets that operate in dollars from those that operate in pesos. For instance, the tourist sector operates in dollars, the sugar sector in pesos, and the two do not meet through the financial system.

The segmented markets created through partial dollarization prevent the development of more normal means to finance enterprises, distort relative prices, and render it virtually impossible to measure the true profitability of enterprises or even assess the state budget. The official exchange rate, which fixed parity between the peso and the dollar, generates large, hidden subsidies.[39] As George Carriazo, Minister Rodríguez's successor as the Deputy Director of the *Centro de Investigaciones de la Economía Mundial*, argued as early as 1996, Cuba must move to unify its exchange rate regime and, thus, unify its now bifurcated economy.[40] Cuba's multiple exchange rate regime has already lasted much longer than Russia's, and thus may have caused more damage.

The multiple exchange rate regime helped to decapitalize the sugar industry, leading to its de facto bankruptcy. On 10 April 2002, the government announced that it would shut down 45 per cent of Cuba's 155 sugar mills.[41] Sugar exports are paid for in dollars, but the government insisted that state enterprises in the sugar sector be paid in pesos at a parity exchange rate between the peso and the dollar. For example, in 2000 the international price that Cuba received for a pound of sugar was approximately $0.10. At the prevailing exchange rate available to those Cubans who received remittances, the producer would receive 2 pesos but, at the official exchange rate, that producer received only 0.10 pesos – or one-twentieth of the real worth of the products. On the other hand, the sugar industry had to purchase some imported inputs in dollars. No wonder state industrial and agricultural enterprises in the sugar sector performed poorly, given that their revenues remained in pesos while some of its inputs switched to dollars.[42] It did not help that between 1997 and 2002 the government cut back peso investments in the sugar sector by 54 percent at the same time that its peso investments in all sectors grew 8 per cent.[43]

The multiple exchange rate regime also transferred de facto subsidies to those Cuban consumers who can purchase imported petroleum or food products in pesos and thus have little incentive to constrain their consumption.[44] A beneficiary of remittances can lawfully import such goods at will to satisfy personal tastes at the same time that severe energy and food shortages plague consumers in the peso economy.

To capture the dollars from tourists and those remitted from abroad, the government created dollar stores. In 1996, dollar stores already sold goods worth $640 million; by 1997, half of all Cubans had some access to hard currencies.[45] In fact, most of the shoppers at these dollar stores are Cubans who obtain dollars in various ways – either legally or illegally. Some products are then re-sold in illegal markets. These stores are well supplied with products, often imported from abroad, in stark contrast with peso stores whose shelves are nearly bare. Access to dollars has become the principal determinant of inequality between Cubans today. Partial dollarization also generates powerful incentives to Cuban enterprises to obtain dollar resources, typically by selling their products to the dollar stores or to enterprises that operate in dollars even if the result is an inefficient allocation of national resources.[46]

Partial dollarization also distorts the labour market. Workers have a strong incentive to shift from peso generating to dollar-generating occupations such as those in the tourism sector. It is now common to find university graduates working in menial jobs to serve international tourists. Workers in tourism receive part of their compensation in dollars. The result de-values education. Another effect on the labour market is the direct result of remittances: people who do no or little work live well if they receive remittances.

Long-term sustained reliance on remittances may further weaken Cuba's already battered work ethic. Karl Marx wrote about the communist principle in the *Critique of the Gotha* Program: 'From each according to his ability, to each according to his needs.' That same text indicates that Marx would write the socialist principle, that is, the standard for work incentives in the transition away from capitalism, as: From each according to his ability, to each according to his effort.[47] Since the early 1990s, the Cuban version could be adapted as 'from each according to his connections, to each according to his luck.'

The remedy to some of these distortions is the unification of the exchange rate, making the already existing 'convertible peso' Cuba's currency. The value of this peso would float subject to central bank intervention. The long-standing official dollar–peso US$1 = 1 parity would be abandoned. The government has been reluctant to adopt such policies because they necessarily imply a certain additional loss of political control.

Oligopoly formation The government's reorganization of state enterprises has created a second cluster of institutional problems, whereby Cuba's quasi-private state enterprise policy creates tight oligopolies to favour the already favoured. This is evident in the tourism sector where partial privatization reforms are most extensive. By the end of the 1990s, two quasi-private state enterprises, Cubanacán and Gran Caribe, monopolized 91 per cent of the supply of five-star hotels, jointly with their respective international partners. Another quasi-private state enterprise, Horizontes, controlled 66 per cent of the supply of two-star hotels and 47 per cent of the supply of four-star hotels, also jointly with its international partners.[48] The government used its discretion to carve out non-competitive niches for its firms even in the most dynamic sectors, weakening competition and creating oligopoly rents.

The Cuban government reorganized some of its more lucrative state enterprises and assigned them to favoured insiders without a competitive bid or meritocratic process. The state owns these enterprises but managers set their own compensation at levels far above those prevailing in the public sector. This Cuban-style partial privatization poses a high risk that privileged managers will fully privatize these state assets for their own benefit at some future point.

The government has also tolerated lawless behaviour on the part of many enterprises. Cuba's domestic financial imbalances at the enterprise level are most readily evident through what some Cuban authors call 'the chain of non-payment,'[49] that is, Enterprise X finances itself by failing to pay what it owes to Enterprise Y, which in turn fails to pay Enterprise Z, and so on. Such illegal behaviour on a massive scale creates enterprise liquidity but threatens the country's financial system. In 2000, enterprise non-payments amounted to a sum equal to one-fifth of GDP.[50] Contract enforcement would provide better discipline for enterprises and reduce the likelihood of further abuse.

Levels of corruption in Cuba had been low before 1990. Since 1990, instances of corruption are reported in the Cuban press with regularity. In 1998 alone, the Cuban Communist Party conducted 1,159 investigations of corruption involving its members, most of whom were high officials. Among the officials most commonly accused and found guilty of corruption are those involved with the quasi-private state enterprises in tourism and other dollar-generating sectors.[51] The combination of new markets, strong state intervention in shaping those markets, and extremely wide executive discretion is a formula for corruption in many transition states.

The formation of oligopolies is sometimes justified as an attempt to retain Cuba's main economic assets in the hands of nationals as the transition accelerates.[52] It surely serves to protect the power and income of the national elite. This is the nationalism of the powerful appropriating public property for private gain – the antithesis of the values of revolutionary socialism. If this process persists, Cuba will find itself fully immersed in crony capitalism.

Suboptimal foreign direct investment regime A third set of problems has arisen regarding the regime for foreign direct investments. As already noted, Article 15 of the 1992 Constitution permits foreign direct investment in the most indirect way. Cuba has received remarkably modest and oscillating flows of foreign investment for various reasons. Its economy is small and weak. US policy no doubts deters some potential investors. But Cuba's Constitution is hardly a good example of reliably rooted property rights. Law 77 (1995) cannot guarantee more rights than the Constitution itself. The Constitution must be changed, not in this instance to alter the political regime but to make it possible for the socialist regime to generate better economic results. Property rights cannot be just an exception to a uniform policy of state ownership, subject to the discretion of the executive committee of the Council of Ministers, and still expect substantial foreign investment, which has been the motor for Cuba's economic recovery.

The government could also use its Law 77 to authorize foreign investments in local firms wholly owned by the international enterprise, instead of insisting as a practical matter on joint ventures. The government would gain information and expertise in coping with foreign firms of different sizes, styles, and investment capacities. The scarcity of foreign investment is caused more by the restrictive fashion in which the government interprets the law than by the law itself. The desire to retain political control seems to be one obstacle to changing the current use of Law 77.

Cuba's approach to foreign direct investment also fosters non-competitive oligopolies. The executive committee of the Council of Ministers tends to grant concessions per product line or geographic site, thus making it unnecessary for foreign firms to compete against each other. The above-cited example of oligopoly in tourism applies to Cuban quasi-private state enterprises and to their international partners. These non-competitive outcomes deprive Cuba of the opportunity to receive better terms from foreign firms and from benefiting from likely efficiencies from greater competition. The government foregoes such benefits for the sake of retaining executive discretion in the allocation of sectoral and territorial resources.

Moreover, the 'chain of non-payment' described above also affects joint ventures operating in Cuba. Some foreign firms suffer from this institutional climate, so lax in contract enforcement and timely payment of bills. At the international level, many Cuban state enterprises and other government agencies do not honor their obligations to international suppliers. Some of these also invest in Cuba, since lawfully authorized forms of investment include 'investment through supplies'.

Cuba stopped servicing its international hard-currency debt in 1986. Since the 1990s, it has made commendable efforts to clear up arrears in its multilateral debts and it has brought down some of its debt with certain governments. The total hard-currency debt initially peaked at $11.1 billion in 1999, dropped to $10.9 billion in 2001, and has since continued to rise.[53] But Cuba replicated at the international level what its enterprises do within the country, namely using nonpayment of suppliers as a means to obtain international financing. This reason is simple: Cuba could not obtain convertible-currency funds in any other way. This is not a sustainable long-term strategy but it has already sustained the Cuban government for a considerable period of time.

Non-payments to international suppliers grew by 73 per cent from 1997 to 2001, thereby financing Cuba's economic recovery. In 2001, non-payment of international suppliers amounted to 19 per cent of all of Cuba's international hard-currency debt. And the value of the non-payments that year far exceeded the value of all of Cuba's goods exports.[54] Many of these international suppliers are the same firms that already invest in Cuba or that might invest if there were a more secure property rights regime.

The partial-reform equilibrium that marked Cuba's political economy at the start of the twenty-first century is driven by strong political incentives. The multiple exchange regime gives the illusion of control even as severe distortions work their way through the Cuban economy, contributing to the sugar industry's bankruptcy. The formation of strong oligopolies rewards elite cadres, prevents substantial denationalization of the means of production, and preserves state control while elements of privatization take root. The cost is a severely anti-competitive regime, with the prospect of increasing levels of corruption. The foreign investment regime maximizes executive discretion in the allocation of resources at the cost of foregoing many potential gains from foreign direct investment. These three sets of policies are obstacles to Cuba's efficient and sustained long-term economic growth prospects. All inflict harm on its economy and all deserve reform. Since entrenched vested interests have been created through these processes, only President Castro's strong leadership can address this 'reform' in the context of Cuba's current political system.

Adopting new socialism-compatible economic reforms

In addition to correcting the adverse results of some of its economic reforms of the 1990s, the government should also deepen the economic reform programme. In this section as in the previous one, I impose on myself the restriction that these new, deeper reforms should be compatible with the socialist system enshrined in Cuba's Constitution and defended by the ruling party.[55] This section discusses four topics. The first three are liberalization measures (illegal markets, deregulating agricultural markets, small Cuban private business firms), and the fourth (pensions) bears on long-term fiscal health. Each recommendation extends procedures already employed or readily available within Cuba's current socialist framework.

Illegal markets One phenomenon impelling Cuba's economic reforms in the early 1990s was the growth of the illegal market. With the economic collapse, Cubans fended for themselves, ignoring economic regulations. Government and communist party officials and ordinary citizens alike engaged in massive lawlessness. Starting in the late 1980s, Cuban officials somewhat tolerated illegal markets as a means to cope with adversity that complemented the legal economy. A 1989 survey of 'grey' (semi-legal) and 'black' (illegal) markets showed that Cubans searched mainly for services in these markets. From 1989 to 1993, however, they increasingly searched for food and household essentials, bidding prices up by a factor of 25 to 30 – an inflation rate that official prices sought to repress.[56] Individual desperation deepened.

The government and the party could not imprison millions of Cubans. They had repressed illegal economic activities before the late 1980s and did so more selectively after 1990.[57] The preferred strategy after 1990 was to find a new equilibrium. State security had better things to do than to chase peasants trying to sell their products. Agricultural private markets, legalization of holding and using dollars, and self-employment were responses, in part, to the state's accommodation of the behavior of its people and its effort to re-establish the rule of law to the extent possible.[58] The size of the illegal market abated, though it did not disappear. Aspects of this state response have been common, of course, to other communist or once-communist countries.

Agricultural markets Following the same principles, the Cuban government can liberalize other aspects of economic behaviour to further shrink the size of the illegal market. Fully liberalizing agricultural markets is one example. Such measures would likely increase output substantially, make the most important component of illegal markets disappear, and relieve the Interior Ministry from having to arrest peasants and ordinary citizens for simple food retail transactions.

Previous sections have shown that the sugar cane UBPCs suffered from various ills but one of them surely included earning revenues in relatively unchanging and low prices for their agricultural production while remaining under excessive state control. Sugar cane UBPCs were in practice prevented from diversifying into other crops while being paid low prices in pesos. State agricultural marketing boards exercised oligopsony power to set prices and output levels. That is one reason why the sugar cane UBPCs were not profitable in the immediate aftermath of their creation. Lo and behold, many UBPCs became profitable when the government liberalized some agricultural prices in late 1994, granting access to market prices to UBPCs engaged in non-sugar production as well private farming cooperatives and individual farmers.[59] These rural enterprises performed well for the remainder of the decade.

Production of fruits and vegetables increased substantially between 1994 and 1998 due to market prices and agricultural deregulation. By 1998, many product lines of agriculture had recovered to their 1989 levels. However, agricultural marketing boards still showed the heavy hand of the state, by paying at prices appreciably below those prevailing in the free agricultural markets – prices at which producers were compelled to sell by law. Even in the late 1990s the Ministry of Agriculture continued to behave towards peasant producers as if they were state employees, issuing excessive regulations and interfering.[60] Yet, the experience of China demonstrates that the deregulation of agricultural markets can generate substantial improvements in economic performance, feed the cities, provide for exports, and contribute significantly to economic growth. Remaining regulations would uphold market-conforming rules and enforce health codes. Full agricultural liberalization would most likely greatly increase food output, end illegal markets in food, and lead to a more efficient allocation of resources.

Small businesses Cuba's approach to property rights in directly productive activities is unusual by world standards. It permits and promotes state firms and foreign firms, but prohibits privately owned national firms. Since the 1960s, the government has permitted individual farmers to contract for some labour through state agencies. It promoted private agricultural cooperatives. In the 1990s, the liberalization of self-employment, as noted, permits paying relatives but not hiring non-relatives. The creation of UBPCs might have been an interim step towards wider entrepreneurial autonomy. In the early to mid-1990s, communist party and government officials as well as academics discussed the utility of authorizing small and medium-sized private Cuban firms.[61] The economic recovery begun in 1994 seemed to some decision-makers to make such a further opening unnecessary, however.

The case for authorizing small and medium-sized Cuban enterprises in the private sector remains strong. In the early 1990s, underemployment in the state sector approximated a fifth of that labour force – that is, some 800,000 workers.[62] Cuba's self-employed have been creative and productive in many endeavours, notwithstanding government barriers and a weak economy.[63] However, in this sphere, too, a partial reform equilibrium has created problems: Cuba lacks a private wholesale market thus forcing private entrepreneurs to rely on illegal markets to obtain their supplies. Some of this illegal entrepreneurship comes at the expense of state enterprises. The severe constraint on the potential growth of small business firms also fosters an illegal labour market. Cuban scholars find that, for each lawfully registered self-employed worker, 3.5 workers have not registered; many of the latter are not relatives. In 1995, that meant that over one million Cubans were self-employed, a figure which dropped to about 600,000 in 1997.[64] Authorizing small business firms would reduce the incentive to engage in such illegal behavior.

Carranza, Monreal and Gutiérrez have made a good case for the role of small and medium-sized enterprises within the political framework of a socialist Cuba.[65] They recommend imposing capital and employment constraints on the size of Cuban enterprises that could be owned and operated privately. They also recommend relying on provincial and municipal governments to regulate small and medium-sized Cuban firms, lifting the weight of micro-regulation from the national government.[66] Carranza, Monreal and Gutiérrez note the advantages of scale that such modest-sized firms would have in many lines of production and services. These firms would have no claim on government subsidies. Although each firm would employ few workers, the growth in the number of such firms could reduce overt and hidden unemployment and improve efficiency. They would pay taxes. They are suited to certain dynamic activities such as software technology development or service operations in which the Cuban economy is severely deficient.[67] Such small business firms could make a significant economic contribution. Authorizing them would imply some further loss of political control but one that the current socialist system can well manage.

Pensions Cuba faces a daunting problem in financing old-age pensions. Cuba's demographic profile has been below the population replacement rate since 1978. By 2015, about one-fifth of the population will be age 60 or older; that proportion will reach one-third in 2035 and remain at that level for decades to come. One out of every six Cubans is likely to be over age 75 in 2050. This is, of course, a consequence of long-term improvements in education, health, nutrition, and in the greater capacity of adults to control their reproductive lives. Absent emigration, the population is scheduled to start shrinking in 2025; with emigration, its shrinkage could begin by 2015. This means that Cuba's system for pension financing will reach crisis proportions soon.[68]

Cuba authorizes women to retire at age 55 and men at age 60. It provides a defined-benefit system. In 1998, 1.4 million people were already in receipt of pensions.[69] In practice, some adjustment has been taking place because pensions are paid in pesos. Their purchasing power value falls as the economy dollarizes. But this approach to pension policy adjustment is profoundly inegalitarian and arbitrary. It would be greatly preferable to raise the age for retirement and pension eligibility, eliminate the gender differential, increase the rate of contributions from all workers in the state and private sectors, and shift gradually towards a defined-contribution system. No Cuban political regime can escape making such reforms.

Conclusions

Cuba's economic reforms introduced in the first half of the 1990s were successful. The government responded pragmatically and effectively to the economic crisis. The reforms stopped the crisis, set the basis for economic recovery, stabilized both fiscal accounts and the political system, and retained, albeit frayed, a social safety net. The political regime persevered and changed little, remaining highly centralized and dependent on a key leader. It continued to invest in health and education and it made significant movements towards energy self-sufficiency. These results gained political support at a time of great peril for the regime. Substantial support remains for state socialism and gradual approaches to economic reforms along with official skepticism of market-oriented reforms.

Yet Cuba suffered an economic debacle from which it has yet to recover. It may not reach the 1985 GDP per capita levels until this century's second decade. The economy is populated by industrial dinosaurs, and Cuba remains an ineffective exporter of agricultural products. Its balance of payments is unsustainable because it is financed through the non-payment of international financial obligations. Its fiscal situation is out of balance because inflation is repressed and partly hidden through illegal markets and dualistic markets. There is no sustainable equilibrium in its domestic or international accounts.

Furthermore, several of Cuba's economic reforms were only partial. Partial-reform equilibrium is a long-term recipe for disaster, because it delays microeconomic reforms indefinitely. Such equilibria in the reform or privatization of state enterprises open the window for high levels of corruption as well as for state capture by quasi-private interests and their foreign partners for private gain. Cuba is vulnerable to these ills because its procedures governing quasi-private enterprises risk the unlawful privatization of public assets and create oligopolies that already choke off inter-enterprise competition. The government has been reluctant to sell off state enterprises to foreigners. Its nationalist political preference, explicit or implicit, for insider privatization could easily lead to crony capitalism.

Socialist Cuba could exit this partial-reform equilibrium. It would be straightforward to liberalize its agricultural markets within its current socialist system, thereby increasing output and curtailing illegal markets, to the delight of the Finance and Interior Ministries. These measures would also improve the fiscal balance. Cuba could set a stronger institutional basis for property rights in sectors where quasi-private enterprises already operate. It could register significant efficiency, productive, and learning gains from liberalizing markets for small nationally owned private businesses and deregulating its foreign direct investment regime much further. Cuba should unify its exchange rates to eliminate severe distortions in its economy and take steps now to address the fiscal time bomb embedded in its pension policies.

In 1990, Cuba launched an experiment in political economy by adopting some market means in order to rescue its socialist political system. Yet it embraced fewer such changes than have the most successful socialist governments – China and Vietnam. Nor has Cuba learned sufficiently the lessons of a wide array of political regimes that, though no longer socialist, have much to teach it. Cuba is proud of its internationalism. Now is time the for Cuba to learn from comparative experiences in ordes to generate prosperity and improve its people's prospects for human development.

Notes

1 This essay is part of a project sponsored by the Inter-American Dialogue. The purpose of this essay is to reflect on the process of economic reforms in Cuba, connecting the Cuban experience to those of other communist or once-communist countries. These other experiences are analyzed by companion papers, whose authors are cited from time to time. I also make a special effort to cite Cuban sources wherever possible. I am grateful to the Weatherhead Center for International Affairs, Harvard University, for its general support of my work. I am also grateful to Shahid Javed Burki, Daniel Erikson, Jeffry Frieden, and Omar Everleny Pérez Villanueva for comments on earlier versions. All mistakes are mine alone.

2 *Granma Weekly Review*, 1 July, 1990, 1.

3 Ibid., 27 May, 1990, 2–3.

4 The statistical yearbook for 2001 changed the baseline for calculations in real prices without connecting the old and new time series, hence the need for separate tables. Subsequent statistical yearbooks follow the revised baseline.

5 I have not found a better inflation indicator for these years. Nonetheless, the price deflator most likely underestimates 'true' inflation. It fails to take fully into account the illegal or 'black' markets, takes no account of time waiting as a measure of inflation actually felt by the population, and it probably also underestimates the effect of dual dollar/peso markets on living standards.

6 For further discussion, see Jorge I. Domínguez, *To Make A World Safe for Revolution: Cuba's Foreign Policy* (Cambridge, MA: Harvard University Press, 1989), chapter 4.

7 Comisión Económica para América Latina y el Caribe, *La economía cubana*, Table A.2 (hereafter, CEPAL). See also *Granma*, 21 December 2002, for the Economy Minister's report to the National Assembly, and http://www.cubagob.cubaweb.cu/des_eco/mep/cuba2000.htm

8 Oficina Nacional de Estadísticas, *Anuario estadístico de Cuba, 2002* (Habana, 2003), Tables II-14 and XIV-3 (hereafter *AEC 2002*). Infant mortality in Washington, DC, was 10.6 in 2001, http://www.census.gov/statab/ranks/rank17.xls

9 Centro de Investigaciones de la Economía Mundial, *Investigación sobre desarrollo humano y equidad en Cuba 1999* (Havana: Caguayo S.A., 2000), 59, 82, 100.

10 Viviana Togores and Anicia García, 'Consumo, mercados y dualidad monetaria en Cuba,' Table 4. Centro de Estudios de la Economía Cubana, Universidad de La Habana.
11 Ángela Ferriol Muruaga, 'Política social cubana: Situación y transformaciones', *Temas*, 11 (1998): 91.
12 Calculated from *AEC 2002*, Table II-3.
13 Ángela Ferriol Muruaga, 'La seguridad alimentaria en Cuba', in Ángela Ferriol Muruaga *et al* (ed.), *Cuba: Crisis, ajuste, y situación social 1990–1996* (Havana: Editorial de Ciencias Sociales, 1998), 94.
14 Silvia M. Domenech (ed.), *Cuba: Economía en período especial* (Havana: Editorial Política, 1996), 15.
15 Computed from *AEC 2002*, Table XII-11.
16 Calculations from Oficina Nacional de Estadísticas, *Anuario estadístico de Cuba, 1996* (Havana, 1998), 99. Hereafter *AEC 1996*.
17 Cuba's policies resemble Bulgaria's (see Christopher Hartwell's chapter in this volume), which at the start of the 1990s continued to subsidize enterprises to sustain the Bulgarian Socialist Party in power. In Bulgaria, as in Cuba, the economy had not collapsed prior to the end of the Soviet Union, and the well-educated population was tolerant, perhaps supportive, of the communist regime. Cuba's policies also resemble those of Uzbekistan, which continued to invest in health care and education and relied extensively on subsidies, also to sustain a political regime that changed little.
18 Darío Machado, '¿Cuál es nuestro clima socio-político?', *El militante comunista*, 9 (September 1990): 6, 7.
19 Calculated from *AEC 1996*, 98.
20 Calculated from *AEC 1996*, 98–9.
21 Noel Chaviano Saldaña, 'El tipo de cambio en la economía estatal cubana', in *Economía y reforma económica en Cuba*, ed., Dietmar Dirmoser and Jaime Estay (Caracas: Editorial Nueva Sociedad, 1997), 309.
22 Computed from *AEC 2002*, Table IV-4.
23 For an early assessment of these reforms, see Carmelo Mesa-Lago, *Are Economic Reforms Propelling Cuba to the Market?* (Coral Gables, FL: North–South Center, University of Miami, 1994), chapter 3.
24 Armando Nova González, 'El cooperativismo en la agricultura cañera de 1993 a 2000', *Economía y desarrollo*, 129 (June–December 2001): 49.
25 Ibid., 54.
26 See, for example, Fidel Castro's remarks at the conclusion of the 1986 Third Congress of the Communist Party of Cuba, *Informe central: Tercer Congreso del Partido Comunista de Cuba* (Havana: Editora Política, 1986).
27 Computed from Oficina Nacional de Estadística, *Anuario estadístico de Cuba, 2000* (Havana, 2001), 103. Hereafter, *AEC 2000*.
28 Carmen D. Deere *et al.*, *Güines, Santo Domingo, Majibacoa: Sobre sus historias agrarias* (Havana: Editorial de Ciencias Sociales, 1998), 369–70.
29 *AEC 2002*, Table V-1. Cuban statistics on unemployment fail to account for widespread underemployment. See Centro de Investigaciones de la Economía Mundial, *Investigación sobre desarrollo humano y equidad en Cuba, 1999*, 67–9. In 2002, the official open unemployment rate was 3.3 per cent. *Granma*, 20 December 2002.
30 Oficina Nacional de Estadísticas, *Anuario estadístico de Cuba, 2001* (Havana, 2002), Table IV-4, hereafter *AEC 2001*. For discussions regarding entrepreneurship in Cuba and the barriers to its development, see Philip Peters and Joseph

Scarpaci, *Cuba's New Entrepreneurs: Five Years of Small-Scale Capitalism* (Arlington, VA: Alexis de Tocqueville Institution, 1998); Benjamin Smith, 'The Self-Employed in Cuba: A Street-Level View', *Cuba in Transition*, vol. 9 (1999); and Ted Henken, 'Condemned to Informality: Cuba's Experiments with Self-Employment during the Special Period (The Case of the Bed and Breakfasts)', *Cuban Studies*, vol. 33 (2002): 29.

31 *AEC 2000*, 128, 137; *AEC 2001*, Tables VI-1, VI-8; CEPAL, Table A.30; CEPAL, *Cuba: Evolución económica durante 2002 y perspectivas para 2003*, LC/Mex/L.566 (United Nations), Table 17.

32 *AEC 2000*, 128, 241, 248, 256; *AEC 2002*, Tables XI-13, XII-1, and XII-11.

33 *AEC 2002*, Tables VI-8 and VII-1.

34 More than half of the joint ventures launched between 1990 and 1993 have already been dissolved. Omar Everleny Pérez Villanueva, 'Foreign Direct Investment in Cuba: Recent Experience and Prospects', in Pedro Monreal (ed.), *Development Prospects in Cuba*, (London: Institute of Latin American Studies, 2002), 52.

35 Helms–Burton has had opportunity costs, however. In its absence, foreign direct investment in Cuba might have grown more rapidly. The international firms that might have invested in Cuba could have been larger, generated better financial terms, improved their technological process, and possessed better access to international markets.

36 Humberto Blanco Rosales, 'El factor gerencial y el perfeccionamiento de la empresa estatal cubana', *Economía y desarrollo*, 126 (January–June 2000): 11–39.

37 George Carriazo Moreno, 'Cuba: Cambios económicos', *Economía y desarrollo*, 120 (June 1996): 23.

38 Omar Everleny Pérez and Alejandro Beruff, 'Desempeño de la economía cubana: Primer trimestre de 1996', *Economía y desarrollo*, 120 (June 1996): 36.

39 Vilma Hidalgo de los Santos, Pavel Vidal Alejandro, and Lourdes Tabares Neyra, 'Equilibrios monetarios y política económica', *Economía y desarrollo*, 127 (July–December 2000): 79.

40 Carriazo Moreno, 'Cuba: Cambios económicos', 27.

41 *Granma*, 20 December 2002. For an analysis of the reasons leading up to this productive catastrophe, see Jaime Sperberg Fuentealba, 'El sector azucarero cubano entre reformas y estancamiento', *Cuban Studies* 33 (2002): 30–47.

42 Nova González, 'El cooperativismo en la agricultura cañera en Cuba de 1993 a 2000', 51. See also Lázaro Peña, 'The Sugar Cane Complex: Problems of Competitiveness and Uncertainty in a Crucial Sector', in Pedro Monreal (ed.) *Development Prospects in Cuba: An Agenda in the Making*, (London: Institute of Latin American Studies, 2002), 107–8, 113.

43 *AEC 2002*, Table X-5.

44 Alfredo González Gutiérrez, 'Economía y sociedad: Los retos del modelo económico', in *Cuba construyendo futuro: Reestructuración económica y transformaciones sociales* (Madrid: Fundación de Investigaciones Marxistas, 2000), 202–3.

45 Ferriol Muruaga, 'Política social cubana', 89–90.

46 Hiram Marquetti Nodarse, 'La economía del dólar: Balance y perspectivas', *Temas*, 11 (1998): 51–62.

47 Karl Marx, 'Critique of the Gotha Program', in *Marx and Engels: Basic Writings on Politics and Philosophy*, ed. Lewis S. Feuer (Garden City: Anchor Books, 1959), 115–20.

48 Alejandro Durán Cárdenas, 'Turismo y economía cubana: Un análisis al final del milenio', *Economía y desarrollo*, 127 (July–December 2000): 41–2.

49 International economists sometimes call this process the 'triangular debt', common in the public sector in the developing world.
50 Hidalgo de los Santos, Vidal Alejandro, and Tabares Neyra, 'Equilibrios monetarios y política económica', 75–105.
51 Jorge Pérez-López, 'Corruption and the Cuban Transition', *Cuba in Transition*, Vol. 9 (1999): 453–77.
52 Such enterprise protectionism resembles what the chapters on Russia, Eastern Europe, and Central Asia reveal. It could have the corrupting effects that Vtyurina (chapter 3) describes for Russia and Hartwell (chapter 4) for Bulgaria. Hartwell notes the defence of a similar process on similar grounds in Slovakia.
53 Banco Central de Cuba, *Cuban Economy in the Special Period, 1990–2000*, 14; *AEC 2002*, Table V1.2.
54 Computed from *AEC 2002*, Table VI-2.
55 To be transparent, I favour a peaceful transition in Cuba to a democratic political regime, not just the enactment of economic reforms compatible with the current political system. In this work, however, my political preferences are not pertinent.
56 Alfredo González Gutiérrez, 'La economía sumergida en Cuba', in Dietmar Dirmoser and Jaime Estay (eds), *Economía y reforma económica en Cuba*, (Caracas: Editorial Nueva Sociedad, 1997), 241–3.
57 For discussion, see Jorge Pérez-López, *Cuba's Second Economy: From Behind the Scenes to Center Stage* (New Brunswick, NJ: Transaction, 1995), 97–109, 145–50.
58 I have visited Cuba every calendar year but one since 1991. These sentences summarize many interviews and personal observations.
59 Niurka Pérez Rojas and Dayma Echevarría León, 'Participación y producción agraria en Cuba: las UBPC', *Temas*, 11 (July–September 1997): 69–75.
60 Minor Sinclar and Martha Thompson, *Cuba Going Against the Grain: Agricultural Crisis and Transformation* (Boston: OXFAM America, 2001), 20, 22, 31, 33, 40. See also George Carriazo Moreno, 'Cambios estructurales en la agricultura cubana: la cooperativización', in Dietmar Dirmoser and Jaime Estay (eds), *Economía y reforma en Cuba*, 195–9.
61 I had such conversations with high party and government officials.
62 Ángela Ferriol, 'El empleo. Próximo desafío', in Dietmar Dirmoser and Jaime Estay (eds), *Economía y reforma económica en Cuba*, 361–2.
63 See Ana Julia Jatar-Hausmann's excellent account in *The Cuban Way: Capitalism, Communism, and Confrontation* (West Hartford, CT: Kumarian Press), chapter 7.
64 Lilia Núñez Moreno, 'Más allá del cuentapropismo en Cuba', *Temas*, 18 (1998): 45–6.
65 This project was incubated and developed at the Centro de Estudios sobre América (CEA). One year after the publication of this book, and possibly because of its impact, the Communist Party Central Committee intervened in the CEA, removed its leaders, and compelled its leading scholars to leave the CEA and disperse. I know these scholars personally.
66 Their recommendation approximates to the township and village enterprises that, as Burki notes, have developed successfully in the People's Republic of China.
67 Julio Carranza Valdés, Luis Gutiérrez Urdaneta, and Pedro Monreal González, *Cuba: La reestructuración de la economía, una propuesta para el debate* (Havana: Editorial de Ciencias Sociales, 1995), 89, 94–5, 154.
68 Alberta Durán Gondar and Ernesto Chávez Negrín, 'Una sociedad que envejece: Retos y perspectivas', *Temas*, 14 (April–June 1998): 60; Ricardo Donate-Armada, "The Aging of the Cuban Population," *Cuba in Transition*, 11 (2001): 481–8.
69 CEPAL, 269.

Part II

Rush to Market

3

Russia's Reforms: Lessons from the Old Patron[1]

Svetlana Vtyurina

Introduction

The collapse of the Soviet Union and the subsequent emergence of modern Russia rank among the most significant historical events of the late twentieth century. Russia's sudden transition towards a flawed yet recognizable free-market democracy marked an enormous societal transformation which has had vast geopolitical repercussions. Even after the fall of the Soviet state and the break-away of 14 satellite republics, Russia remained the largest country in the world, with an immense territory of 6.5 million square miles, vast natural resources, a population of 143 million, and a central role in international affairs.

While the Bolshevik Revolution of 1917 led to the construction of Russia's communist economy based on the authoritative blueprint of Marx's vision, the transition towards a market economy in 1991 required a new set of rules and institutions. Changing the political establishment proved easier than building a new economic system based on market principles. As Edward Hewett commented during the Gorbachev years, 'economic theory is of little help here. Western economists know a great deal about how to manage a market economy, but very little about how to create one.'[2]

Though geographically distant from Russia, the fortunes of Cuba were tightly entwined with the fall of the Soviet Union, because the Cuban economy had received considerable Soviet support from the 1960s to the 1980s. Despite obvious differences in size and population, the countries were bound together by ideology and the geopolitical alliance forged during the Cold War. Both countries embraced communism through homegrown revolutions that contrasted sharply with the experiences of much of Eastern Europe, where command economies were imposed by conquest.[3] Cuba's proximity to the United States also strengthened the military and security alliance for the purposes of Soviet espionage and Cuban defence. Until the 1990s, Cuba benefited greatly from enormous Soviet

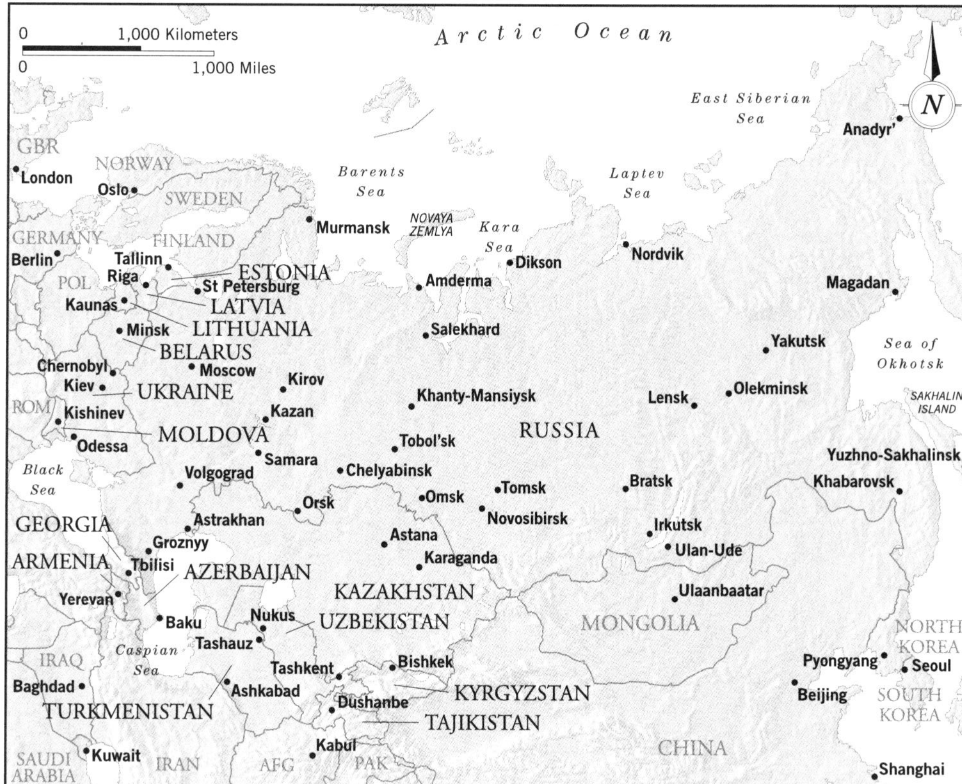
0 1,000 Kilometers
0 1,000 Miles
Arctic Ocean
East Siberian Sea
Barents Sea
Laptev Sea
Kara Sea
NOVAYA ZEMLYA
Sea of Okhotsk
SAKHALIN ISLAND
Black Sea
Caspian Sea
N
GBR
London
NORWAY
Oslo
SWEDEN
FINLAND
GERMANY
Berlin
POL
Tallinn
Riga
Kaunas
ESTONIA
St Petersburg
LATVIA
LITHUANIA
Minsk
BELARUS
Moscow
Chernobyl
Kiev
UKRAINE
ROM
Kishinev
Odessa
MOLDOVA
Murmansk
Amderma
Dikson
Nordvik
Anadyr'
Magadan
Salekhard
Yakutsk
Kirov
Kazan
Khanty-Mansiysk
Lensk
Olekminsk
RUSSIA
Tobol'sk
Samara
Volgograd
Chelyabinsk
Yuzhno-Sakhalinsk
Khabarovsk
Bratsk
Tomsk
Omsk
Orsk
Novosibirsk
Astrakhan
GEORGIA
Groznyy
Astana
Irkutsk
Ulan-Ude
ARMENIA
Tbilisi
Karaganda
AZERBAIJAN
Yerevan
KAZAKHSTAN
Ulaanbaatar
Baku
Nukus
UZBEKISTAN
MONGOLIA
Tashauz
NORTH KOREA
IRAQ
Pyongyang
Seoul
Tashkent
Bishkek
Baghdad
Ashkabad
KYRGYZSTAN
Beijing
SOUTH KOREA
TURKMENISTAN
Dushanbe
TAJIKISTAN
Kabul
CHINA
SAUDI ARABIA
Kuwait
IRAN
AFG
PAK
Shanghai

Map 2 Russia

subsidies and a preferential sugar-for-oil trade relationship. Moreover, Cuba was also allowed to sell excess oil at market prices as a means of obtaining hard currency to finance the needed imports. In the period from 1986 to 1990, Cuba received approximately US$2 billion annually in non-repayable subsidies, in addition to US$2.3 billion a year in Soviet loans.[4] The relationship also included technical assistance and educational exchange. The termination of oil-for-sugar swaps came in 1989 when the Soviet Union demanded cash for its oil, as its economy was crumbling under the weight of fiscal deficit and mounting external debt. After the break-up of the Soviet Union in late 1991, Russia terminated all the remaining economic and technical assistance. While Cuba had adjusted to changing circumstances by trying to maintain an established political and economic system, Russia embarked on a search for new models.

It is difficult to overestimate the impact of Russia's collapse on the Cuban economy. By 1993, the island's GDP had shrunk by one-third, and the Cuban government faced an economic crisis of daunting proportions. A number of free-market measures were introduced, including the legalization of the US dollar, some agricultural reform, and the authorization of selected small businesses to operate independently of the state. Today, more than a decade since Russia cut off aid, Cuba's GDP is still 15 per cent below 1989 levels. In 2001, Russia ended its lease on the Lourdes intelligence base in Cuba, depriving the government of a further estimated $200 million in annual fees. Disputed Russian debt also casts a shadow over Cuba's future, with Russia claiming nearly US$20 billion for loans and credits extended during the Cold War era, equal to Cuba's annual GDP.[5] In short, the historical legacy of the Soviet–Cuba alliance is key to understanding the economic predicament facing Cuba today. Beyond the deeply felt economic trauma, the Russian experience during transition offers important perspectives for the future development of the Cuban economy.

Russia's political context

While this essay focuses primarily on the economic facets of the Russian transition, the enormity of the political shift from Communist Party rule to electoral democracy also played an important role in shaping policy choices. Thus, Russia's political context must also be considered. Russia represented perhaps the most complicated case among the socialist bloc countries that moved away from central planning in the 1990s. Russia faced exceptional obstacles to the implementation of market reforms, stemming from its size, diversity, culture, geopolitical role, extreme economic centralization, excessive investment in defence and space sectors, high degree of monopolization, and an overreliance on the production and export of natural resources. As the largest country in the world by territory, Russia had to coordinate reforms in 89 regions and across 11 time zones.

The putative blessing of abundant natural resources also allowed the government to procrastinate on the reform effort. Furthermore, for most of the 1990s, Russia successfully leveraged its former superpower status to receive sizable loans from the West while delaying reforms. Although economically weak, Russia's military capacity seriously concerned the West. Wary of igniting chaos and discontent in a country loaded with nuclear warheads, many western donors were too willing to overlook inadequacies in the reform implementation.

To further complicate matters, Russians lacked experience with many of the fundamental elements of a market economy, such as free markets, free enterprise, private property and the rule of law. After nearly four generations of communism, the Russian people were accustomed to fixed prices and common property, with a few exceptions, such as the existence of private food markets (*rynki*), small pieces of land, country houses (*dachas*) and gardens (*ogorodi*).

Russia's 1917 communist revolution occurred much earlier than those of Eastern Europe and the Baltic States, or, for that matter, Cuba. Whereas many other countries embraced communism as a rejection of mafia capitalism, or had it imposed by external powers, Russia's Marxism was not only older and internally generated, but also emerged in a country with weak capitalist roots. Nonetheless, Russians did respond quickly to the incentives created by the transition to a market economy.[6] Unfortunately, rent-seeking, corruption, mafia activity and capital flight were all common features of Russia's early capitalism. By 2004, the country has, nonetheless, achieved economic stabilization and demonstrated stronger institutions. Yet, these features were largely absent from Russia's early move to a market economy, and they still lack a strong and sustainable base.

Russia's economic transition was accompanied by two other major historic shifts: the establishment of democracy and the dissolution of the Soviet Union into 15 distinct republics. The political transformation of the Soviet Union, where Russia was the largest republic, was set into motion when Comrade Mikhail Gorbachev was named the General Secretary of the Communist Party in March 1985. The country had suffered through more than two decades of economic and societal stagnation, first under the leadership of Brezhnev, and then under Andropov and Chernenko. Corruption and enrichment among the party elite was widespread and the growing, albeit anonymous, dissent against the Soviet system was increasingly evident. Gorbachev's ascension was marked by his promise to 'shake up the society' and to 'pull it out of hibernation'.[7] In the late 1980s, the new policies of 'perestroika' (transformation) and 'glasnost' (free expression) earned him respect in the West even as it deepened schisms within the Communist Party of the Soviet Union. However, while citizens were encouraged to demand justice and reforms from the bureaucracy, Gorbachev lacked a credible strategy to address the tensions fuelled by vast disparities in social development and living standards among the country's regions and ethnic groups.

During this time, Boris Yeltsin emerged as one of the most controversial figures in the Soviet leadership. In 1987, Yeltsin delivered a speech highly critical of Gorbachev's 'perestroika' programme at the Central Committee Plenum, and was ousted from the top ranks of the Communist Party. Harnessing his newfound notoriety, he remained a force to be reckoned with in the party system.

As political schisms appeared internally, Russia's external environment was also changing. By 1990, the West was joyfully celebrating the fall of the Berlin Wall and the democratic revolutions across Eastern Europe. In stark contrast, the mood in the Soviet Union was characterized by crisis and disorientation in the rapidly changing global and historical landscape. Changes soon began to manifest themselves at home. In March 1990, the USSR's Third Congress of People's Deputies abolished Article 6 of the Constitution, which designated the Communist Party to be the 'leading and directing force of the Soviet society', instituted the Office of the Presidency, and appointed Gorbachev as President of the USSR in an uncontested election. In early summer 1990, the Congress of the Russian Federation Republic elected Yeltsin as the Chairman of its Supreme Soviet, and he used this opportunity to create the position of the Presidency of the Russian Federation Republic.

Over the next year, tensions between communist hardliners, Gorbachev's reformist tendencies, and the republics' push for independence began to mount. The breaking point finally came on 19 August 1991 when a group of top-ranked Party members formed a 'State Emergency Committee' and claimed power as the country's governing body. Effectively acting as a junta, the group declared that the USSR was in mortal danger, because Gorbachev's reforms had led the country to the brink of chaos. But the attempt to seize power soon fell apart. Scores of people rallied in the centre of Moscow, protesting near the Russian Parliament, and Yeltsin clambered on top of a tank to denounce the coup. The junta was forced to abandon power, and the stage was set for the dismantling of the Soviet Union and resulting independence of the empire's 15 republics. President Gorbachev relinquished his duties in December 1991 and Yeltsin remained the President of Russia, having triumphed in the country's first democratic presidential election in June of that year.

The coup cast Yeltsin as a champion of democracy against totalitarian forces, but in October 1993, Yeltsin himself initiated a violent coup against the parliament that opposed his economic policies. He subsequently imposed his own constitution. To consolidate power, he and his aides created the 'Family', described by one commentator as 'a murky clique of Yeltsin [family members], associates and government officials who spanned the allied worlds of big business and political power'.[8] The 'Family' used its political strength and media power to elect Yeltsin to his second term in 1996. As Yeltsin's term was nearing completion, he appointed Vladimir

Putin as his Prime Minister and then resigned just before the 2000 elections. Putin, a former KGB officer and a member of the administration of the first mayor of St Petersburg, became the Acting President and in March 2000 won presidential elections by a comfortable majority.

From the beginning of his term, Putin appointed several liberal economists from his hometown of St Petersburg to the economic team and cautiously continued to pursue market-oriented reforms. He also manoeuvred between Russia's regional governors and oligarchs without noticeably reducing their power. Over time, however, Putin started to visibly expand his administrative apparatus, attend carefully to the opinions of a group of his former KGB colleagues (the so-called '*siloviki*') and distance himself from the 'Family'. He also appointed his own regional governors and struck a deal with the business elite that required them to stay out of politics in exchange for a promise not to revisit their previous shadowy privatization deals. Simultaneously, the state took much of control over media outlets. Putin also forced the exile of two of the most influential oligarchs, Berezhovsky and Gusinsky, to preclude their political ascendance. The aforementioned developments led many observers to conclude that the Russian President was running a 'managed' democracy. In 2003, this perception strengthened further as he endorsed the arrest and jailing of Mikhail Khodorkovsky, Russia's richest businessmen and the CEO of its largest oil company, Yukos.[9] The arrest was also followed by government seizure of Khodorkovsky's shares in the company, making many cast doubt on the security of property rights in Russia. Khodorkovsky, besides being a questionable 'advocate for democracy' due to the murky business deals in his past, had been irritating Putin for some time by heavily funding opposition parties in the Duma, courting the US, and presenting himself as a potential contender in the upcoming 2004 presidential elections.

Understandably this revolt of the Kremlin against big business introduced new uncertainty into Russia's political and economic future. At the same time, one conclusion is clear as ever: Russia continues to chart its own course on the long road from communism to liberal democracy and market economy, which has further diverged from the path taken by the successful reformers of Central and Eastern Europe. Some observers, nonetheless, consider the Khodorkovsky case to be an isolated incident that does not jeopardize the hard-won macroeconomic stabilization and the implementation of further reforms. Others suggest that, while Russia's course may not have shifted drastically, its bureaucracy is thriving, and it will grow more fraudulent and less pluralistic in the near term.[10] This debate is likely to persist in the future, as Vladimir Putin continues his second four-year term in the office following his landslide victory in the 2004 presidential elections.

On the eve of the elections Putin appointed a radically restructured new government, which suggests that he will push hard in his second term for reforms that were stalled in the first.[11] While this had excited many investors and economists, it did not seem to lift ordinary Russians out of the pervasive apathy towards political changes in the country. Together with the outcome of the elections, this seems to indicate that the general populace credits Putin with bringing stability to the sprawling country after the turbulent years of President Yeltsin. Indeed, after the elections Putin promised to continue to preserve stability and fight to increase the standard of living of the Russian people through implementing gradual reforms rather than suffering a series of painful jerks and jumps.

Regarding the country's liberal opposition, at the outset of transition it existed and posed some challenges to the administration in 1992–93 and 1996, but unfortunately it forced no changes from the Kremlin and has since been largely co-opted. Most sincere reformers exited the political system by the late 1990s, unable to counter the Kremlin's monopoly on power or compete against the money offered to it first by the West and then by oligarchs. Those liberal elements that remained within the system have adapted to the rules of the game, joining the 'payroll' of vested interests. While this practice may seem reminiscent of western-style lobbying, in the absence of clear rules and transparency, it only decayed the parliamentary system, and most votes in Parliament were cast according to the 'request' from the interested party.

The 2003 parliamentary election marked another important watershed in post-communist Russian politics.[12] Not only did it weaken the opposition further, as pro-Kremlin parties triumphed at the polls, but, most importantly, it brought ultimate defeat to what was left of the liberal opposition. Such a result could be explained by the fact that these parties, the Union of Right Forces and Yabloko (Apple), have lost the public's trust due to their unfulfilled promises and close ties with the oligarchs. The rest of the opposition will also find it extremely difficult to recover from such a setback. Critics have suggested that this outcome could, perhaps, be harmful to Russia's development as a democratic society, since a lack of checks and balances could make this system inflexible and suppressive.

Economic situation before the collapse of the Soviet Union

Despite lingering problems, Russia has clearly made substantial headway since the eve of 19 August 1991, when the country's economy was in a shambles. By the end of the 1980s the Soviet Union was running fiscal deficits in excess of 6 per cent of GDP as a result of enormous military expenditures, the subsidization of prices, and tremendous economic waste and theft.[13] With limited opportunities to borrow, deficits were financed by monetary emission, which, in turn, led to inflation and shortages. Inflation exceeded 100 per cent in 1989, the result of monetary emission and the government's loss of nominal wage control, while keeping prices constant. In short, too much money was chasing too few goods. The accruing foreign debt, which was used to partly finance the budget deficit, added to the severity of the situation. By 1989, debt was equivalent to almost 59 per cent of GDP and high debt service costs deterred further foreign borrowing. External trade shocks, mainly a significant decrease in the price of oil in 1986, further complicated the situation and the current account deficit reached 4 per cent of GDP by 1989.[14]

Falling output, a result of the collapse of industrial production in state-owned enterprises following shifts in demand and failures of supply planning, further aggravated the situation. In 1991, output fell by 12.8 per cent.[15] While official statistics recorded unemployment levels as negligible, morale and productivity was low and the workers' overall mood could be summarized by the famous Soviet expression 'they pretend to pay us, we pretend to work'.

Constant shortages and growth in real incomes created a growing demand for consumer goods and services, resulting in the vigorous expansion of the underground economy. The official and unofficial sectors intertwined, because every person and every enterprise that had an opportunity did business 'on the side', typically during official work hours and employing state assets. This informal business accounted for more than 10 per cent of labour time and up to one-third of household incomes by the mid-1980s.[16]

Perhaps sensing better than others that the economic collapse was imminent, the ruling Communist Party elites, the Nomenklatura, moved to extract the most benefit out of the state assets. Describing the situation at the time, one observer noted that 'the greater the economic chaos and confusion, the greater the opportunities for personal enrichment'.[17] The Law on Cooperatives introduced by President Gorbachev in 1986 and the later Law on Enterprises (1990) theoretically represented a step towards private ownership of businesses, but in reality allowed the spin-off of state property and assets. This was especially evident in export industries, where the Nomenklatura, state enterprise managers, and newly emerged 'businessmen' prospered tremendously through transfer pricing and the abuse of a dual exchange rate system. Subsequently, numerous quasi-state trading companies and banks were established to carry out these groups' interests. Thus, Russia's economic transition of the 1990s did not 'invent' corruption; rather, it vastly expanded the opportunities for illicit activity that was already taking place under communism.

The West was also well aware of the economic difficulties, and in early 1990 it summoned the International Monetary Fund (IMF) and the World Bank to organize conferences on how to revive the Russian economy. During the Gorbachev years, both Soviet and western economists also proposed plans on how to stem the country's devastating crisis. But the full political collapse of the Soviet Union caught many observers by surprise, and the subsequent turn towards a market economy proved to be a combustible mix in the Russian environment.

The path to economic reform

The failed coup d'état of August 1991 delivered the final blow to the Soviet house of cards. With the republics breaking away, budgetary, trade, payment, and delivery systems in the new countries were in total disarray and needed immediate restoration. Russia initially appeared to benefit from retaining the ownership of a vast amount of natural resources, but it also assumed the Soviet Union's foreign debt obligations, which amounted to $60 billion at that time.[18]

The IMF played a key role in shaping Russia's economic reform programme, with considerable input from the United States. The final model chosen was based on the general principles of the neoliberal economic model, known as 'the Washington Consensus', while integrating some of the lessons from Eastern Europe's early experiences with transition. Russian President Boris Yeltsin at first favoured Chinese industrial policy, given his bias towards authoritarianism and his background as a construction engineer, but the international advisors prevailed in advocating the monetarist neoliberal policies.[19]

The proposed reform model contained four main elements. The first was macroeconomic stabilization, which entailed tightening fiscal and credit policies, and addressing internal and external imbalances. The second was price and market reform, which consisted of removal of price controls, trade liberalization, and creation of competitive factor markets. The third was enterprise reform and private sector development, including establishing and clarifying property rights, facilitating entry and exit of firms, and restructuring of enterprises. The fourth was institutional reform, which foresaw redefining the role of the state, legal and regulatory reform, reform of government institutions (tax administration, budget and expenditure control, monetary control) and the social safety net.[20] This framework became a foundation for Russia's programme with the IMF and the World Bank.[21] While the main reform objectives were determined and generally agreed upon, the issue of *sequencing and speed* emerged as key points of contention.

The struggle for stabilization

Fiscal policy Russia faced three main challenges in stabilizing the macroeconomy: establishing an effective tax system, improving fiscal management, and grappling with the problem of barter and non-payment. The government established a tax system in the beginning of the transition period, but to date has struggled to make it truly efficient. Underpaid government employees used tax and customs collection as a means of survival through extortion and acceptance of bribes at expense of state revenues. Local governments' ability to set taxes at excessive levels on top of the already high federal tax added to the distortion. In many regions, combined tax rates reached over 100 per cent, creating an intolerable environment for business. Tax evasion was widespread and tax collection levels were extremely poor.

On the expenditure side, fiscal management was complicated by the continuation of Soviet-era budget practices, such as explicit and implicit subsidies to state and quasi-state enterprises as well as households. Enterprise managers often lobbied for such subsidies, preaching social catastrophe if they could not pay their workers. The subsidies eventually became an unsustainable drain on the country's balance sheets. A serious non-payments crisis also haunted Russia throughout the mid-1990s. High non-payments to large natural monopolies were compensated, or offset, by tax evasion by those companies, which subsequently put an extraordinary burden of implicit subsidy on the budget.

To further complicate matters, barter emerged as a common means of payment by the mid-1990s. This was especially true among state enterprises, as cash collection levels were extremely low, and some workers were paid with local products – including cement slabs and women's undergarments. Barter also stemmed from the inability of wasteful enterprises to sell their unwanted products, and from the abuse of the system by commodity-producing companies that sought significant tax write-offs on inflated prices. The presence of barter in the Russian economy persisted until after the 1998 crash, when state finances were tightened and money became the dominant form of payment. Its share in industrial sales has dropped to 20 per cent in 2001 from 50 per cent in 1998 and the downward trend continued thereafter.[22]

Inadequate tax collection, high expenditure obligations, and subsidies resulted in tremendous fiscal deficits, as seen in Table 3.1. As a result, arrears accumulated to public sector employees (such as teachers and doctors) and pensioners, in some cases reaching annual salary levels. Efforts to improve the macroeconomy were undermined by the government's ability to attract financing for its deficits by issuing government securities at very high rates, with the participation of foreign investors after 1996. This policy was a key factor leading to the 1998 financial crisis that resulted in a complete drying up of any sort of financing.

The 1998 crisis may have been a 'blessing in disguise' because it made Russia's leaders finally acknowledge that such fiscal policies were unsustainable and that they had to take steps to place hard budget constraints on state enterprises, streamline the tax system and follow overall prudent fiscal policies, resulting in the establishment of the Oil Stabilization Fund. Russia achieved its

Table 3.1 Russia: inflation, growth, fiscal deficit, and FDI, 1991–2002

Year	*Growth (%/GDP)*	*Fiscal balance (%/GDP)*	*Inflation (%)*	*Net FDI (US$ Billion)*
1991	–12.8 to – 5.0	–6.0	91.4	—
1992	–14.5	–10.4	1734.7	0.7
1993	–8.7	–6.5	878.8	0.9
1994	–12.7	–11.4	307.5	0.63
1995	–4.1	–4.8	198	2.07
1996	–3.6	–8.9	47.9	2.53
1997	1.4	–7.9	14.7	4.78
1998	–5.3	–8.0	27.8	2.5
1999	6.3	–3.3	85.7	2.81
2000	10.0	2.7	20.1	2.48
2001	5.0	3.0	18.6	2.39
2002*	4.3	0.6	15.1	2.13

Sources: IMF, *World Economic Outlook*, September 2003.
Notes: [1] Enlarged government overall balance, on commitment basis.
*Estimates.

first primary fiscal surplus (before debt-interest payments) of 3 per cent in 1999. The first overall budget surplus of 2.7 per cent was reached in 2000 and has been sustained ever since. Although a significant accomplishment, the Russian experience demonstrates the drawbacks of delaying fiscal discipline.

Monetary policy In the early 1990s, Russia's central bank was thrust into a completely new role: the nascent market economy required an independent but accountable Central Bank to maintain a low inflationary environment through the available instruments, such as prime interest rates, reserve requirements and open market operations. In the 1993 Constitution, the Central Bank gained independence from the government to conduct monetary policy and also took complete control of money issuance.

The Central Bank moved quickly to establish much higher salaries, attracting more qualified staff than in other government bodies, and soon outpacing the Ministry of Finance in terms of technology and expertise. However, independence did not translate into accountability and the Central Bank made some very bad policy choices during the early transition period. The Bank initially maintained a loose monetary policy by providing cheap directed credits to enterprises through monetary emission, causing both inflation and currency collapse, while helping many connected individuals to enrich themselves with state money. The Central Bank mistakenly resisted tightening monetary policy through interest rate increases, instead holding interest rates below inflation rates, pushing inflation higher and allowing gains from cheap credits. This also prompted a significant demonetization, as the population bought hard currency and commodities with their rubles instead of holding money in savings accounts. The deficiencies in the supervisory role of the Central Bank were made evident by its tolerance of banks' shoddy accounting practices and double book keeping designed for tax avoidance, which obviously led to an inadequate oversight of the banking sector in the early to mid-1990s.

By the mid-1990s, high inflation levels became so unsustainable that monetary policy had to be significantly tightened and interest rates were set as high as 150 per cent. Significant fiscal deficits crowded out private investment and further contributed to high interest rates. Six-month ruble-denominated government obligations (GKOs) were yielding 212 per cent just before the 1996 presidential elections, and only decreased to 144 per cent thereafter. The 1998 financial crisis brought such policies to an end. As the government defaulted on approximately $70 billion (in nominal terms) of its GKOs and financing dried up, it had to pursue very strict fiscal and monetary policies, and interest rates decreased considerably. When monetary policy became somewhat loose again in 1999, inflation skyrocketed to 85.7 per cent, as seen in Table 3.2. At present, inflation lies in the range of 12–15 per cent, which is a consequence of a passive sterilization policy by the Central Bank and its decision to keep the ruble depreciating, as well as of continuing increases in utility tariffs and other administered prices.

The toxic combination of poor policy choices, weak supervisory practices, resistance to banking reform, dubious cross-shareholdings of quasi-state banks, and high employee salaries soon made the Central Bank a political target in the post-Yeltsin era. In 2001, the Parliament and the government seriously considered stripping the Central Bank of its independence, and in 2002, the Parliament passed several amendments to the Central Bank Law that require increased monitoring of the Bank. In addition to the Parliament's Audit Chamber, supervision is now handled by a new National Banking Council consisting of members appointed by the government, the President, and the Parliament. This increased political oversight may generate new conflicts of interest at the Bank. The new management team at the Central Bank, which assumed its position in 2002, however, does bring hope for a more responsible monetary policy and banking sector reforms in the future. Unfortunately, the free-wheeling policies adopted by the Central Bank during the early years of transition have seriously hampered the financial reform process in Russia.

Growth As shown in Table 3.2, Russia's loose monetary policy severely undermined growth, as the growth cycle appeared to be highly correlated with the inflation pattern, except in the period 1999–2002. However, a range of other factors also affected Russia's growth rate at this time. In 1992, GDP plummeted by 14.5 per cent – a much greater fall than was initially anticipated. The massive contraction stemmed from a variety of factors, including structural changes, a sharp increase in unregistered output, foreign trade shocks and reduction of implicit trade subsidies, the

Table 3.2 Russia: growth and inflation, 1991–2002

Year	*1991*	*1992*	*1993*	*1994*	*1995*	*1996*	*1997*	*1998*	*1999*	*2000*	*2001*	*2002*
Growth	–12.8	–14.5	–8.7	–12.7	–4.2	–3.6	1.4	–5.3	6.3	10.0	5.0	4.3
Inflation	91.4	1734.7	878.8	307.5	198	47.9	14.7	27.8	85.7	20.1	18.6	15.1

Source: IMF, *World Economic Outlook*, September 2003.

collapse of defence production and consumption, and the end of wasteful socialist investment. The severe collapse in output may have been exaggerated due to systemic overreporting of production during the Soviet era.[23] However, there is little doubt that the decline was extraordinary and had a severe impact on the Russian economy.

Few observers expected that Russia would suffer from seven years of continuous recession, but there were a number of reasons for this phenomenon. They include the gradual pace of structural adjustment, high and persistent inflation until the mid-1990s, low foreign direct and domestic investment, limited export growth in non-commodity sectors, large fiscal deficits, the absence of a functioning banking system and corruption. Russia marked its first year of growth in 1999, due to a drastically tighter fiscal policy, higher oil prices, a surge in exports and a revival of domestic production following the depreciation of the ruble. While this trend continued for the next two years, Russia's prospects for steady growth remain impeded by four factors: (1) failure to diversify an economy dominated by large commodity-producing firms; (2) the banking system's inability to channel money to sectors with high growth potential; (3) low productivity; and (4) inadequate implementation of reforms. Unless these issues are properly addressed soon, growth will not reach levels sufficient for a noticeable increase in the living standards of the Russian population.[24]

Price and market reforms

Prices The liberalization of prices was one of the most controversial and complex decisions that faced the Yeltsin government during the early years of transition. In 1992 the government liberalized 80 per cent of wholesale prices and 90 per cent of retail prices in value terms, but indirect price controls continued to be imposed on state trade, which limited the effect of price adjustments. As a result, shortages disappeared only gradually, and there were notable price disparities between the state and private sectors, as well as between formal and informal trade, and between regions, the latter due to the locally imposed controls.

Despite several aforementioned complications, on the whole deregulation of consumer prices was fairly straightforward. This was not the case, though, for freeing commodity prices, especially in terms of energy and metals, which ended up being extremely contentious because of the practice of transfer pricing. Managers of energy and commodity companies were interested in low state prices for commodities so they could buy domestically for their private accounts and sell abroad at a much higher price. Prices for essential foods, public transport, utilities and agricultural procurement were also kept below cost recovery levels. Although intended to lessen the burden on the population, low commodity and agriculture prices were beneficial to rent-seekers.[25]

These disparities led to inflation of 1,500–2,500 per cent by the end of 1992 (Table 3.2). Hyperinflation resulted not only from initial price adjustment and incomplete price liberalization but also from insufficient fiscal and monetary tightening early on. The monetary overhang, a legacy of the pre-transition years, exacerbated the situation. Hyperinflation was extremely harmful in social terms, wiping out personal savings, and devastating the elderly and other vulnerable groups. Confidence in the already weak ruble suffered, resulting in the flight to foreign currencies. The volume of money as a percentage of GDP plummeted. 'Payments' dollarization of the economy grew dramatically, and the dollar remains the preferred store of value in Russia.[26]

Trade In tandem with price liberalization, trade was completely liberalized in January 1992. This led to trade off-the-lots or from small kiosks in the streets, and a parallel underground industry of racketeering blossomed alongside a phenomenon known in the West as 'providing protection' but termed 'providing the roof' (*krysha*) in Russia.[27] Illegal business related to crime skyrocketed, while law enforcement officials focused their efforts on gaining personally from the emerging black market. After a few very turbulent years, especially for street traders, the situation stabilized. Large stores and shopping malls were built and small traders were permitted to operate under the license and from the premises of a kiosk (*palatka*), and they have become an integral part of Russian life. Russia's economy today is frequently perceived to consist mostly of a few large industrial groups (FIGs) and hundreds of thousands of kiosks.[28] Unfortunately, the growth of small and medium-sized enterprises (SMEs) has been hampered by administrative hurdles to establishing a business and by a lack of affordable credit.

Exchange rate When the ruble was allowed to float in 1992, it initially plunged (Table 3.3). Another serious currency crisis occurred in 1993, known as 'Black Tuesday'. A currency band was introduced in 1995, pegging the ruble to the US dollar to avoid destabilizing fluctuations in the exchange rate. The dollar was a natural choice for the peg, due to the high level of dollarization of the Russian economy and the dollar denomination of much of its foreign debt and commodity exports. While the introduction of a band helped to stabilize prices, the policy was undermined by loose fiscal policy. The IMF initially advocated this exchange rate arrangement, and was later summoned to bail Russia out of the crisis it produced. Similarly, the IMF's advice on capital account liberalization, such as allowing foreign participation in the government debt market, was given prematurely. The exchange rate stability provided a sense of false security, which together with high interest rates on government securities attracted very significant short-term foreign investment flows. When debt servicing became unsustainable in 1998, the government defaulted and abandoned the exchange rate band. This was a devastating event, as foreign capital surged out of the country and the ruble fell fivefold. Currently, the Central

Table 3.3 Russia: exchange rate, 1991–2002

	Year											
	1991	*1992*	*1993*	*1994*	*1995*	*1996*	*1997*	*1998*	*1999*	*2000*	*2001*	*2002*
Exchange rate (Rubles per US dollar)	0.0017	0.22	0.93	2.21	4.56	5.12	5.78	9.71	24.62	28.13	29.17	31.35

Source: IMF, *World Economic Outlook*, September 2003.

Bank of Russia maintains a floating exchange rate arrangement in principle, while in reality it manages its exchange rate, which is not unusual for a country with fragile economic stability.

Having liberalized the current account for tourism and trade and capital accounts for some private inflows, there is still no full currency convertibility in Russia because the Central Bank requires exporters to surrender a part of their foreign exchange earnings and maintains restrictions on certain current and capital account transactions. Although full liberalization of the external account is warranted in order to encourage trade and investment activity, this should be coordinated with the further strengthening of the domestic financial system and of the legal and regulatory environment. Only in this way will the authorities ensure a continuous flow of foreign exchange while minimizing the growth of un-hedged foreign exchange positions.

Imports and exports Russia's import liberalization went rather smoothly and caused little controversy. Since the initial shortages were so grave and domestic production was so distorted, all sorts of imports were welcome. However, as in other areas, lawlessness and corruption were rampant. Over-invoicing of imports allowed significant capital flight. Corruption in customs deprived the state of its due trade tax revenues as well as endangered the population through the influx of expired foodstuffs. Protectionism was high in some areas, which dissuaded foreigners from importing capital goods to set up production in Russia, because it was much cheaper for Russian traders to import ready-to-use goods. This hindered domestic production and made foreign goods rather expensive.

By contrast, export liberalization was highly controversial, especially with regard to commodity exports like energy. First, efforts to raise trade tax revenues through export tariffs and quotas were undermined by powerful interest groups that bribed officials to escape taxes and payments for quotas. Powerful exporters also lobbied hard for regulation and access privileges to quotas and licenses for personal gain, taking advantage of low commodity prices in the domestic market. Deregulation was strongly opposed by everyone with access to these exports, including enterprise managers, traders, bankers and state officials. According to popular rhetoric, the full liberalization of exports would lead to mass exporting and consequent shortages of key commodities because local currency had little value. In reality, such limited liberalization created great opportunities for rent-seeking while there were still persistent and severe energy shortages across the country.

Energy price subsidization eventually created too much pressure on the budget. Initially, there were also fears that liberalized energy prices would force many enterprises to go bankrupt or raise their product prices drastically, thereby driving up inflation. In reality, enterprises that could not pay their electricity bill were unproductive and stayed afloat only because of state subsidies; they should have been either restructured or closed in the first place. Schools and hospitals were, in turn, cheated of transfers from their regional governments since they were running budget deficits and could not pay their obligations. Energy price liberalization continues to be a key issue on the agenda of the Putin government, balancing the need to cut subsidies and raise tariffs while still guaranteeing sufficient and affordable energy for household consumption.

Enterprise reform and restructuring

Privatization The flaws in Russia's privatization process are notorious, and they included insider trading, backroom dealing, crony capitalism, and asset stripping. Although clearly necessary, the creation of private property through the privatization of state-owned assets in Russia generated new social and economic distortions. The process had two main objectives: the improvement of economic efficiency in a significant number of crippled enterprises,[29] and the redistribution of formerly state-owned property to create the massive middle class of private owners that was widely perceived as necessary for social and political stability.[30] What went right and wrong in terms of the speed, sequencing and beneficiaries of Russia's privatization process remains controversial today, but there is little doubt that the process was severely tarnished.

Land ownership emerged as a key issue early in the process. Communist and agrarian parties and other vested interests were against almost any type of agricultural land privatization, arguing that it would lead to monopolization by rich Russian owners, or, worse, foreigners. After more than ten years of transition, leasing state land by individuals or collectives will likely remain in general practice. In 2001, Russia passed a new law allowing for privatization of some of the agricultural land by Russians and urban land (except at the country's borders) by citizens and foreigners, but considerable administrative hurdles to land privatization prevented a successful transfer of ownership. It was, however, the privatization of state enterprises that ended up posing the major challenge to Russia's economic future as a capitalist state.

Enterprise privatization in Russia was conducted in two stages: a voucher stage and a 'money' stage. The voucher stage, characterized by free distribution of formerly state-owned property to every citizen, was concerned mainly with social justice, while the 'money' stage was intended to increase efficiency, attract managerial expertise, and generate significant state revenue. While efficiency and social justice may seem like competing concerns, they were compatible in this particular case. Such a massive transfer of resources to the private sector, in the name of efficiency, would not have been politically feasible without the provision of some minimum benefit for the Russian population, which for decades was considered the owner of the country's property and resources.

In 1992, the Russian government distributed 150 million privatization vouchers – one per person – with each voucher having a nominal value of 10,000 rubles in 1 January 1992 prices. The vouchers could be invested in any enterprise identified for privatization at auctions open to the public. Enterprise employees were granted a privileged position, able to choose from several options during the privatization of their company, which could include the amount of shares, the price, and the quantity that had to be bought with vouchers. The voucher stage of privatization had an expiration date of 1 January 1994, but was only fully completed in July 1994. The 'money' stage was intended as a continuous process. Different methods were used, depending on the size of the companies.[31] For reasons of national security, about 30 per cent of all enterprises, mostly energy companies and components of the military-industrial complex, were not subject to privatization according to normal procedures. On paper, the results of voucher privatization looked impressive. By end of 1997, 130,000 formerly state-owned enterprises (out of a total of 267,000 non-agricultural enterprises) had become privately owned or stock corporations.[32]

However, the reality sharply contradicted the apparent success of voucher privatization, and social obligations to citizens were fulfilled in name only. While every citizen had an opportunity to receive a voucher, the process was hampered by poor organization, a lack of financial transparency, and the failure to educate the public about its options. This diminished the intended outcome by excluding the majority of the population from the process. Few individuals foresaw potential earnings in buying vouchers at face value on the street for resale to investment funds or enterprise insiders. Many of the shares purchased with vouchers simply 'burned' – that is, got lost in the process of enterprises re-writing their books. Relatively few owners recognized the value of the shares or legally pursued their ownership rights.

Some people invested vouchers in newly created funds that financed enterprises. However, no investment fund could hold more than 25 per cent of total shares in a single enterprise, which limited their influence. Seeking to protect their control, enterprise insiders opposed ownership by these funds, forcing many of them into bankruptcy from speculative activities in short-term investing. The funds merely provided a quick way to waste vouchers. As enterprise managers moved to thwart privatization, employees were coerced into choosing a privatization option that allowed managers to buy a controlling block of shares. As a result, the newly privatized enterprises, with no capital and old management, did not look very different from the original pre-transition enterprises. The goals of achieving financial stability, increasing economic efficiency and creating a competitive environment remained largely unfulfilled.

In July 1994, the second, or 'money', stage of privatization began with the purpose of attracting investment capital and strategic investors with managerial expertise and interest in improving the economic efficiency of enterprises. By presidential decree, larger companies were transformed into stockholding companies. Unfortunately, investment bids and efforts to sell assets of bankrupt enterprises were under-utilized approaches. Instead, starting in 1995, stockholder companies were mainly created through buyouts of leased companies. By 1997, this stage of privation had fallen short of its aspirations. Only 15,000 enterprises had been privatized, compared to 122,000 between 1992 and 1994. Privatized companies tended to be small (less than 200 employees) and 58 per cent operated in the trade and service sectors.[33]

There were, however, some notable exceptions. In August 1995, a presidential decree authorized the sale of federal shares in 23 of the largest stockholding companies, including four commodity-producing and -exporting companies that were giants of Russian industry. Some of the largest ones included oil companies – Lukoil, Yukos, and Sidanko – and the world's largest nickel producer, Norilsk Nickel. This now-infamous operation was termed 'loans-for-shares', where the government pledged shares as collateral for loans from a few private banks. In 1996, the government failed to repay these loans and the banks gained control of the shares. The enterprises were sold in this scheme for bargain prices. One classic example was the sale of 5 per cent of the shares in Russia's premier oil company, Lukoil, for around $35 million, while its equivalent market price (offered to foreigners) was on the order of $250 million.[34] Many other sales show similarly disturbing disparities between the sale and actual market price. Worse, many of the banks offering loans were essentially bankrupt, and kept afloat only with government deposits. Therefore banks received precious shares, while the state received loans originating from government deposits. While it was perceived that, given the lack of capital, banks would rush to the market to sell their shares to foreigners, this did not materialize. Instead, banks used their shares to strengthen control over these very profitable enterprises and to form financial and industrial giants, which now dominate the economy.

When this 'loans-for-shares' ordeal came to light, it scandalized the Russian public. In 1996, the Accounting Office of the Russian Parliament concluded that the projected revenues to the state from the 'money' stage of privatization were under-collected by a factor of 280. The government came under a lot of fire, but largely prevailed in the many suits filed against it.

While the Russian government is principally at fault for the flawed privatization, external advisers like the IMF, the World Bank and the US administration must share some blame for the debacle. The uncertainty of President Yeltsin's re-election in 1996 gave the international community reason to approve loans to counter popular discontent. During the 1990s, the Clinton administration viewed the stability of Boris Yeltsin's rule as the linchpin of US–Russia policy. This political concern often prevailed over economic prudence in matters of lending and finance to Russia.

Noreena Hertz, who advised the Russian government on privatization with the World Bank in 1991, argues that external advisers did not sufficiently consider the human costs during the first stages of privatization. Rather, their goal was simply the removal of assets from state control so that 'communism would never reappear'. Political realities were considered to be of secondary importance. With country engagement limited to brief meetings in Moscow, the top external decision makers lacked familiarity with what was happening on the ground, leading to misconceptions about the Russian situation.[35]

In summary, Russia's privatization process accomplished the redistribution of the state-owned property, but with the exceptions of real estate and small-scale enterprises, it was unfair, corrupt, and fell short of creating many profitable domestic industries. For the average Russian, 'privatization' is a dirty word, and the process is commonly referred to as 'prihvatization', an adaptation of the word '*prihvatit*', meaning 'to grab and go'. Moreover, while private enterprise ownership was created in the atmosphere of shadowy laws, this did not lead to the adoption of strong laws protecting property rights after the privatization process was complete. Under such circumstances, the 2003 Khodorkovsky affair only underlined the insecurity of property rights and the discretion available to the state. It has once again ignited fears of re-nationalization despite the government's assurances that this would be detrimental to the economy and the society.

Banking The development of a well-functioning banking sector is one of Russia's major challenges. In Soviet times, banks were principally used to channel money to wherever it was requested, with no practice of credit appraisal and no notion of collateral. After 1991, Russia's banking system had to be rebuilt from scratch, with a 12 per cent cap on foreign ownership and the exclusion of foreign banks from retail activity. An estimated 2,500 banks emerged in Russia during the first two years of transition. While some banks succeeded in turning a profit, most failed to channel national savings to the productive sectors of the economy and stimulate economic growth. Instead, the activities of Russian banks included a number of schemes that contradicted basic principles of market economics.

The Russian government initially used private banks for many of its transactions. One new bank practice entailed 'borrowing' government funds at very low interest rates to exchange them for hard currency, lend to importers for a short term at a much higher interest rate, and deposit the received money back into government accounts. The interest rate, the depreciating ruble and high inflation combined to make this scheme very profitable, but it delayed pensions and government employee salaries when banks lacked the money to pay on the government's behalf. In addition, many private deposits vanished from banks through ponzi schemes that eventually bankrupted the banks and innocent depositors alike. Many Russians believed claims that interest rates of 300 per cent were possible in a normal economy and were devastated when their savings were lost. While this is a widespread phenomenon in countries that lack a developed financial sector and a strong legal system, in Russia it further fuelled popular discontent toward the capitalist transition.

The brief stabilization of 1995–96 reduced the opportunities for easy profits, and many larger banks started buying shares in enterprises, leading to the loan-for-shares scandal and to the creation of financial industrial groups (FIGs). Banks also profited by buying government bonds at astronomical interest rates, resulting from the government's significant financing needs. This kept lending to the private sector, especially to SMEs, at very low levels.

The 1998 financial crisis brought Russia's banking system to its knees. As the government defaulted on its domestic debt and the ruble devaluation forced settlement of expensive exchange rate contracts, the banks' capital depleted. Several hundred banks went bankrupt and had their licenses revoked. As in 1992, ordinary citizens lost their ruble savings to inflation, but this time their dollar deposits also vanished because there was no deposit guarantee plan in place. Consequently, individuals, retail and corporate customers diverted their accounts to the State Savings Bank, which at present has a near-monopoly, holding 53 per cent of total deposits (69 per cent of household deposits) in the system.[36] In 2004, more than six years after the crisis, the situation has improved as many banks became profitable and more transparent, and the government has prepared a blueprint for further reform of the financial sector. Yet tangible results in the establishment of a viable banking system in Russia are still to be seen.

Institutional reform

Russia's economic transformation failed to adequately address the task of institution building, and today it is generally accepted that the neoliberal approach underestimated the significant need for institutional, legal and regulatory reforms early in the transition. In the absence of functional institutions, shady privatizations, banking crises, ponzi schemes, tax evasion, corruption, economic and general crime thrived in Russia. A functional market economy requires a state that enforces the laws adopted by the legislature, and a judiciary that protects its citizens from damages by fairly meting out justice. The pre-existing link between political power and the administration of justice must be severed. While Russia changed much of its legal system in the 1990s, the country remains a 'shadowy world of flexible laws', where the creation of 'a decent system of law and order to make ordinary Russians more secure is still far off'.[37] Weak governance, rent-seeking, and the government's inability to enforce the law coherently continue to hurt Russia's prospects for faster growth and development.

Russia's insufficient attempts at institutional reform highlight a deeper debate about the pace and sequence of reforms in transition economies. Some economists argue that the fast pace of reform is essential, while others support gradualism in order to reduce social costs.[38] Quick reform implementation in the absence of a functional institutional framework significantly reduces the benefits of reforms and creates opportunities for rent-seeking and opposition to reforms by vested interests. But gradual adjustment also allows ample time to build and mobilize opposition to reform.[39]

Whatever the economic merits of each approach, the strategy undertaken in Russia's case was driven mainly by political considerations alien to the external advisers. Still, the US administration, the IMF, the World Bank, and other international actors certainly share some of the blame for Russia's woes. Perhaps their two most serious mistakes were neglecting the Russian population's perception of the policies they prescribed, and placing too much trust in the group of reformers they chose as partners in the reform process. The policy prescriptions proceeded directly from the Washington Consensus, and were not tailored to the fairly objective cultural and psychological characteristics of the Russian people. US advisers worked closely with a select group of reformers – dominated by Yeltsin – overlooking many Russian experts and often collaborating with professionals who used their positions for personal enrichment. To be fair, western advisers could not have been expected to fully master the complex and unstable political situation in Russia, nor predict the corruptibility of individual technocrats. Nevertheless, the Russian experience indicates that broader consultation with a diverse group of policy makers, greater attention to public opinion, and a more flexible policy-making approach would have vastly increased the chances for a more successful transition.

Social consequences of reforms

The majority of Russian people suffered a substantial degree of hardship throughout the reform period created by the hyperinflation of 1992, a plunge in real incomes, the loss of savings in 1992 and 1998, and the lack of an affordable energy supply, among other factors. Chronic unemployment added to the stresses of Russian populace. While official unemployment fluctuated at sustainable levels of 5–13 per cent during the reform period (see Table 3.4), these data exclude many people who stayed with their enterprises without collecting salaries in order to secure state pensions and maintain career standing. In addition, many Russians work in two jobs, engage in unofficial activities, and often rely on their families for support. Russia has a large informal sector, which, depending on the season, employs around 10 million people or up to 13–15 per cent of the total working population.[40] In addition to the troubled labour market, the

Table 3.4 Russia: unemployment (%)

	Year											
	1991	*1992*	*1993*	*1994*	*1995*	*1996*	*1997*	*1998*	*1999*	*2000*	*2001*	*2002*
Unemployment	0.10	5.20	5.29	6.88	8.14	9.26	10.81	11.64	12.63	10.42	8.97	8.00

Source: World Bank, *World Development Indicators Database*, 2001; IMF, *World Economic Outlook*, 2003.

social consequences of the transition were also felt in the areas of income distribution, social assistance, health and education.

As income fell and inequality increased, Russia's Gini coefficient of income inequality rose from 0.26 in 1991 to 0.40 by 1997, where it remained throughout 2001.[41] True inequality may be higher still since underreporting of income is widespread. Privatization contributed to the drastic increase in inequality, by producing unequal distribution of ownership that undermined the goal of creating a large, stable middle class. In 2004, private ownership is spread too thinly and financial resources remain in the hands of a powerful few. The stock market, while technically developed (one of a few bright spots), lacks depth, its capitalization is small, and trading is concentrated among a few large investors.

The fall in the average level of income and the growth in inequality are the two main reasons for the rise in the poverty indicators during the transition. By the turn of the century, an estimated 35 per cent of the population lived below the subsistence minimum.[42] While living standards declined across the board, single parent families and single older retirees were particularly hard hit, especially women. The transition also posed a challenge to Russia's social safety net. The Soviet system of social assistance had three categories of beneficiaries: individuals with special achievements (nomenklatura apparatchiki, cosmonauts, academics, Soviet reality writers, scientists), social insurance recipients (pensioners, temporary unemployed, and workers under hazardous conditions), and social safety net beneficiaries (mainly children and the disabled). The last category had the lowest priority and was financed from the budget on a residual basis.

In the early 1990s, Russia's fraying social safety net was ill-equipped to confront sharpening socioeconomic problems, including a rise in unemployment, increased poverty, new influxes of refugees and migrants, and non-payments of state salaries and pensions. At present, 70 per cent of Russia's population receives social benefits, but the level of assistance has not increased over the transition period, as shown in Table 3.5. The current system continues to greatly benefit the urban population, providing both monetary and 'shadow' benefits (housing, medical care, transportation and vacations). Not surprisingly, most promised social payments actually do not take place, or are provided in meager installments. The truly needy receive only one-third of the total sum of available funds and the current system provides benefits rather than security, contributing to social inequality.

Health care had been proclaimed as one of the main achievements of the Soviet regime, but in reality the sector suffered from focusing more on inputs (such as hospitals and beds) than on efficient utilization of resources and actual health standards. Despite some improvements in the last few years, health indicators dropped precipitously during the 1990s. Transition resulted in a deterioration of men's and women's reproductive health,

Table 3.5 Russia: state social expenditures as percentage of GDP, 1992–2002

	Year										
	1992	*1993*	*1994*	*1995*	*1996*	*1997*	*1998*	*1999*	*2000*	*2001*	*2002*
Health	2.5	3.1	3.2	2.3	2.8	3.3	2.6	2.4	3.2	3.2	3.5
Education	3.5	4.1	4.5	3.1	3.9	4.3	3.6	3.2	2.9	3.2	3.5
Social Policy	1.1	0.9	1.1	1.1	1.3	1.2	1.2	0.9	1.1	n/a	n/a

Source: IMF Statistical Database.

evidenced by an elevated number of pregnancy and birth complications, the high abortion rate (60 per cent), high maternal mortality, and the spread of sexually transmitted diseases.[43] Life expectancy declined sharply at the beginning of transition (from 64.4 years in 1989 to 57.3 years in 1994), with the steepest decline among males.[44]

There are several causes for the decline in public health during the transition period. First, experts posit that the new difficulties and general uncertainty associated with transition are behind epidemics of mental illness and alcoholism during the 1990s, which are themselves linked to lower life expectancy, homicide and suicide. Secondly, the quality of care received by the masses deteriorated during the 1990s, owing to both economic factors and governmental negligence. There were acute shortages of medical supplies and equipment, and low state salaries failed to motivate the public doctors upon which low-income people and pensioners relied. Also detrimental to the poor, the government maintains a general subsidy on pharmaceuticals that cheapens drugs for the middle and upper classes, but is insufficient to make drugs affordable for the most needy. The HIV/AIDS epidemic is another factor in Russia's declining public health that threatens to become a full-blown health care crisis. Negligence has complicated this problem, as the state's response to the crisis has been one of delayed acknowledgement and general inaction.

By contrast, Russia's relatively high levels of education will help the country to maintain stable economic growth. The adult literacy level stands at 99.5 per cent, and the number of students in higher education is 327 per 10,000 people.[45] By these parameters, Russia is superior to many economically developed countries. Indeed, the Russian education system is still widely perceived as world class, especially in the field of information technology.[46] Nonetheless, Russian education inherited problems from Soviet times, including inadequate spending on technology, low teacher salaries, 'residual' financing of education, and 'overproduction' of specialists in certain fields.

Russia's spending on education was maintained at about 3.6 per cent of GDP during the transition period and stood at 2.9 per cent of GDP in 2000 (Table 3.5), far below the region's better performers, such as the Czech Republic (5.1 per cent), Slovakia (5.0) and Lithuania (5.4). In addition, educational inequality in Russia surged during the 1990s, especially between rural and urban areas, and between poor and affluent regions. Newly decentralized management has meant that local authorities now struggle to balance education financing against other regional needs. Russian students' scores on international tests have decreased, and vary widely by school. The 'elite' education is provided by private schools as well as by state schools in favoured municipalities, while 'mass' education is provided in small towns and villages that constitute the majority of schools in the country. Due to the withdrawal of federal financing and limited ability to self-finance, these schools have suffered the most.

While the level of teachers and professors grew 25 per cent between 1989 and 1996,[47] there is a shortage of qualified teaching personnel, especially in the most popular disciplines, such as economics and jurisprudence. Moreover, the increase in the number of teachers comes at the expense of expenditures on textbooks, school supplies and school maintenance. Due to the low salary levels (averaging $100 per month), many teachers either leave the state education system or become indifferent to the quality of education they are providing.

In the final analysis, Russia's transition was clearly beset with failures in the social, political and economic realms, but important successes have also emerged. The discontinuation of shortages and the current abundance of food and consumer goods represent a remarkable break with the Soviet past. The ability to make personal employment decisions and the freedoms of travel, speech and expression are invaluable outcomes of the transition. Yet daily life remains a struggle for most Russians, evidenced by the falling social and health indicators. The paucity of knowledge about the free market, especially financial markets, as well as the failure of many state reforms during the 1990s, leave a deep distrust of the state and the free market in the minds of many. The complex mix of achievements and challenges in Russia provides ample lessons for Cuba.

Russian lessons for Cuba's future

The collapse of the Soviet Union certainly influenced the trajectory of the Cuban economy. Financial assistance through loans and implicit oil subsidies from the Soviet Union and the Council of Economic Assistance (CMEA) came to an end in 1992, forcing Cuba to start adjusting to new circumstances. There are similarities in the way in which both countries were forced to confront external shocks and domestic economic declines, and distinct parallels exist between the events in Russia in 1991 and in Cuba shortly thereafter. Many elements of Cuba's reforms are reminiscent of pre-transition Russia, such as private food markets, special stores, limited self-employment, cooperatives, skill mismatch in the labour market, a dual exchange rate, and a black market for goods. During the 1990s, Cuba's economic performance in some areas even appeared favourable compared to contemporary Russia. The main difference remains that the acceptance of market principles for the new economic order in Russia came with a complete change of political ideology, whereas Cuba's reforms had been implemented partially and under the same government.

Political transition The liberalization of the Cuban economy in 1993 was commenced by the political establishment of Fidel Castro, in power since 1959.[48] While some Cubans became more open in countering the official line of thinking, naturally many are still in favour of preserving the most obvious achievements of the communist regime: free education and health care. In June 2002, the Cuban government moved to formally enshrine one-party socialism in the constitution as the permanent system of government. This suggests that socialism in Cuba might not be supplanted any time soon by another political or economic system.[49] Nonetheless, as partial opening of the economy is already bringing economic benefits to Cubans, many are presumed to be increasingly supportive of further liberalization. While the political establishment remains in power, Cuba may be best suited for an economic model like the one successfully employed in China and Vietnam. This model allows for further market-oriented reforms, including the establishment of small and medium-sized enterprises, and openness to trade and investment.

As the example of Russia shows, the evolution of political transition is difficult to predict. Cuba reflects this fact, where dramatic regime change does not appear imminent. Cuba may lack the necessary elements for change that were present in Eastern Europe and Russia, such as a structured and organized opposition that presents a viable alternative to the current regime. The cohesiveness of the political elite will be an important variable in determining Castro's successor. If Cuba's political elite remains united, then Cuba is more likely to undergo a process of slow reform initiated from the above. In the event of fractionalization and power struggles at the top, it could be possible to have a more rapid and radical change coming from below. It would not be surprising if Cuba's future leader, while favouring more liberal economic ideas, nonetheless, emerges from the Party ranks, as occurred in Russia. It is worth noting that both Yeltsin and Putin emerged from the Soviet bureaucracy to guide Russia's fragile new democracy.

Fiscal and monetary policies Like Russia, Cuba possesses the ability to conduct responsible macroeconomic policies when there are few other options. Fiscal and monetary tightening was evident soon after 1993 as 'adjustment by brute force', when monetization of fiscal deficits was no longer possible from a social point of view.[50] In the early 1990s, Cuba boasted a much better record on the fiscal front, as its fiscal adjustment was much faster and sharper than Russia's. Establishing a tax system was also an important development, although its level of efficiency must increase. With limited statistical information, however, it is difficult to judge the effect of monetary and fiscal policies on growth in Cuba.

The Russian experience does provide several key lessons. Fiscal reform must commence early on with the objective of increasing budget revenues by expanding the tax base and reducing the informal economy. The government and the Central Bank must resist pressure from inefficient state enterprises for subsidies and credits under the pretence of preserving social stability. In addition, laid-off workers should be guaranteed subsistence while job creation in the private sector is encouraged to take root. While there is no doubt that fiscal and monetary management will be complicated by significant structural changes, prudence is, perhaps, the most valuable aspect in formulating appropriate policies.

Liberalization In the early 1990s, Cuba liberalized most agricultural prices (except for a few essential foods) and other prices in between 25 and 30 per cent of the economy. Such relaxation of controls, but not their full elimination, gave rise to a large unofficial private sector and deprived the state of its trade revenues. Full price liberalization (while protecting the most vulnerable groups in society) would be more appropriate, because it would create productive free trade markets beneficial to entrepreneurs and generate tax revenues for the state. While it could be argued that full liberalization of domestic prices will create hyperinflation as a result of peso devaluation, it needs to be recognized that Cuba is already at a stage of partial price deregulation. By pursuing full deregulation of prices, accompanied by tight fiscal and monetary policies, Cuba would only have to contend with a short-term surge in inflation. While shock therapy is politically unpopular, many successful reformers have chosen to 'bite the bullet' in order to achieve impressive results early in the transition and build support for a continued reform effort. The unpalatable alternative is to follow Russia's example of a prolonged period of high inflation resulting from loose fiscal and monetary policies. Experience in Russia also shows that price liberalization works best in concert with improving regulation of trade, suppressing economic crime, rooting out corruption among officials, and creating a strong legal environment.

In 2004, external liberalization in Cuba remains limited to legalizing the possession and use of hard currency, remittances from abroad, tourism and some foreign direct investment (FDI). This has greatly helped the country's balance of payments as inflows of foreign exchange cover interest on foreign debt and help finance imports. However, as in the pre-transition and early-transition Russia, this limited liberalization and the existence of a dual or triple exchange rate system is bound to distort prices and induce speculative arbitrage opportunities. Cuba's exchange bureaus, legalized in 1993, differ substantially from their Russian counterparts. Even if Cuba's trade is based on market demand and supply, the existence of a black currency market and the circulation of triple currencies point to significant distortions in the current system. On the other hand, special stores where dollar holders can buy goods unavailable elsewhere are very reminiscent of Russia's pre-transition stores called '*Berezkas*' ('Birch trees'). Russia's '*Berezkas*', like Cuba's dollar stores, were harbingers of negative social repercussions, such as sharpening inequalities and the ascendance of informal, or 'black', markets.

Over the past decade, Cuba has become an economy with high 'payments' dollarization and most likely it will remain so in the foreseeable future. On the supply side, despite limited trade with the United States, dollar-denominated remittance flows are very high, of the order of US$500 million to US$1 billion annually.[51] On the demand side, Cuba's continued status as a net importer of energy (priced in US dollars) will prolong its need for dollars. Cubans also share Russians' choice of the dollar as their preferred currency, reflecting the country's weak macroeconomic and structural fundamentals, including unclear government policies and past irresponsible fiscal policies. While Russia has made progress, Cuba still exhibits an unsustainable exchange rate policy, a politically constrained Central Bank, and an inefficient banking sector. The dollarization phenomenon, however, is very common in other emerging market and developing countries. It is not considered to be a major impediment to development when the macroeconomic environment is still vulnerable and structural reforms are yet to be completed. In cases where countries have experienced extreme price volatility and capital flight, dollarization has often played a key role in the re-monetization of the economy. However, in the longer term, if the country reaches 'financial' or 'real' dollarization, while maintaining a fixed exchange rate, this could create risks in the financial sector, mostly in currency loan portfolios. It can likewise undermine the ability of the central bank to serve as 'lender of last resort'.[52]

Cuba's decision on the appropriate exchange rate arrangement could be guided by the following considerations: the size of the economy and its openness, trade linkages, the pattern of external shocks, history of inflation, willingness to give up monetary policy, flexibility of fiscal policy and labour markets, the level of international reserves and debt denomination. Since Cuba is a small island economy, the transition could start off with a hard peg to the US dollar (supported by a high level of remittances) to control for inflation during the liberalization of prices. However, as time goes by and inflation subsides, greater exchange rate flexibility may be warranted to avoid building dangerous imbalances as happened in Russia.

Given Cuba's high dependence on both export and import industries, it will be vital to develop an institutional framework to steer these industries, like a tariff system and quality regulation so that they are able to compete on the international level. Since Cuba is a net energy importer, the issue of the unification of domestic and world market prices is also valid. As the government will most likely continue to subsidize private and commercial energy consumption, Cuba would be well-served by improving energy consumption patterns, putting hard constraints on energy use above necessary levels and eliminating waste through public awareness campaigns.

Employment and income distribution The decision to create a private sector by legalizing self-employment had different origins in Russia and Cuba. In Russia, it reflected a conscious move towards a market economy and an attempt to generate economic growth. In Cuba, it was prompted by the grave condition of state finances, in light of the need to cut subsidies and close down inefficient state enterprises. Thus, Cuba's shift toward self-employment provided a way to avoid a large rise in joblessness while generating some tax revenue. However, many restrictions persisted, especially in professional fields, and the Cuban government has vacillated between removing and creating obstacles to self-employment, especially in the restaurant industry. By contrast, Russia has made significant progress, with levels of non-state employment at 70 per cent in 1997, compared to Cuba's 25 per cent.[53] While the output growth in Cuba has been considerable since the partial legalization of self-employment in 1993, the government's ambivalent policies have weakened the country's potential for growth, contributed to income and social inequalities, and will continue to do so in the absence of a stronger and less arbitrary legal framework. If laws to regulate private activity were adopted in the future, Cuba would do well to create a conducive and broad-based tax system with relatively low tax levels and strong administrative capacity.

Education and health Education is trumpeted as one of the most treasured achievements of the Cuban socialist system, but the island's partial shift to a market economy has deeply devalued the work performed by the educated classes. Working in the dollarized sector of the economy, taxicab drivers or bed and breakfast entrepreneurs can earn considerably more than a professor, diminishing the value placed on university education. This is reflected in the marketplace. From 1990 to 1999 university enrollment declined by 58 per cent, at least in part because young people see little value in higher education compared to dollar-earning activities in Cuba's service sector. As in Russia, the Cuban government's decision to fix the already-reduced quotas for university enrolment as a cost-cutting measure has also accelerated this trend.[54] Similarly, distortions in the labour market have greatly increased instances of skill mismatch as people forego certain real sector professional training and switch to business activities. In Russia, despite some difficulties, the education system has remained relatively intact because Russian people understood its value in the market economy and did their best to educate themselves and their kin. Russia offers three basic lessons in education that may be applicable to Cuba in the future. First, spending on education should be maintained at the highest possible level and left under the authority of the federal government. Second, basic educational standards required by all school types (public, private, parochial) need to be set across the board. Lastly, teachers' salaries must remain sufficiently competitive to attract talented candidates and instill a desire to teach well.

Cuba's health sector appears to face severe challenges. As state expenses are growing in this area, mortality rates for seven contagious diseases have increased in the period 1994–2000, and daily nutritional supply continued to decrease.[55] While the number of physicians increased twofold in the period 1989–2000, thousands work in other occupations, where they can earn several times the salary paid for their profession. Unfortunately, Russia's performance does not provide an enviable example of maintaining public health during economic transition, despite the fact that state spending on health was generally maintained. Russia's experience does indicate that, for example, fixing prices of pharmaceuticals at the expense of the budget, while providing benefits to those who do not need them, only further deprives health and social assistance programs of much needed funds.

One lesson that must be garnered from Russia's transition is that health and education services provide important underpinnings of social stability that are extremely important to the population. Dramatic deterioration in the nation's health resource capacity can hobble the move to the market economy, deplete valuable popular support for reform, and take many years to restore. Squandering this progress is a mistake that a country like Cuba can ill afford.

Social assistance Russia's social assistance programmes offer a cautionary lesson to Cuba. When economic transition causes a rise in poverty, it is a consequence of many socioeconomic factors that are not easily resolved. Nonetheless, the government can conduct a policy that will reduce poverty and lessen its effects. One key priority must be the development of an effective labour market by supporting active employment programmes and linking the minimum wage to the inflation rate. The resolution of these problems often does not need to wait for times of high economic growth; income redistribution towards the least paid categories of workers and the legalization of informal incomes can occur even during periods of economic stagnation. Yet, even in the rosiest transition scenarios, those segments of the population at high risk of poverty will require financial assistance through social programmes. Russia's experience shows that social programmes should target the neediest population groups early in the transition.

Cuba faces a problem of ever-growing pension and social assistance deficits, while real pensions and transfers to individuals continue to decline. The government is said to be considering a significant reform of the pension scheme that may increase the age of retirement, implement workers' contributions and incorporate the growing private sector.[56] This would be a good start, which ideally should be followed by the creation of a multi-tier pension system, which allows people to diversify risks across countries, regions, and assets. Social assistance should also be streamlined to cover the neediest at levels adequate to maintain a minimum living standard corresponding to the macroeconomic developments in the country. Controlling inflation is also essential to a functional pension system.

Privatization In 2004, some private sector activity is allowed in Cuba, but it is largely limited to family-owned micro-enterprises. Such small enterprises, as well as medium-sized ones, should be given a greater role in the economy as they have significant potential to drive economic growth. Cuba's liberalization measures were also targeted at restructuring unprofitable state enterprises in order to improve efficiency and reduce reliance on state subsidies. Yet there are still 1,500 potential enterprises to be privatized in Cuba, which could generate US$20–40 billion, according to the pricing strategy applied by Poland, Czechoslovakia, Hungary and East Germany.[57] In 1998, the Cuban government approved a new law to decentralize 95 firms that together employ 115,000 workers, but a substantive privatization process is clearly not on the economic agenda at present.

Cuba's path to privatization remains unknown, but Russia's example shows that voucher privatization does not provide for an increase in investment capital and managerial expertise. Therefore, Cuba would most likely benefit from a fair and transparent 'money' privatization (dissimilar to most of Russia's experience in this area), which would create employment opportunities and generate revenue for the state. While Cuba will probably want to avoid a lengthy and protracted privatization process, appropriate sequencing would begin with privatization of small and medium-sized businesses, followed by high export-potential enterprises, while the government creates the optimum conditions for a full privatization strategy. The Cuban government will simultaneously want to strengthen or put in place new social safety nets to mitigate the adjustment costs for laid-off workers.

Given that Cuba's factories are large, cumbersome and inefficient, privatization will not be an easy task. Cuba will also need to deal with substantial external debt and a plethora of individual claims for properties expropriated following the 1959 revolution. The issue of property rights will be a prominent one. Clear rules should be established and implemented rigorously. The most relevant example of how this was done more or less successfully could be derived from East Germany's experience. In the agricultural sector, two-thirds of state lands have been redistributed to cooperatives. Cuba's policy of granting limited managerial autonomy and economic independence to cooperatives is a good start in raising productivity and production. However, so far progress has been slow because a genuine sense of independence will not be present until these cooperatives are allowed to break their linkages with state companies and truly do business on their own.[58] Legislation passed in November 2002 was intended to give greater autonomy to small-farmer cooperatives, but the actual effects remain to be seen.

Cuba must also recognize that privatization alone does not guarantee success and efficiency in the economy, and Russia's example is a testament to how the process can go awry. The Cuban experience thus far suggests that changing the incentive structure could be more sensible than changing the ownership structure – at least during the early stages of transition. This notion is especially supported by the fact that in the absence of state-regulating mechanisms (e.g., commercial codes, antitrust laws, a reliable tax system), the managers of newly privatized firms have huge incentives to search for short-term benefits, as occurred in Russia.[59] Joint ventures between foreign investors and the state in Cuba have worked well to make private and public incentives compatible, while simultaneously keeping out organized crime. Thus, consideration could be given to expanding this structure to the rest of the state enterprises before appropriate institutions are created and privatization could be conducted transparently and beneficially to the state and the population. At the same time, experiences in other countries suggest that issues of governance may rise in such structures as state elites are tempted by substantial kickbacks from foreign investors in return for concessions being asked from the state. In this case, transparency in awarding contracts would be key to a successful functioning of joint enterprises.

Banking Russia fell far short of establishing an efficient banking system to ensure high and sustainable rates of growth, which in turn should lead to a flow of national savings into productive activities. The political pull of nationalism simply outweighed the powerful argument for allowing foreign banks to come into the country to set up their branches or buy into the existing domestic banks. Foreign banks can bring new technologies, products, ideas, and professionals that are lacking in the domestic market, as well as providing comfort and security to those domestic depositors who have little faith in the native system. Ignorance of banking principles, together with the desire to make quick gains at the expense of the population or the budget, significantly retarded Russia's growth and development. Yet foreign banks only enter a country once a strong legal system is in place to protect their interests, which includes the enforcement of laws such as property rights, collateral, and bankruptcy.

Cuba's economic policy makers will have to cope with this tension between the nationalistic desire to keep banks 'Cuban' and the benefits of opening to foreign expertise. Along with the development of an efficient banking system, Cuba should aim to develop a domestic capital market with an adequate regulatory structure, allowing the population's savings and remittances to be channeled into productive business activities as well as creating a source of borrowing for the government. As a part of capital account liberalization, foreign participation in this market should be well sequenced with other reforms in the financial sector and with the macroeconomic developments in Cuba – a difficult task for countries adapting to rapid change.

Institution building Without question, the creation of institutions has proven to be one of the weakest parts of Russia's transition. Flaws in tax administration, banking laws and the legal system have produced many undesirable outcomes, including corruption and a widespread lack of respect for the law. Institution building requires a strong state role with proper incentives for law enforcement. Maintaining decent pay and moderate benefits for civil servants in relatively stable state jobs should be emphasized. But safeguards must be in place to ensure that essential government bureaucrats do not to seek additional personal enrichment by abusing their state-given powers. Codes of conduct and a merit-based recruitment system can help to prevent a culture of corruption from taking root. This, however, may not be enough, as modest benefits will only attract lower level employees to government jobs. High government officials that are capable of upholding standards of fairness and transparency can set examples throughout state organizations. Controlling corruption at the upper echelon is crucial for limiting the temptation for rent-seeking during the transition period. This requires an adequate division of power and the establishment of independent regulatory institutions. This is much easier said than done, and would require exceptional will, determination and honesty from those in power. If Cuba can win the battle against corruption, its economic reform process will have gained a vital early advantage over that of the former Soviet Union.

Foreign advice and expertise The challenge of properly harnessing the benefits of foreign expertise has been exceedingly difficult and controversial for many transition economies. In many areas, foreign expertise can help build institutions and create strong businesses. This expertise can vary from technical assistance (in setting up tax, legal, regulatory and supervisory systems as well as a Central Bank) to FDI and outright foreign ownership. While Russia made good use of the former, FDI and ownership have been impeded by weak legal and governance systems. The experience of successful reformers illustrates that foreign capital and expertise are extremely important for the country's development and growth, particularly in the development of the banking system. Even today, it appears that Cuba has realized the value of foreign expertise and investment and opened doors in the tourism, mining, energy, transport, and communications industries. Foreign firms, for their part, have promoted fundamental changes by training thousands of Cuban employees in managerial, financial, and marketing skills. FDI helped to bring in foreign currency and reduce fiscal deficits, which ultimately resulted in subsidies being slashed almost sixfold over the period 1990–2000. While FDI levels remain low in Cuba, at just US$39 million in 2001, both countries appear to be forging ahead on this front.[60]

Despite the clear advantages, foreign involvement in the domestic economy often emerges as a political stumbling block during the reform process. It is not uncommon to have a substantial domestic opposition to foreign investors. In Russia, such opposition stems from the excessive lobbying of domestic producers who do not want to lose market share to more efficient foreign enterprises (automotive and banking sectors stand out as particularly clear examples of this phenomenon). Hostility also stems from the perceived role of external advisors in advocating reforms with negative repercussions. However, this tension between nationalism/protectionism and the benefits of foreign expertise and capital could be resolved with policies that explain the advantages of foreign involvement. In the Russian oil sector, for example, Russian companies need US technology and experience, and the US companies cannot afford to be sidelined in such a potentially profitable market as Russia.[61] Hopefully, such practice could be translated into other areas, especially the banking sector, as total FDI in Russia as of 2002 was only US$23 billion, while it was $45 billion in Poland and an eye-popping US$448 billion in China.[62] Cuba also can greatly benefit from the involvement of international companies in its many sectors, especially in energy refining.

Conclusion

Despite considerable progress over the last decade, the outcome of Russia's transformation from a centrally planned economy to something approaching a normal market economy remains vigorously debated. In the past several years, analysts' sentiments have veered from joyous (1997) to hopelessly grim (1998) to cautiously optimistic (2000) and even exuberant (2002). In 2004, Russia's political and economic growing pains continue to perplex the international community, provoking both accolades and consternation.

Of course, in the early 1990s it was clear that some sort of change was necessary in the Soviet Union given its grave economic conditions, yet nobody precisely knew what would trigger this change and what form it would take. Political change came first, when the failed coup d'état of August 1991 precipitated the end of the Soviet Union. The rapid pace of events left little time to develop an economic reform programme suited to Russia's eccentricities, and the Russian reformers were left with little option but to accept proposals from the Washington-based international financial institutions to guide the country's systemic transformation. The results were mixed at best; and, in many cases, the failures were far more dramatic than the successes – culminating in the financial crisis of 1998 which brought the economy to a halt. While the primary responsibility for the outcome of the transformation still lies on the shoulders of the Russian reformers and politicians, there is little question that they found willing handmaidens in their partners from the international community.

This chapter argues that Russia's situation going into this transformation was quite unique, due to its size, the abundance of natural resources, geopolitics, culture and history. Although Russia could have drawn somewhat on the experience (albeit very recent) of several Eastern European countries, it would have been difficult to replicate any other transition model. This fact suggests that the Russian example may have limited usefulness when considering the economic future of Cuba. Yet due to its outsized role in the study of economic transition, the Russian example deserves careful analysis because the results of the reforms give vivid lessons on their consequences for the economy and the society and provide examples of good and bad policy choices. As some analysts have argued, 'If there is one outstanding lesson from the Russian experience, it is that economic culture is much harder to change than the ownership or planning system'.[63] The relevance of this insight must not be ignored in the Cuban case.

Cuba, having started on the path of economic liberalization in 1993, may benefit from the insights provided by the Russian experience, which can aid in the assessment of Cuba's economic reform both today and following the rule of Fidel Castro. Russia's dramatic political and economic transformation left a deep impression on the Cuban government and its people. Today, more than a decade later, Russia's experience can provide important lessons for Cuba – both positive and negative. By learning from Russia's example while avoiding the country's shipwrecks, perhaps Cuba can outshine its former patron.

Notes

1 The views expressed in this essay are solely those of the author and do not represent the views of the International Monetary Fund, the Russian Federation, the Inter-American Dialogue, or any other affiliated party.
2 Edward Hewett, 'Is Soviet Socialism Reformable?', originally cited in M. Donald Hancock and John Logue, *Transitions to Capitalism and Democracy in Russia and Central Europe: Achievements, Problems, Prospects* (Westport, CT: Praeger Publishers 2000).
3 Willem H. Buiter, *From Predation to Accumulation*? (Oxford: Blackwell Publishers, 2000).
4 Ernesto Hernandez-Cata, 'The Fall and Recovery of the Cuban Economy in the 1990's: Mirage or Reality', *International Monetary Fund Working Paper* 01/48 (April 2001).
5 'Cuba's Foreign Debt', *US Department of State Fact Sheet,* 24 July 2003, http://www.state.gov/p/wha/rls/fs/22743pf.htm.
6 Jerry Hough, *The Logic of Economic Reform in Russia* (Washington, DC: The Brookings Institution, 2001).
7 Peter Reddaway and Dmitri Glinski, *The Tragedy of Russia's Reforms: Market Bolshevism against Democracy* (Washington, DC: Endowment of the United States Institute for Peace, 2001).
8 Daniel Treisman, *Russia Renewed?* (Washington, DC: The Brookings Institution, 2001).
9 Martin Wolf, 'Putin's Clampdown Could Put Prosperity at Risk, *Financial Times,* 5 November 2003.
10 Stefan Wagstyl, Andrew Jack and Arkady Ostrovsky, 'We Are Living in a Different Country Now... There Will Not be Repression, But a Creeping Bureaucratic Coup', *Financial Times*, 3 November 2003.
11 'Sliding to Victory', *The Economist*, 13 March 2004.
12 'Putin ascendant as opposition melts away', *Oxford Analytica*, 20 January 2004.
13 Anders Åslund, *Building Capitalism: the Transformation of the Former Soviet Bloc* (Cambridge: Press Syndicate of the University of Cambridge, 2002).
14 United Nations, Economic Commission for Europe, *Economic Survey of Europe in 1990–1991* (New York: United Nations, 1991).
15 This figure varies with data source. These data are from F. Gerard Adams and Libor Krkoska's *Lessons of the East Asian Transition Experience for Transformation in*

Eastern Europe: China and Vietnam vs. Czech Republic, Hungary, Poland and Russia (Netherlands: Kluwer Academic Publishers, 1996).

16 Thane Gustafson, *Capitalism Russian-style* (Cambridge: Press Syndicate of the University of Cambridge, 1999).

17 Michael Dobbs, *Down with the Big Brother: the End of Soviet Empire* (New York: Knopf, 1997).

18 'The Soviet Economy on the Brink', *The Economist*, 16 March 1991.

19 'Yeltsin was advised otherwise by the international community since it did not put concrete indicators of success such as economic growth or a level of construction above monetary factors as inflation, money supply and budgetary stringency;' Jerry Hough, *The Logic of Economic Reform in Russia.*

20 Lawrence Summers, 'The Next Decade in Central and Eastern Europe', originally cited in Jerry Hough, *The Logic of Economic Reform in Russia.*

21 There were four programmes with the IMF in the period of 1992–9. While the committed amount was around US$21.5 billion, disbursements amounted to US$11.3 billion, as only two programmes (1992–3, 1995–6) were completed. There were also numerous loans from the World Bank aimed at facilitating structural reforms.

22 International Monetary Fund, *Russian Federation: 2001 Article IV Consultation and Post Program Monitoring – Staff Report* (Washington, DC: International Monetary Fund, 2002).

23 Åslund, *Building Capitalism.*

24 'Russia's Economy: Scratch and Sniff', *The Economist,* 16 February 2002.

25 Throughout this essay rent-seeking is defined as 'profits in excess of competitive level', Richard Brealey and Stewart Myers, *Principles of Corporate Finance,* 6th edition (New York: McGraw Hill).

26 'Payments' dollarization refers to a situation in which the dollar is used as a means of payment. 'Financial' dollarization is defined as a situation in which the dollar is used to index deposits, loans, and other financial contracts. 'Real' dollarization is a situation in which the dollar is used to index wages, prices of goods, and other real contracts. Alain Ize and Eric Parrado, 'Dollarization, Monetary Policy and the Pass-Through', *International Monetary Fund Working Paper*, 02/188, November 2002.

27 In this context, 'providing the roof' means that instead of engaging in outright banditry, crime groups would have an agreement with businesses (usually small) to provide protection from rival crime groups in exchange for a certain payment.

28 FIGs are defined as holdings headed by large commodity-producing companies (oil and other major raw materials), a bank (usually performing a treasury function for the holding), and several other companies predominantly in automotive, metal, agriculture, timber and coal businesses. In this sense they are reminiscent of Korean *chaebols* as well as German industrial conglomerates which are dominated by the cross-shareholding of each other's shares by companies and banks.

29 Jerry Hough, *The Logic of Economic Reform in Russia.*

30 Much of the quantitative information on this topic is obtained from Victor B. Supyan's 'Privatization in Russia: Phases and Effects', in Paul J.J. Welfens and Evgeny Gavrilenkov (ed), *Restructuring, Stabilizing and Modernizing the New Russia* (Berlin: Sringer-Verlag, 2000).

31 Ibid. All companies were divided into three groups according to the following criteria: (1) small companies, with fewer than 200 employees, were to be sold at voucher auctions or leased by their employees with the right of a complete

buyout; (2) companies with more than 1,000 employees should be transformed into public stockholding companies; and (3) medium-sized enterprises could choose between employee buyout or public stockholding status.

32 Ibid. They included 20,000 large enterprises, each employing thousands of workers. The privatization of small-scale enterprises in the service sector was very impressive with the new private sector accounting for more than 70 per cent. Privatized enterprises utilized more than 60 per cent of the productive capital in manufacturing, produced 75 per cent of Russia's gross domestic product, and employed about 70 per cent of the national labour force. About 40 million citizens became stockholders in privatized enterprises, nearly 1 million were owners of their own small businesses. Some 2,560 commercial banks were created, along with millions of retail trade companies, consulting services, repair, construction and food-producing enterprises.

33 Ibid.

34 Jerry Hough, *The Logic of Economic Reform in Russia.*

35 Noreena Hertz, 'Silent Takeover: Global Capitalism and the Death of Democracy', originally cited in Jules Evans 'The new New Deal', *Euromoney*, vol. 33, no. 401, (September 2002).

36 Renaissance Capital, *The Russian Banking Sector: a Crisis of Stagnation*, September, 2001, and Intefax Rating Agency (various reports).

37 'Russia's Economy: Scratch and Sniff'.

38 World Bank, *Transition, The First Ten Years: Analysis and Lessons for Eastern Europe and the Former Soviet Union* (Washington, DC: World Bank, 2002).

39 Ibid. 'While it was found to be quite difficult to shed light on the desirability of progressing rapidly on all reform fronts, the results of transformation among various reformers show that the quicker full liberalization is achieved, the higher the growth. Here, however, country-specific factors such as external shocks, politics, policies and initial conditions play a very important role.'

40 *Demoscope Weekly: Russian Demographic Barometer*, issue 69–70, June, 2002, www.demoscope.ru.

41 Independent Institute for Social Policy, *Inequality and Poverty in Russia in Transition* (Moscow: Independent Institute for Social Policy, 2002).

42 Anthony Shorrocks and Stanislav Kolenikov, *Poverty Trends in Russia during the Transition*, May 2001, http://www.wider.unu.edu/conference/conference-2001-1/Shorrocks_Kolenikov.pdf.

43 Ludmila Kamsiuk, *Population and Society: Reproductive Health of the Population of Russia* (Moscow: Center for Demographics and Ecology, RAN, Roscompechat, October, 1999).

44 Ibid.

45 This section draws on Anatoli Suvorov's 'What is Happening with Russian Education?,' *Demoscope Weekly: Population and Society*, 14 October 2002, www.polit.ru.

46 'Russia: IT Explosion Helps to Fuel Boom Times', ed., Julian Marshall, *Euromoney*, vol. 33, no. 401, (September 2002).

47 World Bank, *Transition, The First Ten Years.*

48 This section draws on Daniel P. Erikson's and Peter Wolf's *Cuba: What Next?* (Washington, DC: Inter-American Dialogue, Conference Report, October 2002).

49 'Cuba: Opposition Splits Strengthen Government Position', *Oxford Analytica*, 7 November 2002.

50 Hernandez-Cata, 'The Fall and Recovery of the Cuban Economy in the 1990's'.

51 Paolo Spadoni, 'The Role of the United States in the Cuban Economy', paper presented at the Thirteenth Annual Meeting of the Association for the Study of the Cuban Economy, Miami, 7 August 2003.
52 Eduardo Levy-Yeyati, 'Monetary Operations and Government Securities Markets', in Malcolm Knight, Arne B. Petersen and Robert T. Price (ed), *Transforming Financial Systems in the Baltics, Russia, and Other Countries of the Former Soviet Union* (Washington, DC: IMF, Publication Services, 1999).
53 Ibid.
54 Philip Peters, *Survival Story: Cuba's Economy in the Post-Soviet Decade* (Virginia: Lexington Institute, May 2002).
55 United Nations Development Programme Report, 2000.
56 Carmelo Mesa-Lago, *The Cuban Economy at the Start of the 21st Century: Evaluation of Performance and Debate on the Future* (Washington, DC: Association for the Cuban Economy, 2001).
57 Toe A. Babun, Jr., 'Preliminary Study of the Impact of the Privatization of State-Owned Enterprises in Cuba', *Cuba in Transition*, vol. 9 (1999).
58 Jose M. March-Poquet, 'What Type of Transition is Cuba Undergoing?', *Centre for Research into Post-Communist Economies*, Vol. 12, No. 1 (2000).
59 Ana Julia Jatar-Hausmann, 'What Cuba Can Teach Russia', *Foreign Policy*, Volume 53, Number 2 (1999).
60 'Cuba: Economic Summary,' *U.S. Department of State Fact Sheet*, 30 July 2003, www.state.gov.p/wha/rls/fs/22902pf.htm.
61 Sheila McNulty, 'Russian Oil Becomes More Attractive', *Financial Times*, 2 October 2002.
62 Martin Wolf, 'Putin's Clampdown Could Put Prosperity at Risk'.
63 M. Donald Hancock and John Logue, *Transitions to Capitalism and Democracy in Russia and Central Europe: Achievements, Problems, Prospects* (Westport, CT: Praeger Publishers, 2000).

4
Eastern Europe: Different Paths, Different Results

Christopher A. Hartwell

Introduction

The challenge of economic transition in Eastern Europe was a daunting task. The shift required sweeping political and economic reform with limited knowledge about the policies necessary to successfully complete such a transition. Yet the experience of these countries over the past decade, which encompassed vast differences in policy choices and the sequencing and timing of reforms, provides a wealth of information that can play an important role in shaping the economic future of Cuba and other remaining socialist countries. Cuba today occupies a position similar to many of the former Soviet satellite economies before the fall of the Berlin Wall, and this essay argues that many of Eastern Europe's lessons will prove highly salient to the Cuban experience.

While certain aspects of Eastern Europe's transition were familiar – many countries, such as the East Asian Tigers, had gone from autarky and import-substitution to global integration and liberalization during the post-Second World War period – the sheer breadth and scale of the transformation were historically unparalleled. As a result, considerable debate emerged both within and outside of the region about what economic policies were optimal for a successful transition from communism to capitalism. The 'Washington Consensus' represented the prevailing school of thought on global economic policy, advocating for the rapid retreat of the state from the economic arena. However, the Washington Consensus was only a backdrop for the debate, and the question of what was to be done in Eastern Europe remained a local issue.

In the early years of the transition process, the debate was separated into the 'shock therapy' and 'gradualist' schools of thought, which proposed different timetables for transition. Supporters of 'shock therapy' believed that the window of opportunity to transform an economy closed rapidly; thus, an entire package of reforms – including price and wage liberalization, macroeconomic adjustment, enterprise reform and privatization – should

Map 3 Eastern Europe

be bundled together and implemented as quickly as possible at the onset of transition. In effect, the advocates of shock therapy believed that the plumbing of an economy had to be ripped out all at once. By contrast, the gradualist school believed that a slow and deliberate sequencing of reforms was preferable to a rush to the market.

The choice between shock therapy and gradualism partially explains the divergent growth patterns of Eastern European countries during the 1990s (see Figure 4.1). Undoubtedly, the choice of reform path was not the only factor affecting economic performance; initial conditions, geographical location, and intrinsic comparative advantages also played important roles.[1] Still, policy choices were an important factor for Eastern Europe, and will certainly be important for Cuba in the future. Thus, the experience of Eastern Europe should be assessed by examining what strategies explain the differing performances since the initial shock. Can a successful reform strategy and the attendant policies be transferred elsewhere, and are there policies that should be unequivocally avoided?

This chapter will focus on this final question, principally by examining the contrapositive to distill policy lessons for a transformation of Cuba's socialist economy. While much has been written about the successful transition economies (most notably Poland and the Czech Republic) and their policies, far less research has been done on the laggard countries in the region. Examining why a country's transition policies *fail* to achieve growth and how this failure could have been prevented will yield important lessons for Cuba if the country embraces new market mechanisms. This essay will briefly examine the Czech Republic – a country generally

Figure 4.1 'Shock therapy' vs gradualism, 1990–2001[2]

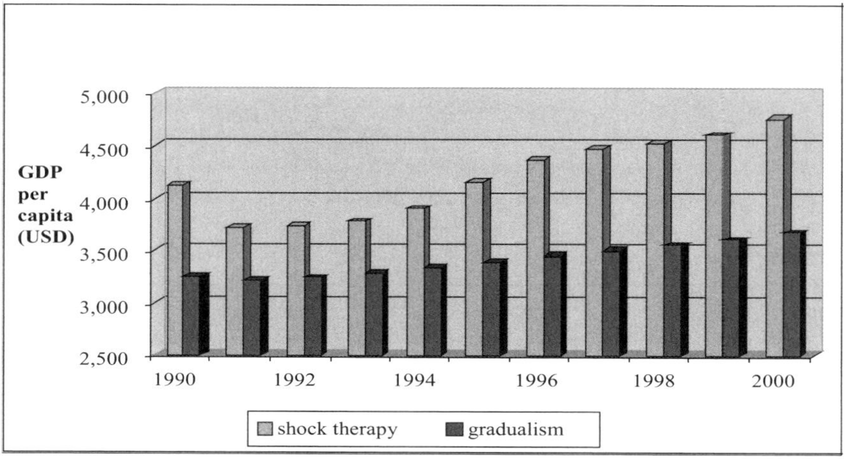

recognized as successfully managing the transition process – and then proceed to analyze the more turbulent transition experiences of Slovakia and Bulgaria, assessing their policy shortcomings. The final section of the chapter will reflect on potential lessons for Cuba if the government decides to embrace a more market-oriented approach to economic policy making.

The Czech Republic: shock therapy exemplar

The Czech Republic's transition has long been singled out as the embodiment of the 'shock therapy' reform strategy. Once the communist regime ended in 1989, the Czechoslovak Federal Republic (CSFR) attempted an ambitious set of reforms modelled on Poland's example. Under the supervision of Finance Minister Vaclav Klaus, Prague followed austere fiscal and monetary policies, including devaluation, institution of a fixed exchange rate, current-account convertibility, and a mass privatization scheme based on voucher distribution.[3] In general, the Czechs eschewed arguments about the 'proper sequencing' of reforms and successfully enacted policies simultaneously throughout the macroeconomy. The stabilization programme resulted in one of the lowest rates of inflation in the region (9.1 per cent by the end of 1995), coupled with low unemployment (2.9 per cent) and a moderate current account deficit (2.7 per cent of GDP). Growth rebounded in the latter half of 1993, reaching impressive rates until the crisis year of 1997, and GDP per capita also demonstrated an impressive increase (see Figure 4.2).

Having stabilized the economy in the first few years following the fall of communism, the Czech Republic's principal macroeconomic problems stemmed from its early success in creating an attractive environment for

Figure 4.2 Czech Republic: GDP growth, 1991–2001

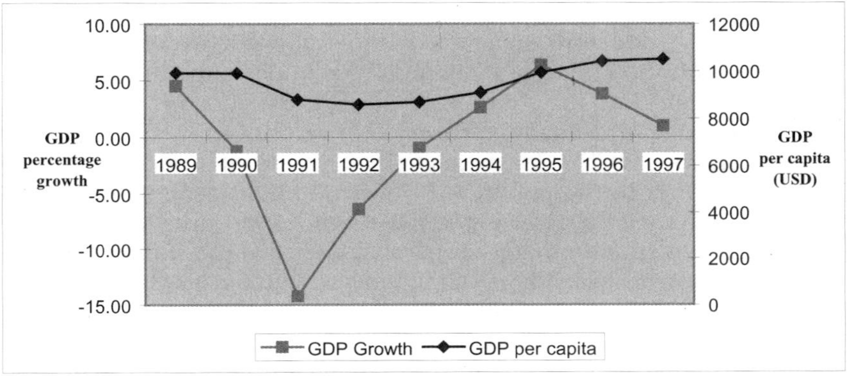

Source: World Bank, *World Development Indicators, 2001*.

investment. The country was soon swamped with foreign capital flows that threatened both the stability of the exchange rate and the country's inflation management policies. The Czech Republic utilized a pegged exchange rate system in order to temper inflation. This form of inflationary control through exchange rate targeting worked well enough from 1991 to 1995, but by 1996 the continued attractiveness of Czech markets and high levels of capital inflows led to increased domestic demand and real appreciation of the currency. Due mainly to the presence of the peg and its susceptibility to speculative attack, the country was hit disproportionately hard by the Asian financial crisis of 1997.[4] Of course, the issue of appropriate exchange rate regimes is not limited to countries in transition; it is salient for all emerging markets (indeed, even for advanced industrial economies such as the UK and Spain in 1992). However, the crisis also demonstrated that the Czech Republic was moving beyond the initial transition phases and into the next stage of challenges in macroeconomic management.

The Czech Republic was far from perfect in its reform strategies or in its policies, and today Czechs are widely perceived as having one of the most corrupt governments and business environments in Central Europe. The anti-corruption group Transparency International rates the country of 52 out of 102, tied with Slovakia and Morocco, and behind countries such as Ghana and South Korea. Furthermore, the private sector, while a major share of the economy, has undergone precious little restructuring. The source of both of these ills lies principally in the machinations and shenanigans surrounding the voucher-based privatization process which was introduced almost immediately after the collapse of communism.

Unlike the other countries in this survey, Slovakia and Bulgaria, the Czech Republic was not hampered by political considerations or communist-era nostalgia to retain some industries under the hand of the state; indeed, Finance Minister Klaus had a concerted plan to privatize as much of the state's assets as possible. But the Czechs chose a flawed method. The first round of privatization in Czechoslovakia was intended to transfer assets to the private sector in a rapid manner. It was based on three initiatives: the restitution of property nationalized under communist rule;[5] privatizing the smallest-scale businesses through the auctions of shops and service facilities; and finally, large-scale privatization of the large state-owned enterprises. The large-scale privatization was implemented by issuing vouchers to the public, with over 6 million people in the CSFR receiving free shares of 2800 enterprises in industry, agriculture, and services.[6] The first round of large-scale privatization successfully completed the distribution of shares shortly after independence in 1993. Preparations for a second round of voucher-based sales began in 1994.

While the vouchers succeeded in dispersing ownership, they failed to induce the enterprise restructuring necessary to reform the dilapidated communist-era heavy industry. The problems associated with 'Investment

Privatization Funds' bear special warning for a country like Cuba considering economic reform. These funds were intended to improve corporate governance and force enterprise restructuring, but remained controlled by state-owned banks that were only too eager to extend soft credits. In the absence of hard budget constraints, private entities began to exhibit the same inefficiencies as state-owned enterprises, and the problems of unproductive firm investment were compounded by rising wages for a labour force insulated from the layoffs that market forces would normally require.[7]

In short, the Czech Republic underwent a highly successful macroeconomic stabilization programme, but this success was undermined by slow movement on the microeconomic front, in particular in enterprise restructuring. If anything, the Czech case argues for even swifter action than was actually undertaken. If the state-owned banks had been cut loose earlier and the financial system tackled along with trade and price liberalization, the Czech Republic would have been much less vulnerable to speculative attack in 1997. However, in contrast to the countries we will examine below, the Czech Republic has worked diligently to correct some of the mistakes made early in the transition process. By 2000, the financial sector's lagging status had been corrected with a painful but necessary effort by the government to strip out liabilities of banks and put the remaining financial assets on the auction block for strategic investors.[8]

More than anything, the experience of the Czech Republic underlines that transition is a process, not an event, and the points at which it faltered during the 1990s coincided with periods of 'structural inaction'.[9] Yet as of 2002, the country was once again a star performer in the region and the leading economy of those invited for EU accession. As the IMF succinctly stated in July 2002, 'the Czech economy has... left behind the baggage of transition'.[10] For Eastern European countries like Slovakia and Bulgaria, however, the baggage was still on the carousel.

Slovakia: two paths in one

Slovakia's economic transformation has differed from most other economies in Central and Eastern Europe, and stands in stark contrast to its neighbour and former federal partner, the Czech Republic. The effects of the macroeconomic reforms in Czechoslovakia were not distributed evenly throughout the country, and the eastern republics of Slovakia were hit disproportionately hard by transition due to their reliance on Soviet markets and subsidies from Prague to sustain industry. In 1991, the first year of the stabilization programme, Slovakia's GDP fell by 14.6 per cent, as compared to 11.5 per cent in the Czech Republic.[11] This decline abated somewhat but continued through 1993, with a further decline of 4 per cent. Unemployment also skyrocketed following transition, with Slovakia's unemployment rate rising from virtually zero unemployment in 1990 to 12 per cent in 1991, compared to 4 per cent in the Czech Republic.[12]

These regional disparities began to stir discontent in the Slovak Republic that manifested itself in the newly acquired electoral process. The general parliamentary election of June 1992 revealed a deep rift between the Czechs and the Slovaks, as the Czechs elected a majority of right-centre parties to federal and national parliament, while the Slovaks moved in precisely the opposite direction. The victory of leftist parties in Slovakia expressed the populace's desire to take a more gradual approach to reform than that which the Czechs had been proposing, with critics charging that the reforms of Finance Minister Vaclav Klaus in Prague were 'tailored to the Czech economy' and thus inappropriate for Slovakia.[13] Moreover, the elections revealed a further split between west and east, as policies of the western-educated Klaus seemed to conflict with the Soviet background of many Slovak municipal leaders.

Given the dim prospects of mutually acceptable compromise, the winning parties in the Federal parliament drafted an agreement to peacefully separate the Czech republic and Slovakia into two sovereign entities.[14] On 1 January 1993, the Velvet Revolution parted Czechoslovakia into two nations, and, at one stroke, Slovakia was faced with running its own economy independent of Prague – and without the subsidies and redistribution that was the hallmark of the CSFR. In part to assert its newfound independence in economic policy, the government of Vladmir Meciar and the Movement for a Democratic Slovakia (MDS) immediately translated the popular sentiment for gradualism into reality with the issuance of a 'Strategy of Economic Revival'. The new strategy placed emphasis on providing fiscal stimulus to the macroeconomic indicators before fully undertaking the microeconomic transition. Microeconomic reforms, including privatization and industry restructuring, were to rely on the tight leadership and financial assistance of the state. This contrasted sharply with the Czech Republic, which acted to sever ties between state and market and introduce hard budget constraints at the earliest possible moment.

Slovakia initially appeared to find a balance between reform and caution absent from the Czech reform process, and the country hit a turning point earlier than many of its neighbours (with the exception of Poland), as GDP began to recover by 1994 through an export-fuelled boom (see Figure 4.3). Liberalization of foreign trade helped to reorient Slovakia towards western markets, as exports surged 23 per cent in 1994 and single-handedly brought the country out of recession. Several factors drove export growth, including the initial devaluation of the koruna, which bolstered the country's export advantage, with current account surpluses in 1994 and 1995. Similarly, the recovery of Slovakia's trade partners spurred export growth in the intermediate goods that the country produced, and this process was aided by the government's completion of several regional agreements that shifted the trade orientation away from ex-Council for Mutual Economic Assistance (CMEA) members.

In addition to the expansion of exports, the Slovak government under Vladimir Meciar deliberately undertook large infrastructure investments in order to stimulate the economy. Essentially following a Keynesian 'pump-priming' scenario, large public works projects such as highway construction – crucial for Slovakia's integration into Western Europe – and dam and nuclear plant construction were hastened into fruition through a massive infusion of public funds. During this period, fiscal stability was maintained through an increase in total government revenue achieved by increasing the value-added tax, the maintenance of a stable tax base, and the continued recovery of the economy. This created the perception of a 'virtuous cycle', as economic growth increased government revenues that were then invested in public works projects. Apparently successful in the good times of 1994–95, Meciar's plan relied on Slovakia's expansion and the collection of sufficient revenues. However, as events unfolded, this strategy soon became unsustainable.

Although shock therapy had been applied to the macroeconomy, microeconomic reforms were abruptly abandoned in 1994 in favour of a gradualist approach. As part of government's plan for enterprise reform, Meciar announced the cancellation of a second wave of privatization that had been originally slated for 1995. The privatization process in the Czech Republic resulted in dispersal of ownership but little real change in corporate governance, but voucher privatization in Slovakia was quantitatively and qualitatively different, as less property and properties of generally poorer quality were included in the first wave.[16] At the time, the economic turmoil of transition generated considerable popular resentment. For

Figure 4.3 Slovakia: GDP growth, 1991–2001[15]

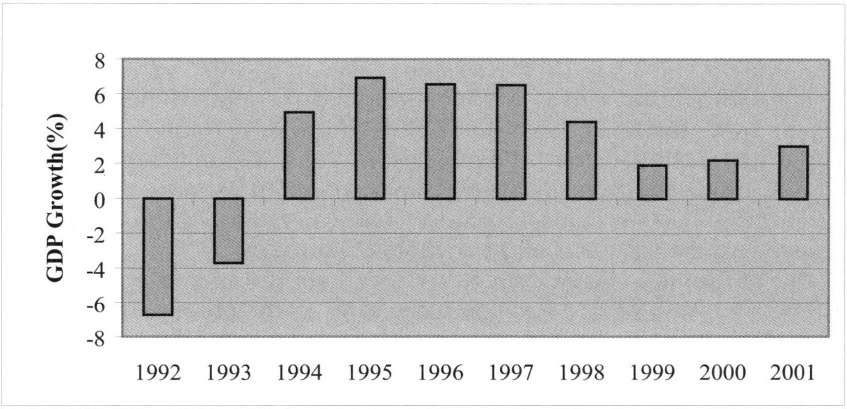

example, in 1994, polls revealed that 72 per cent of the population agreed with the statement that 'democracy didn't meet their expectations', while 71 per cent thought that they were better off under communism. Thus, as part of a broad realignment in favour of gradualist policies, Meciar implemented a change in the privatization process through Act No. 369, canceling the privatization of 50 state-owned companies and announcing that no further voucher privatization would take place in Slovakia. Instead, as outlined in the government's Policy Statement of 10 January 1995, direct sales to interested bidders would predominate, carried out through the National Property Fund (NPF).[17]

With the failures of the Czech voucher experience becoming increasingly apparent, the change to direct sales appeared to be a prudent choice, as the state aimed 'to sell enterprises to those "strategic" buyers who would be able to rejuvenate them – usually management or domestic investors'.[18] In theory, direct sales to outside owners should have led to better corporate governance and increased access to skills and capital, while also raising government revenue.[19] However, rather than establishing enterprise restructuring as an explicit goal, the National Property Fund and Meciar's government instead utilized the direct sales process to foster a Slovak business community. In the words of NPF Presidium Chairman Štefan Gavorník, the key question was 'to whom Slovakia will belong.' The nationality of company ownership, rather than a fair sales price or the managerial capacity of the purchasing group, was held to be the most important factor.[18]

With the bar set so low for privatizing state assets, the direct sales method was also characterized by incompetence and corruption, perhaps even exceeding the Czech example, which was diffuse enough to allow few opportunities for corruption by the state. In practice, the direct sales method was highly opaque and lacked any form of public accountability, as the National Property Fund stopped providing information on either the criteria for selection or even on the projects themselves. Instead, the NPF directed its energies into other roles, with broad powers to offer incentives to buyers, reduce prices by up to 50 per cent as compensation for buyer investments, and lengthen the terms of payment up to 20 years. Given the secret nature of the privatization process and the arbitrary nature of the sales terms, sales tended to be concentrated towards political insiders and those who favoured the ruling coalition. Thus, loss-making enterprises moved from inefficient managers under communism to inefficient (and often disinterested) managers under quasi-capitalism. This was hardly a way to ensure the success of the economic transition.

One of the most blatant examples of the sort of chicanery that occurred in the second wave of privatization came early in the process. In 1994, the managers of the politically connected ironworks firm Východoslovenské Železiarne (VSŽ) acted to incorporate a new company, 'Manager'. Essentially a shell company with no real assets or productive capacity, Manager quickly sprang into action. Only three days after the company's founding, it obtained approval for the privatization of 9.53 per cent of VSŽ's shares at 200 Slovak korunas per share, even though the market value at that time was three times higher. This provides just one example of how insiders took advantage of the privatization process to buy assets at below cost, and retain control at the expense of restructuring.

Deals such as the VSŽ privatization occurred far too often, a particularly troubling development for the prospects of future enterprise growth, as fully 57 per cent of the state's assets during this period were privatized through direct sales, while a mere 5 per cent were offered for public tender. Furthermore, the government made no bones about playing favourites with the privatization process. Former Economics Minister Jan Ducky claimed in a prominent Slovak business magazine that 'each government in the world gives to those who cooperate with it', while the honorary chairman of a coalition partner in the government said that 'fair privatization does not exist, as we all know... the only criterion is loyalty'.[21] The subsequent murder of Ducky in February 1999 fueled suspicions about corrupt business practices and illustrated how an undercurrent of lawlessness coursed through Slovakia's privatization process

As the process progressed, however, problems other than plain old corruption became apparent, as many Slovak managers simply lacked sufficient funding and the know-how to achieve a successful privatization.[22] The performance of companies that were sold using the direct sales method reflected this shortcoming. In a case study of Slovak companies, the World Bank found that companies privatized in this wave were more likely to show deterioration in productivity and profitability, while those privatized in the CSFR wave showed consistent improvements in quality of services and increased productivity.[23]

Slovakia's managerial deficiency stemmed in part from its initial conditions. Czechoslovakia had perhaps the least vibrant private sector of any of the Visegrad Group, which comprised Czechoslovakia, Poland and Hungary. Czechoslovakia's public sector share of GDP in 1989 stood at 99.3 per cent. While this saturation had abated somewhat at independence, the private sector in Slovakia still only accounted for 32.4 per cent of GDP in 1993.[24] In short, Slovakia lacked the institutions and knowledge needed to function in a capitalist economy, and the NPF's focus on maintaining domestic ownership further undermined efforts to turn state assets into profitable private companies.

The absence of indigenous knowledge in transforming enterprises was exacerbated by the fact that the Slovaks were basically going it alone, a direct consequence of the policies of the Party for a Democratic Slovakia (HDZS) government of Vladimir Meciar. Foreign direct investment was in relatively short supply for Slovakia compared with the leading countries in the region (especially compared to its highly touted neighbour – see

Table 4.1). Investment opportunities and synergies in the country were ignored by design, as low levels of FDI were the inevitable result of a privatization process that specifically favoured domestic buyers and producers over foreign investors. Building a Slovak business community was a primary goal of the privatization process. The results dramatically illustrate this flaw. Although 'purposeful participation' of foreign investors was an avowed goal of the government, only 5 of 367 privatization decisions favoured foreign applicants in 1995 – slightly more than one per cent. The political hurdles for foreign investors persisted in 1996, when foreign applicants won only two of 400 decisions.[25]

However, the government's bias against foreign investment was not the only reason for the FDI drought, as many investors naturally shied away from the country's increasing international isolation and uncertain business climate.[26] Moreover, Slovakia was in a very competitive environment for FDI at the onset of transition, as economic expansion in the US and Western Europe provided a ready source of capital, and investors were seeking to gain the best return on their investments. The low labour costs and chance for reward throughout Eastern Europe enticed many investors into the region, but as years progressed, the countries that had a steadfast commitment to developing a market economy – and thus greater chance of growth – were separated from those that did not. As Slovakia diverged from other high-performance transition economies, markets viewed the country as a greater risk for FDI and favoured investment in nearby Hungary or the Czech Republic. This competition meant that foreign know-how, which could have benefited the Slovak economy, instead went to other countries in the region.

Sailing into trouble The Slovak government placed its emphasis on achieving high rates of GDP growth while ignoring the institutional reform that was needed. But by 1996, the lack of progress on privatization and the stagnation in developing institutions to handle a market economy was starting to hinder the macroeconomy, at precisely the same time that the external economic climate was worsening. Unemployment had been a persistent thorn in the side of the economy, rising to 12 per cent through 1996 and 1997. Worse still, more than 70 per cent of those unemployed classified as 'long-term', because they had not worked for six months or more. Regional disparities in unemployment also plagued Slovakia, with relatively low levels near the capital, Bratislava, but nearly a quarter of the workforce unemployed in the eastern part of the country.

The government's fiscal situation had also deteriorated since 1994–95, due to irresponsible fiscal management during boom periods, which exacerbated the effect of the cyclical downturn. Crony privatization resulted in only a trickle of revenue compared with the book value of the enterprises sold, and the poor performance of the privatized industries affected the tax revenue. As the tax base weakened, past government investment projects

Table 4.1 FDI per capita in Eastern Europe (millions of US$)[27]

	1990	*1993*	*1994*	*1995*	*1996*	*1997*	*1998*	*1999*	*2000*	*2001*
Albania	n/a	18	17	22	27	14	13	12	42	58
Bosnia	n/a	n/a	n/a	n/a	n/a	n/a	27	24	40	35
Bulgaria	**0**	**5**	**12**	**11**	**13**	**61**	**65**	**100**	**123**	**86**
Croatia	n/a	26	25	26	115	121	225	359	257	343
Czech Republic	**7**	**63**	**84**	**248**	**138**	**126**	**361**	**615**	**485**	**478**
Hungary	30	227	112	435	223	214	201	196	163	240
Macedonia	n/a	n/a	10	5	6	8	59	16	87	217
Moldova	n/a	3	3	15	6	22	21	11	39	41
Poland	2	45	49	95	116	127	165	188	242	207
Romania	n/a	4	15	18	12	54	90	46	46	51
Slovakia	**n/a**	**34**	**51**	**48**	**67**	**41**	**127**	**72**	**384**	**274**
Slovenia	2	57	64	89	97	189	125	91	88	222
Yugoslavia	n/a	n/a	n/a	n/a	n/a	70	11	13	3	20

were further draining the government's finances. The budget deficit rose from 1.9 per cent in 1995 to 4.4 per cent in 1996, and eventually reached 5.6 per cent in 1997.

In order to finance the deficit, the Slovak government resorted to a two-pronged strategy of heavy borrowing and the issuance of government debt with attractive rates of interest. External borrowing skyrocketed during 1997 and 1998, and the government began to accrue shorter-term debt; by the end of 1998, gross foreign debt had reached 62 per cent of GDP, half of which had less than one year's maturity.[28] Government-issued debt also had the deleterious effect of crowding out private investment. In order to induce banks to hold government securities, interest rates on Treasury bills consistently moved in the 20–30 per cent range by 1997, and commercial banks were 'only too glad' to accept them.[29] This mechanism provided the government with a short-term boost of liquidity, while reducing funds available for the private sector. For example, growth in credit to enterprises and households slowed to 5 per cent in 1997, compared to growth of over 30 per cent in net credit to the government.[30] The credit crunch, coupled with moves by the central bank to reduce bank refinancing, forced the private sector to borrow from abroad. As the government's external debt ballooned, private sector indebtedness to foreign creditors more than doubled, rising from 61.9 billion korunas to 132.4 billion korunas, leaving a combined government and private foreign indebtedness equal to half the economy in 1997.[31] Nearly 43 per cent of all public external debt was denominated in dollars.

In order to prevent the fiscal problems from affecting the real economy, the Slovak National Bank (NBS) abruptly shifted gears in 1996, moving from an expansionary monetary policy to a highly restrictive one. However, NBS had only limited room to manoeuvre, because the country's fixed exchange rate and exorbitantly high interest rates meant that a further rate increase would jeopardize the government's finance and threaten the country's creditworthiness. High interest rates were already causing debt-servicing problems in the enterprise sector, while the banking sector's loan portfolios were deteriorating.

Slovakia's external situation was also worsening at this point. In particular, the pegged exchange rate which had been in place since 1991 was causing further macroeconomic deterioration. Although nominally fixed against the German mark (60 per cent) and the American dollar (40 per cent), the koruna had appreciated in real terms over 1996, removing the competitive boost that exports received from the 10 per cent devaluation enacted at independence.[32] Real wage increases further harmed competitiveness within the economy, fuelled by the expansionary monetary policy that the NBS had followed through 1994 and 1995, which far outstripped the increases in labour productivity. Deprived of its labour advantage, Slovakia's exports slowed down significantly and the current account deficit widened to 11 per cent of GDP.

Despite these mounting structural flaws, the economy continued to grow through domestic consumption, which rose by an remarkable 20 per cent in 1996. Without massive changes in Slovak economic policies, however, the economy was becoming more and more fragile and susceptible to exogenous financial shocks. The first such shock came in the middle of 1997, as the koruna came under speculative attack in the wake of currency weakness in most emerging markets (to eventually culminate in Thailand and the Asian crisis). The shock was more severe in the Czech Republic, but contagion effects helped push the Slovak koruna to the lower bound of its fluctuation band. In response, the NBS tightened the money supply and kept the exchange rate close to parity with the German and US currencies.[33] Interest rates soon skyrocketed, the NBS lost 18 per cent of its reserves in defence of the koruna, and the banking sector was severely shaken. Indeed, the interest rate increases proved to be too much for the Investment and Development Bank (IRB), one of the three largest banks in the country and a bank in which the state had a 35 per cent share. With a heavy burden of non-performing loans and frozen credit lines, IRB was placed under the forced administration of the state in December 1997.

The failure of IRB presaged a turning point for the Slovakian economy. Continued foreign indebtedness and a sense of growing political instability led Moody's Investor Service to downgrade Slovakia's credit rating in March 1998 to a non-investment speculative grade (later in the year, Moody's also downgraded Slovakia's financial institutions to the lowest grade). Popular discontent within the country over the pace and dispersal of economic benefits mounted throughout the year, and a poll taken by the Institute of Public Affairs (IVO), a Slovak think tank, found that 69 per cent of Slovaks felt that the economy was getting worse, as opposed to a mere 2 per cent who thought they were better off. Slovakia was also descending into a political maelstrom, as the Meciar government began to exhibit authoritarian tendencies during 1997 and 1998, such as jailing opponents and attempting to muzzle the press. This backsliding earned the opprobrium of the West, which passed over Slovakia for first-round inclusion into the EU or NATO in discussions. As the country entered economic freefall in 1998, only a political change was able to turn the tide.

In the run-up to the September 1998 parliamentary elections, the Meciar government was forced to face the impact on public opinion of more damning economic news. On 23 September the Slovak public learned 'that the balance of the government's account with the NBS had but a few thousand korunas in it.'[31] A week before this revelation, inter-bank interest rates rose abruptly, exceeding 50 per cent for the first time since the speculative attack on the koruna in May 1997. These gloomy economic indicators contrasted with continued GDP growth of nearly 5 per cent, and the elections showed the widespread ambivalence of the Slovak populace without revealing a popular mandate for change. Meciar's MDS party won the largest proportion in parliament, securing 27 per cent of the seats. But an opposition coalition of four different parties representing 58 per cent of the votes coalesced to form a new government. MDS was excluded from the talks to determine the shape of the new government.

The governing coalition chose Mikuláš Dzurinda of the Slovak Democratic Coalition (SDK) to be the new prime minister, a seemingly thankless job given the state of the country's finances. Almost immediately, Dzurinda's government instituted a stabilization package focused on halting Slovakia's slide, with the centrepiece being the elimination of the currency peg on 1 October 1998. This occurred in the wake of the ruble devaluation and failures of currency pegs in emerging markets during the Asian crisis.[35] Meciar had refused to devalue the currency throughout 1998 for purely political reasons, and the peg had been rigidly respected despite the resulting severe overvaluation of the koruna. Once left to float, the koruna immediately depreciated by 6 per cent. However, the currency began to regain strength once the new government was formalized by the end of October, ending up at 7.9 per cent, slightly stronger than its former fluctuation band.

In tandem with this drastically needed step in monetary policy, the government sought to impose fiscal order and reinstate financial discipline by reducing governmental expenditures and reforming public finance and revenue collection. The government set a deficit target of 2 per cent of GDP (which was ultimately not achieved in 1999) and implemented expenditure cuts in highway construction, wage freezes in the civil service and education sectors. It also carried out a politically difficult lay-off of non-essential civil servants. In order to stimulate production and entrepreneurship, corporate income taxes were lowered from a rate of 40 per cent to a slightly less repressive 25 per cent. To encourage the growth of small business, enterprises with an annual turnover under one million korunas were licensed but not required to pay tax.

Changes in taxation were part of a bold plan aimed at revitalizing enterprise reforms that had languished under the Meciar government. As a first step, the legal and regulatory framework for enterprises was reworked with an eye towards facilitating liquidation. Bankruptcy laws were amended at the end of 1998 to simplify procedures and allow much greater scope for creditors and debtors to reach a settlement, in hopes of accelerating the restructuring process. According to an OECD report published in 2000, the new bankruptcy procedures disadvantaged some creditors, mainly the state, but created new incentives for the majority to make use of the system. The report also commented that legal changes would take time to filter into business and institutional practices.[36]

With a revamped legal framework in place, President Dzurinda hoped to resuscitate the moribund privatization process, which had been ridden with sweetheart deals while simultaneously prohibiting the privatization of a long list of 'strategic industries'. Dzurinda accomplished a significant revision of the strategic industries identified in the last quarter of 1998, with only six or seven enterprises exempt from partial or full privatization, including the postal service, railways, forestry, and water supply sectors. A flurry of activity and sales followed, including the successful sale of Slovak Telecom in 2000 to Deutsche Telekom for US$900 million. By 2002, even the enterprises still classified as 'strategic' in the late 1990s had been slated for privatization, including Slovakia's Water and Sewerage Works and the power generation utility, Slovenske Elektrarne

The deep restructuring required by many Slovakian firms meant abandoning the policy of creating an autonomous Slovak business community in favour of attracting FDI. In 1999, the coalition government introduced new incentives for foreign investors, including proposals to introduce a ten-year tax holiday to investors in new assets and facilities, known as greenfield investors, and allowing foreign financial institutions to purchase land for their operations. In general, these policies have succeeded in enticing investors back into Slovakia, aided by the change of government and general move towards macroeconomic stability. In addition to the Deutsche Telekom purchase of Slovak Telecom, US Steel purchased the core steel-making functions of VSŽ in 2001, while 36.2 per cent of the Slovnaft oil refinery was purchased in 2000 by the Hungarian company Mol. However, these sales only came after nearly a decade of struggling to find the right balance between maintaining national ownership and harnessing the managerial knowledge that comes with foreign direct investment.

Financial sector issues The Slovak banking system had been steadily deteriorating during the period 1996–98, as the government spent US$571 million in bailing out banks without any concomitant structural reform. In late 1998, Prime Minister Dzurinda's government hastily drafted a plan to rehabilitate four state-owned banks, including the vitally important Investment and Development Bank (IRB), that accounted for about 45 per cent of the banking sector's 782 billion korunas in assets at the end of 1999. One key issue was the need to start the banks on the road to viability by removing non-performing loans from the balance sheets. For this purpose, the government worked with technical advisors from the European Union and the United States to create a debt-resolution agency, Slovenska Konsolidacna. Some US$2.13 billion in bad loans was transferred from the banks to this agency for auction. Fresh capital injection to the affected banks accompanied the transfer of debt to the public sector, with the aim of luring foreign investors to purchase and restructure the dilapidated financial institutions.

Restructuring the banking sector has taken longer than expected, due to the volume of non-performing loans closely linked to loss-making state-owned industries. Nevertheless, the effort to reform the Slovak banking sector has met with tangible success, including the sale of 87 per cent of

Slovenska Sporitelna (Slovakia's largest bank) to Austria's Erste bank in early 2001. Relaxation of FDI and ownership rules allowed increased consolidation of Slovakia's private banks, as foreign investors acquired the domestic banks that were relatively healthy. For example, after its acquisition by Raiffeisen of Austria, Slovakia's Tatra Banka, expanded its operations throughout the country and now ranks third in terms of assets.

Worries for the future While Slovakia's efforts to stabilize the economy and accelerate the microeconomic transition have been mostly successful, it has been at a price. Unemployment has emerged as the largest problem, exacerbated by the stabilization and austerity policies of the Dzurinda government. Restructuring Slovakia's firms and the subsequent waves of privatization swept away the politically motivated employment favoured by Meciar, but the number of unemployed leapt by 69,000 between October 1998 and January 1999. The cancellation of sweeping infrastructure projects proposed by Meciar added to the burden, as unemployment reached 15.1 per cent in the first quarter of 1999. Unemployment continued to climb throughout 2000 as the macroeconomic stabilization package worked its way through the economy, hitting a high of 20.8 per cent in January 2001. Retraining and replacing the workforce remains a major challenge for the Slovak economy, but one that may be easier now that restructuring has begun and FDI is on the rise. Slovakia's continued preparation for EU membership and the corollary access to Western European markets may also help to ease unemployment, especially if the world economy experiences sustained growth in 2004.

In retrospect, Slovakia pursued a two-track policy that combined a big bang in the macroeconomy with gradual microeconomic reform that began to slow the country's growth. Eventually the slow pace of enterprise reform was forced to accelerate when external imbalances became too onerous and the costs of a stalled privatization process became too high. The transition of enterprises and efforts to lay the foundations of a capitalist economy are still underway in Slovakia, but for the most part the fundamentals of a market economy are in place and growth has resumed. However, while the economic parting of Czechoslovakia cast Slovakia in the role of the ugly stepsister to the Czech Republic's Cinderella, other countries in Eastern Europe were left even further behind. The next section illustrates the plight of Bulgaria, a country that continues to trail many of the other economies in the region.

Bulgaria: delayed therapy

Bulgaria's shift to democratic governance was accompanied by a lingering desire for the previous guarantees of a centrally planned economy. During the first four years of the transition, opinion polls showed that between one-third and one-half of the public approved of the old communist system – not a good omen for future success.[34] Despite some small-scale dissent, Bulgaria did not exhibit widespread disenchantment with its economic system, and, like Slovakia, citizens supported leaders who promised to either slow down or halt reforms. This popular sentiment, especially prevalent during the early years of transition, coupled with incomplete political reform, led to a decade of half-hearted policies and partial liberalization that took their toll on the Bulgarian economy.

Resistance to reform had several roots. Much like Cuba in Latin America, Bulgaria was known for its subservience to the Soviet Union. Dependent on its larger patron for critical aid and assistance, it was perpetually consigned to the periphery of development.[38] Government intervention in the economy had been a fact of life for Bulgarians from time immemorial, including even the distant pre-Second World War 'capitalist' experiment there. Bulgarians had little experience with anything else.[39] But perhaps the predominant reason for the public's complacency came from the performance of Bulgaria relative to her neighbours during the Cold War. Bulgaria simply did not experience the major economic crises during communist rule that had plagued other countries in the Soviet bloc. This relative calm was mainly due to Bulgaria's trade with Western Europe outside the CMEA, and small-scale experiments in decentralized management. In addition, the country was blessed with one of the best-educated and most highly trained workforces in the region. Confronted with the choice of relative stability or an uncertain future, the population was bound to choose the status quo.

This is not to say that Bulgaria's economic situation was *a priori* fundamentally sound, however, no matter how much popular support it enjoyed. In reality, the country was hard-pressed to survive the collapse of communism and the end of the Soviet Union's generous aid. In terms of macroeconomic stability, the country's foreign debt burden at the beginning of transition represented a major liability and perhaps its biggest obstacle to reform. While its net debt of US$9.1 billion in 1990 was small on an absolute scale compared to those of Hungary or Poland (who had US$20.2 billion and $44 billion, respectively), it represented 379 per cent of Bulgarian exports, growing to 412 per cent of exports in 1991. An unsustainable burden, the high level of debt led to multiple rescheduling attempts with international banks and sovereign lenders, but the country declared a unilateral moratorium on debt repayment in 1990 before negotiations on rescheduling were completed. This rash move effectively cut off all sources of external financing during the economic transition. Foreign capital markets refused to even touch Bulgaria, and as late as 1999 the IMF reported that the country still had not gained full access to capital markets.[40] The debt rescheduling talks lasted three years after the moratorium, worsening Bulgaria's external position at a time when the slow pace of reform further diverted foreign direct investment.

Bulgaria's inability to pay its debt was a harbinger of other fiscal problems that began to mount during the early stages of transition. The Bulgarian National Bank (BNB) continued seigniorage financing – that is, financing with the capital gain generated by the creation of reserve money, despite its inflationary effects. Loss-making state enterprises continued to be subsidized by state-owned commercial banks, which were in turn subsidized by the BNB. The government thus had a fiscal liability of loss-making enterprises, keeping these businesses afloat for political or other, less legal, reasons. It was politically popular to avoid the surges in unemployment seen in the other countries in Eastern Europe, but sustaining moribund enterprises undermined the balance sheets of the banks and hindered their development. The government became dangerously over-leveraged as a result.

Despite the presence of so many loss-making enterprises supported by the government, the private sector initially made inroads in Bulgaria, growing from 19 per cent of GDP in 1990 to 48 per cent in 1995. The restitution of small urban properties in the early post-communist years played an important role in expanding the private sector.[41] According to early studies of Bulgaria's reforms, privately owned companies outperformed and created more jobs than state-owned enterprises – all without massive subsidies.[42] The enforcement of a hard budget constraint and the effects of competition had brought results, but the private sector remained too minuscule to drive the economy, and was rife with problems in any case. In the absence of a middle class constituency committed to the success of privatization, the government's policy became disjointed and increased financial fragility.

Bulgaria's political system exhibited the same gradualist, patchwork mentality that produced the hybrid of capitalism and state planning in the economic arena. The country had apparently worked through a successful political succession without major upheaval. Unlike neighbouring countries that had popular protests to oust the sitting rulers, Bulgaria's change from the authoritarian 18-year dictatorship of Todor Zhikov to democratically elected Andrei Lukanov occurred with relatively little fanfare. The country lacked a broad-based democratic or dissident movement and the populace was largely inexperienced with political pluralism. In the words of one commentator, by 1992, Bulgaria boasted a 'working constitution and appeared to have a well-functioning electoral system'.[43] However, it soon became apparent that political advances were not translating into economic reforms, and Bulgaria's post-communist evolution behind to lag behind the performance of other transition economies.[44] In fact, it is possible to argue that Bulgaria's political transition occurred in name only. In most cases, the same *nomenklatura* that governed the country during communism retained positions of high power. Popular impetus for change did not manifest itself on the streets like in Budapest or Prague; most Bulgarians were content with the system, unaware of its frailty, or simply had no frame of reference for anything other than a top-down economic system. In the absence of broad popular support for reform, former communists were able to retool themselves as the Bulgarian Socialist Party (BSP) and win the country's democratic elections in 1990 – the first since the Second World War. Consequently, economic reforms proceeded at a snail's pace, with both privatization and price liberalization being notable mainly for their slowness.

In 1991, after nearly two years in power, the BSP were ousted by the ostensibly reformist Union of Democratic Forces (UDF) in an exceedingly close election. However, this was far from a radical change, as one observer noted: 'the BSP and UDF are to a considerable extent fictitious [and] they do not represent deep social separation or patterns of rivalry'. Bulgaria's transition experience was typical for Balkan countries, with broad public support for socialism and no experience with parliamentary democracy.[45] Moreover, the UDF were almost immediately shackled by a loss in parliamentary elections in 1992, which gave a party representing ethnic Turks a pivotal role in close voting.

The UDF attempted a cautious package of reforms, but their rule was not to last. Proving themselves inept at running the country and unable to build support for an economic reform plan, the UDF lost to Zhan Videnov of the Socialist Party in 1994, amidst widespread corruption charges. An eyewitness to the elections of 1994 trenchantly noted that, even though the BSP had been out of office for nearly two years, 'the machinery of government had never been out of their hands'.[46] Meanwhile, Bulgaria's financial woes continued to mount. Much like Russia, the economic life of Bulgaria was beholden to politically well-connected 'groups' in the private sector that concentrated former state assets in their hands. Privatization favoured insiders who were given opportunities to acquire assets at rock-bottom prices. Without restructuring by the new owners, firms retained jobs and created a natural constituency for the Socialists by guaranteeing continued employment. This confluence of factors created a situation similar to the 'crony capitalism' of the Asian crisis, with a comparable outcome.

Bulgaria's banking crisis In 1997, six years after the collapse of the Soviet Union and eight years after the fall of the Berlin Wall, an exogenous shock forced Bulgaria to finally embark on long-delayed reforms. The first half of the 1990s were characterized by half-hearted economic measures proposed by the ruling ex-communists, including the 1995 Law on Prices that effectively ended price liberalization and brought the domestic market back under the purview of the state. However, the country was firmly in the midst of a banking disaster. Eighty per cent of the country's banking sector assets were held by ten state banks, nine of which had negative capital, with more than half their portfolios classified as non-performing. Further, half of the known private banks were technically bankrupt.[47] Two rounds of bank closures did nothing to assuage the fears of the deposit-holding public, and bank runs occurred sporadically as more institutions were placed under conservatorship, administered by the Ministry of Justice. Foreign-exchange deposits were practically non-existent by the end of 1996. Fearful of bank failure, citizens preferred to keep their hard currency out of the banking system.

The simmering troubles in the banking sector exploded into a fully-fledged crisis in 1997. Continued mismanagement of the economy by the Videnov government and the bias against reform led to a drastic fall in real output of more than 10 per cent in 1996, following two years of modest growth for the first time in the post-communist era. With the banking system on the precipice, the Bulgarian National Bank (BNB) took emergency steps that only served to further destabilize Bulgaria's fragile economy. In an attempt to stave off a total banking collapse, the BNB increased liquidity in the system by offering collateralized loans to banks more freely, but at a rate set at a penalty to the central bank's overnight rates – known as the Lombard window. However, when combined with repurchasing of government bonds, this resulted in a massive spike of inflation. In fact, inflation reached an annualized figure of 500 per cent in January 1997, climbing to just under 2,000 per cent for the first quarter just two months later (see Figure 4.4).

Hyperinflation While Bulgaria's economy was far from being a true market economy, the hyperinflation tore through every segment of society, acting as an egregious tax on the poor and those holding currency, and finally exposing the populace to the unsustainability of Bulgaria's economic path. Hyperinflation's power to sever social links and foment political unrest has been widely documented throughout economic history, with

Figure 4.4 Bulgaria: annual inflation (%)

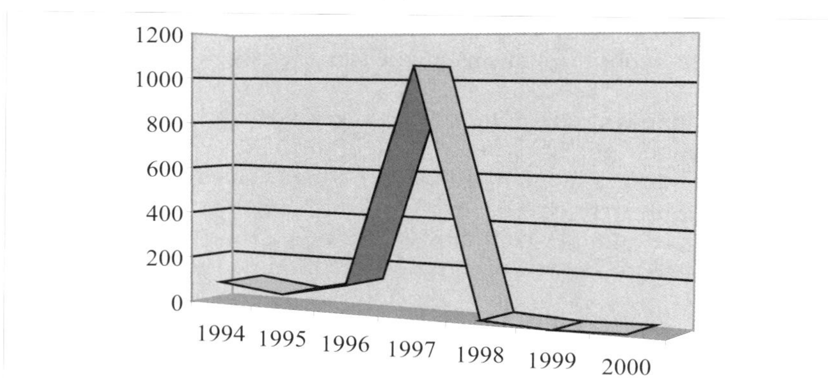

Source: Economist Intelligence Unit Data Service, www.eiu.com.

perhaps the most famous case of hyperinflation, in the Weimar Republic, also the most devastating. In extreme cases, hyperinflation acts to destroy economic institutions, because it renders useless the price mechanisms essential for a functioning market economy.[48] Bulgaria's bout with hyperinflation fuelled public disenchantment with the ex-communist's economic stewardship, creating an opportunity for the free-market opposition to lay a credible claim to the political leadership of the country. Bulgaria, which had eluded large-scale popular unrest in the eight years since the fall of the Berlin Wall, suddenly developed a popular constituency for reform as the crisis of hyperinflation enveloped the ruling party. Street protests and the reinvigoration of the UDF opposition party forced the resignation of Videnov at the end of 1996, and an interim government committed itself to elections in April 1997. The UDF's Petar Stoyanov triumphed in emergency elections and quickly ushered in a credible stabilization package fashioned around a currency board to break the back of inflation, coupled with a plan to end state subsidies and finally complete the introduction of price liberalization.

In the years since the introduction of the currency board, the Bulgarian economy has fallen more in line with other post-communist economies in recovering from an output decline. Output has returned to the positive side, with growth of 3.5 per cent in 1998, 2.4 per cent in 1999 (with growth lower due to after-effects of the Russian devaluation), 5 per cent in 2000, 4.1 per cent in 2001 and 4.8 per cent in 2003. Structurally, Stoyanov's government has stabilized the economy and reinvigorated privatization, including in the beleaguered banking sector. Inflation has been reigned in, climbing from a low of 2.6 per cent in 1998 to 11.4 per cent in 2000, but declining steadily to 7.4 per cent in 2001 and 5.8 per cent in 2002. Meanwhile FDI has skyrocketed to 6 per cent of GDP (or $750 million, from a low of $34 million in 1992). These successes notwithstanding, the Bulgarian public has refrained from showing a clear-cut preference for reform in elections. Due to the hardships of the delayed reform, Stoyanov was ousted in elections in 2001, with BSP candidate Georgi Parvanov taking 54 per cent of the vote. Still seeking entry into the EU, Parvanov has taken a more market-oriented approach than his BSP predecessors, maintaining fiscal discipline and continuing with the structural reforms that have produced non-inflationary growth.

Bulgaria's experience illustrates the difficulties of implementing gradualist reforms. The attempted hybridization of a capitalist and a command economy created ample distortions at both micro and macro levels, opening up incredible opportunities for corruption even if proper market reforms (such as privatization) were attempted. Additionally, the lack of political reform in Bulgaria also allowed rent-seeking behavior to occur, as an inexperienced polity continued to favour those who were stealthily bankrupting the system. While the Bulgarian public initially supported the gradualist approach to reform, this led to the accrual of hidden costs that eventually proved unsustainable and brought considerable hardship to the country.

Bulgaria's banking crisis also challenges one of the fundamental tenets of gradualism: that the transition to a market economy is smoother when relying on institutions initially formed during the era of central planning. Institutions arise endogenously from their specific circumstances, embody the local knowledge and skills present at their creation, and reflect the epoch in which they were born. Even the most flexible and forward-looking of institutions must rely on rules and norms to function, and these are not easily changed. Thus, an institution that is created under communism in anticipation of market reform – such as a banking facility protected by the state, but expecting financial sector liberalization – would be very different from an institution actually created during the period of liberalization. In effect, the gradualist school has preached an 'infant institutions' policy, with the same effect as the 'infant industry' arguments from the 1960s – institutions formed in the absence of competition were handicapped when actually exposed to basic competition and the international markets.

In Bulgaria, the hesitancy and uncertain nature of reform led the institutional mechanisms to flounder, especially in the financial sector. Banks that could have been privatized in order to foster a competitive financial sector were instead left in the hands of the state, forced to lend to unprofitable state-owned enterprises, and left without the capital base needed to impose tougher budget constraints on both public and private enterprises.[49] In the presence of these constraints, the banks were doomed to failure – and the government's attempts to keep the shaky edifice erect only led to the hyperinflation that eventually brought the system down. In this case, Bulgaria's transition was very similar to the problems that other developing countries have experienced throughout the 1990s. The banking crisis echoed Mexico's 'Tequila crisis' of 1994–95, where highly leveraged banks were susceptible to the slightest exogenous shock. The management of the Bulgarian government, with its cosy network of insiders and sweetheart deals, suffered from problems identical to Indonesia and other countries affected by the Asian crisis. In retrospect, Bulgaria's institutions did undergo a shock therapy; it just came after seven lost years.

Policy lessons for Cuba

The Czech Republic, Slovakia, and Bulgaria each followed different routes to economic liberalization, and their range of experiences encapsulates the successes and failures of the post-communist transition in Eastern Europe. While Cuba retained its communist system after the end of the Cold War, and is largely governed by socialist principles today, it is likely that the country's leadership will eventually need to grapple with the challenges of incorporating greater market mechanisms in order to attain sustained economic growth. Like Cuba, many of the countries in Eastern Europe possessed small, well-educated populations accustomed to a system centred on a socialist value system. Furthermore, these countries were close to affluent western markets and indeed were propelled towards assuming membership in key regional institutions, such as the European Union. Cuba will likely feel a similar pull in the future towards the regional infrastructure of the Western Hemisphere, including the multilateral development banks, and perhaps even the free trade agreements that the island rigorously eschews at present. In the area of economic reform, the experiences of Slovakia and Bulgaria are particularly relevant for Cuba. Both countries now appear to be on the road to recovery, but much of the decade of transition has been plagued by policy debacles and missed opportunities. If Cuba finds itself considering a move away from central planning and towards a market economy, several lessons stand out from an examination of Eastern Europe:

- *The intersection between political reform and economic transition*
  In Slovakia and Bulgaria, where communism was relatively popular, reforms have proceeded more slowly and have created more economic and social disruption. This has reinforced the public's preference for communism and delayed the benefits of economic growth that justify moving to a market economy. Public support is a key determinant of the success of an economic transition – especially one that is undertaken concurrent with the transition to democracy. A country's leadership should not sacrifice one for the sake of the other, and, in fact, research on Eastern Europe has shown that the higher the level of democracy, the higher the support for reform.[50] In order to build this broad-based support, full explanation of the benefits of reform should be made to the public at large, with recognition of the short-term hardship and long-term benefits. A successful public relations campaign that keeps the public informed and involved will avoid a situation like that of Bulgaria, where the public clung for seven lost years to the vestiges of the old system and it took another crisis to finally push through reform. The process also entails moving beyond the ideological rigidity that developed over decades to guide economic policy. Strong and persuasive political leadership can play an important role in shaping this dynamic of economic reform.[51]
- *Price liberalization must be comprehensive*
  The cases of Slovakia and Bulgaria suggest that partial price liberalization is a ticket to nowhere. The basic building block of the free market, the true essence of capitalism, is that prices reflect information and the underlying laws of supply and demand. Communist economies, by contrast, have only a tenuous connection between price and quality, or

supply and demand. After the fall of the Berlin Wall, those transition countries that quickly abolished administered prices and price controls were much better equipped to cope with inflationary pressures than the ones that attempted to assuage the pain of transition through controlling prices. Bulgaria's 1995 attempt to retain price controls is a classic example of a country's leadership further repressing the necessary systemic corrections, making the inevitable inflation of transition even worse by sparking hyperinflation. Rational economic actors can adapt quickly to changing situations, and evidence shows that transition economies that abolished price controls early on in their transition learned the price system fairly quickly.[52] Without such price liberalization, the system is doomed to sputter on. The resultant inflation means a greater likelihood that other reforms will fail, as higher prices eat into the political support for continued reform.

- *Microeconomic weakness doesn't mean macroeconomic instability, but neither can be sustained*
  Slovakia grew impressively in 1994 and 1995, despite a non-transparent privatization process that left many enterprises without badly needed restructuring. However, the prospects for future growth were badly damaged by the lack of microeconomic reform and structural transformation, and the slowdown of 1997 and 1998 revealed that long-term growth hinges on successful enterprise reform. Likewise, the structural weaknesses in Bulgaria's banking system were enough to retard the system's growth, finally bursting into a conflagration that threatened to bring down the entire system. Macroeconomic stability is a vital first step towards reform, but the real challenge in building a market economy entails forging new connections and links at the microeconomic level. Even the Czech Republic revealed the difficulties in creating a vibrant private sector – while it was able to move assets into private hands, procrastination in some aspects of microeconomic reform, such as financial sector privatization, reverberated throughout the system and remained a drag on the real economy until corrected. The Eastern European experience shows Cuba that progress must be simultaneously pursued on both fronts – the early gains that emerge from macroeconomic reform alone will prove to be a mirage over the long term unless state enterprise restructuring is also addressed.
- *Corruption is the Achilles' heel of privatization*
  The importance of fashioning appropriate rules and institutions for a market economy is the paramount challenge for transition economies, and nowhere does this challenge manifest itself more than in the privatization process. Privatization has caused much consternation for transition economies, as the need for a rapid transfer of assets to the private sector must be balanced against the competing (and often-entrenched) interests that could unhinge the process. In order to

combat the rent-seeking behaviour of interest groups and avoid the political use of a crucial economic process, the experiences of the Czech Republic, Slovakia, and Bulgaria show that the process needs to have maximum transparency and to be as broad-based as possible. Unfettered corruption has the capacity to strip privatization of its presumed economic benefits, and to undermine the reform process as a whole. Cuba will need the legal safeguards to prevent this history from repeating itself in an era of increasing economic openness, especially given the controversial issue of expropriated properties that is going to further complicate the island's future.

- *Harness foreign knowledge for domestic gain*

  Advanced economies possess a wealth of knowledge about building a market economy and making loss-making enterprises viable. However, socialist countries have traditionally been reluctant to embrace foreign expertise, as a result of strong nationalism, residual hostilities from the Cold War, and concern for developing a domestic private sector. These are indeed important considerations, but this does not mean that foreign knowledge should be shunned; quite the opposite, it should be welcomed. International know-how can increase managerial efficiency, improve corporate governance, and prevent the crony capitalism that has stalked many of the post-communist countries of Eastern Europe. Slovakia remains the example of a country that did all that it could utilizing only domestic managers, and it did a credible job for a people with scarce experience with capitalism. But the needed restructuring was avoided in order to reward political cronies, undermining national competitiveness.

  If Slovakia had followed a policy similar to that adopted by Singapore in the 1970s, which encouraged foreign investment in order to stimulate growth, Slovakia's favourable location and skilled workforce could have been put to better use.[53] Of course, building public support for this approach can be quite difficult, and even developed economies have trouble convincing their populace of the benefits of foreign competition. To date, Cuba has carefully navigated this terrain, harnessing foreign knowledge to develop the tourist and mining sectors while remaining defiantly committed to an independent nationalism. Given Cuba's strong sense of nationalism, the question of 'to whom will Cuba belong' is likely to be one of the thorniest issues for the island if it moves towards a market economy. The island's leadership would benefit from a careful review of the Eastern Europe experience, and could thereby develop a strategy for harnessing foreign knowledge without compromising its sovereignty.

- *The benefits of taking decisive action*

  A successful and complete economic transition will necessarily take many years, but the basic institutions and laws needed to shape the new society can generally only be formed during a very small window of time. The common thread that runs through Slovakia and Bulgaria (and many other failed transitions) is that a gradual approach runs the risk of being co-opted by politics and other special interests. Even in the Czech Republic, a halting approach to financial liberalization and the privatization of the banking sector negatively impacted on privatization and delayed much-needed restructuring in the enterprise sector. If anything, the experience of the past decade of transition bears out the wisdom of the 'shock therapy' school, as even countries that were not disillusioned with communism (such as Slovakia and Bulgaria) could have taken the medicine quickly and then started to move on.

Cuba's economic future will be determined by the leadership and circumstances at the time, and many argue that the country would be well suited to a gradualist approach towards the 'market socialism' practiced in several East Asian countries. However, Eastern Europe also presents a telling example for Cuba, as the island's geographical and cultural orientation is similarly westward-looking. In terms of size, proximity to advanced markets, and rich human and intellectual capital, Cuba has much in common with the Czech Republic, Slovakia, and Bulgaria. Slovakia and Bulgaria both eventually did undertake a shock therapy, but only after years of half-hearted measures that increased the impoverishment of their peoples. Moving away from a planned economy entails managing significant, and often abrupt, change, but the temptation to proceed slowly can result in market distortions that cripple the economy down the road. The Cuban government is no stranger to decisive action. But the question remains whether Cuba will adopt the more comprehensive reform path that has benefited the Czech Republic, or instead engage in the series of adjustments that have hampered the economic development of Slovakia, Bulgaria, and other lagging countries in the region.

Notes

1 For an overview of the literature on initial conditions, see especially Martha de Melo, Cevdet Denizer, Alan Gelb, and Stoyan Tenev, 'Circumstances and Choice: The Role of Initial Conditions and Policies in Transition Economies', *World Bank Working Paper*, no. 1866 (1997).

2 Taken from World Bank, *World Development Indicators 2001*. For the purposes of this chapter, 'shock therapy' countries are the Czech Republic and Poland, while the gradual countries are Hungary, Bulgaria, Romania, and the Slovak Republic.

3 Jan Fidrmuc and Jarko Fidrmuc, 'Macroeconomic Developments in Slovakia and the EU Accession Process', *International Institute for Applied Systems Analysis (Austria) Interim Report*, IR-00-007 (2000).

4 The debate on 'corner solutions' in exchange rate management for transition and emerging markets has been played out elsewhere, and will not be discussed at length here. Suffice it to say, a pegged exchange rate utilized for monetary policy purposes cannot survive in a world of capital mobility, as the Czech

Republic found out in 1997. See Christopher A. Hartwell, 'Feeding the Tigers: Capital Flows to East Asia and the Experience with Globalization', *EMP Financial Advisors Study*, no. 3 (2000).

5 An excellent examination of the lessons for Cuba from the Eastern Europe example comes from G. Douglas Harper, 'Restitution of Property in Cuba: Lesson Learned from Eastern Europe', from *Proceedings of the Annual Meeting of the Association for the Study of the Cuban Economy*, vol. 9 (1999).

6 Josef Kotrba, 'Privatization Process in the Czech Republic: Players and Winners', in Jan Svejnar (ed.), *The Czech Republic and Economic Transition in Eastern Europe* (New York: Academic Press, 1995).

7 Laura Papi, 'Czech Republic – Elections May Delay EU Convergence', *Deutsche Bank Research Report (Global Emerging Markets Research),* June 1998.

8 'Czech Republic: the Financial Sector', *European Union Enlargement Papers,* No. 3 (August 2000).

9 International Monetary Fund, 'Staff Report for the 2002 Article IV Consultation', 12 July 2002.

10 Ibid.

11 Ibid. However, Slovakia's troubles may have come not from the policies but from its industrial composition pre-transition. The country had a higher proportion of heavy industry and armament factories than the more service-oriented Czechs, and would be hit harder by the end of state subsidies and the loss of CMEA markets.

12 Of course, the claim of Slovakia to have zero unemployment under communism is dubious, as statistics from the communist era must be taken with a grain of salt. Also official statistics on unemployment rarely took into account underemployment, and so the jump in unemployment following transition is probably not as large as the official statistics suppose.

13 M.D. Plachtinsky, 'Reforma Škrta Rozpocet', *Práca*, 18 December 1992.

14 František Turnovec, 'The Political System and Economic Transition', in Jan Svejnar (ed.), *The Czech Republic and Economic Transition in Eastern Europe* (New York: Academic Press, 1995).

15 World Bank, *World Development Indicators 2001.*

16 Anton Marcincin, 'Privatization', in Anton Marcincin and Miroslav Beblavy (eds), *Economic Policy in Slovakia 1990–1999* (Bratislava: Slovak Foreign Policy Association, 2000).

17 Ibid.

18 Miroslav Beblavy, 'Industrial Policy', in *Economic Policy in Slovakia 1990–1999.*

19 Simeon Djankov and Gerhard Pohl, 'Restructuring of Large Firms in Slovakia', *World Bank Working Paper* No. 1758 (April 1997).

20 *Hospodárske noviny*, 24 October 1995, 4.

21 Jan Ducky quoted in *Trend*, April 1996. Viazoslav Moric, chairman of the SNS, quoted in Ivan Miklos, 'Economic Transition and the Emergence of Clientelist Structures in Slovakia', in John Gould and Sona Szomolanyi (eds), *Slovakia: Problems of Democratic Consolidation and the Struggle for the Rules of the Game* (Bratislava: Slovak Political Science Association, 1997).

22 Anton Marcincin, 'Privatization', in *Economic Policy in Slovakia 1990–1999.*

23 Simeon Djankov and Gerhard Pohl, 'Restructuring of Large Firms in Slovakia', *World Bank Working Paper* No. 1758 (April 1997). A caveat is provided by the authors, however, who note that successful firms 'may have been privatized early *because* the new owners saw their potential for improvement', blurring the lines of causality.

24 I. Mikloš and E. Žitnanský, 'Ekonomika', in M. Bútora (ed.), *Slovensko 1996* (Bratislava: Inštitút pre verejné otázky, 1997).
25 Ivan Miklos, 'Economic Transition and the Emergence of Clientalist Structures in Slovakia', in John Gould and Sona Szomolanyi (eds), *Slovakia: Problems of Democratic Consolidation and the Struggle for the Rules of the Game* (Bratislava: Slovak Political Science Association, 1997).
26 Robert Anderson, 'Slovakia: Investors Starting to Take More Notice', *Financial Times*, 4 July 2001.
27 Data from the Vienna Institute for International Economic Studies (WIIW) and the Austrian Institute of Economic Research (WIFO). Data Compilation on FDI in Central and Eastern Europe, 2002. http://www.wiiw.ac.at/e/fdi_data.html.
28 OECD, *OECD Economic Surveys: Slovakia* (Brussels: Organization for Economic Cooperation and Development, 1999).
29 Zora Kominkova, 'Money Supply in Slovakia in the Background of Monetary Developments, 1997–2000', *Biatec* (Journal of the National Bank of Slovakia), no. 9, July 2001.
30 International Monetary Fund, *Slovakia: Recent Economic Developments, 1998* (Washington, DC: International Monetary Fund, 1998).
31 Peter Dovciak, 'Deficit in General Government and the Current Account of the Balance of Payments', National Bank of Slovakia, http://www.nbs.sk/INDEXA.HTM.
32 The koruna was allowed to fluctuate around a tightly circumscribed band of +/– 1.5 per cent. In 1996, this band was widened to +/– 7 per cent, in order to deter speculative capital flows.
33 International Monetary Fund, *Slovakia: Recent Economic Developments, 1998.*
34 'Slovak Monthly Report – September 1998', MESA 10 Centre for Economic and Social Analysis (Bratislava), http://www.internet.sk/mesa10/REPORTY/R98_09.HTM.
35 A discussion of the fixed vs floating rate regime can be found in Christopher A. Hartwell, 'Feeding the Tigers: Capital Flows to East Asia and the Experience with Globalization', *EMP Financial Advisors Policy Study*, no. 3 (June 2000).
36 Joaquim Martins and Tristan Price, 'Policy Interdependence During Economic Transition: the Case of Slovakia, 1999–2000', *OECD Economics Department Working Paper*, no. 253 (July 2000).
37 J. Bristow, *The Bulgarian Economy In Transition* (Cheltenham: Edward Elgar, 1996).
38 Bulgarian president Todor Zhikov praised the Soviet Union so effusively that Bulgaria was mockingly referred to as the Soviet Union's 'sixteenth republic', and Zhikov himself offered on two separate occasions to incorporate Bulgaria into the USSR proper.
39 Roumen Avramov and Jerome Sgard, 'Bulgaria: From Enterprise Indiscipline to Financial Crisis', *Centre d'Etudes Prospectives et Informations Internationales (CEPII) Working Paper*, no. 96–100 (July 1996).
40 International Monetary Fund, *Bulgaria: Recent Economic Developments* (Washington, DC: IMF Press, 1999).
41 'Bulgaria Country Briefing', *The Economist*, online edition, http://www.economist.com/countries/Bulgaria/profile.cfm?folder=Profile-Economic%20Structure.
42 See especially Valentijn Bilsen and Jozef Konings, 'Job Creation, Job Destruction and Growth of Newly Established, Privatized and State-Owned Enterprises in Transition Economies: Survey Evidence from Bulgaria, Hungary, and Romania', *Journal of Comparative Economics*, vol. 26, no. 3 (September 1998): 429–45.

43 Ilian Mihov, 'Bulgaria: Ten Years of Economic Transition', in Mario Blejer and Marko Skreb (eds), *Transition: The First Decade* (Cambridge: MIT Press, 2001).
44 Ibid.
45 'The Political Change in Bulgaria: Pre-Electoral Attitudes', *Kultura* (Sofia), 7 June 1990.
46 Paul Swider, "Red Mafia" Fumbles Economic Ball – Opposition Seeks a Return to Power', *Metropole Paris*, 16 (January 1997), http://www.metropoleparis.com/1997/70120203/bulgaria.html.
47 Anne-Marie Gulde, 'The Role of the Currency Board in Bulgaria's Stabilization', *IMF Policy Discussion Paper*, 99/3 (April 1999).
48 Anders Åslund, *Post-Communist Revolutions: How Big a Bang?* (Washington, DC: Centre for Strategic and International Studies, 1992).
49 Roumen Avramov and Jerome Sgard, 'Bulgaria: From Enterprise Indiscipline to Financial Crisis.'
50 Jan Fidrmuc, 'Liberalization, Democracy, and Economic Performance During Transition', *Zentrum für Europäische Integrationsforschung (ZEI), Working Paper* B5 (2000).
51 Frank Wykoff, 'Creating Capitalism: Politics, Reforms, and Economic Performance', *Claremont College Department of Economics Working Paper*, 2001–17 (July 2001).
52 Jerzy D. Konieczny and Andrezej Skrzypacz, 'Inflation and Price Setting in a Natural Experiment', *Stanford Graduate School of Business Research Paper* No. 1695 (July 2001).
53 For an exposition of Singapore's strategy, see Christopher A. Hartwell, 'Competing, With Globalization', *EMP Financial Advisors Study*, no. 21 (December 2001).

5
The Struggle of the Central Asian Republics

Zahid Hasnain

Central Asia is perhaps the most overlooked region in the study of economic transition. Since the early 1990s, 26 countries of the former Soviet Union and communist bloc have begun to construct productive, market economies during a period of dramatic, and often traumatic, change. For five states in particular – the Central Asian Republics (CARs) of Kazakhstan, Kyrgyzstan, Uzbekistan, Tajikistan and Turkmenistan – the challenges of this triple economic, political and geopolitical transformation have been particularly daunting. This chapter will examine the market-led economic reforms of the Central Asian states, and conclude with thoughts on the economic policy challenges facing Cuba and other countries on the verge of transition.

The five CARs occupy an area of roughly 1.5 million square miles, stretching geographically from the Caspian Sea in the West to China in the East, and from Siberia in the North to Afghanistan in the South. Their terrain is varied, with a mountainous east and western deserts, and is rich in natural, agricultural, and mineral resources. The republics have a total population of 55 million in one of the most sparsely populated regions in the world. Uzbekistan is the largest country with 25 million people, followed by Kazakhstan with 17 million. Tajikistan's 7 million people represent the youngest population of any former Soviet country, as its intensely fought civil war left approximately 70 per cent of its people aged younger than 30 years. Kyrgyzstan and Turkmenistan each have about five million citizens.

The region's history has been marked by significant cultural development and endemic conflict. Central Asia initially developed as a link between Europe and China by way of the famous Silk Route, which imported fabric, as well as new technologies, religions, and ideas. The region has been the spiritual home of most of the major religions of the world, and its location at the heart of the Eurasian continent has also made it a focal point of geostrategic power struggles for the past two thousand years. In the nineteenth century the region was the scene of the

Map 4 The Central Asian Republics

so-called 'Great Game', as the Russian and British Empires jockeyed for predominance in Asia. In the twentieth century, the CARs' incorporation into, and later independence from, the Soviet Union were both marked by significant turmoil. After September 11, their strategic location near Afghanistan generated renewed international attention in the context of the US-led 'War on Terror'.

While rich in history, the five states are the poorest of the former Soviet republics, as indicated by Table 5.1. The underdevelopment of the CARs predates the communist bloc's collapse and is not simply a product of the transition away from central planning. However, low levels of industrialization, wealth and infrastructure all contributed to unfavourable initial conditions that have threatened the progress of reform. As with many formerly socialist countries, Central Asia's social development indicators compared favourably to regions with similar income levels, only to undergo marked decline when sudden economic transition led to a drastic decline of GDP (a drop of 20–60 per cent between 1990 and 1995).[1] Social spending, especially in countries like Kyrgyzstan and Tajikistan now saddled with large external debts, has faced the constraints of fiscal discipline required to modernize developing economies.

In Central Asia, dominant political currents have weighed as heavily as economic indicators in shaping the process of reform. Each of the CARs has significant ethnic minority populations, including Russians, and ethnic tensions have long threatened regional security. Border disputes also factor into the ethnic conflict, particularly with respect to strife between Uzbekistan and Turkmenistan, and between the Uzbek and Kyrgyz populations within Kyrgyzstan. Militant Islam is another source of instability that contributed to the bloody civil war in Tajikistan from 1992 to 1997. These nationalistic and religious trends, as well as the political fallout from the

Table 5.1 CARs: economic, social, and demographic features, 1998

	Kazakhstan	*Kyrgyzstan*	*Tajikistan*	*Turkmenistan*	*Uzbekistan*
Per capita GDP (PPP)	1,434	366	179	390	433
Population (millions)	15.7	4.7	6.1	4.7	24.0
Life Expectancy at birth	68	67	68	65	68
Urban Population (% of total)	58	38	32	45	41
Total GDP (in US$ billions)	22.40	1.63	1.32	1.92	10.39

Source: *Walden's World of Information Business Intelligence Report*, by country, 2000–2.

Soviet collapse, have resulted in the significant out-migration of Russians, which has depleted some of these countries, in particular Kazakhstan, of much-needed human capital. More importantly, the combustible nature of Central Asia's social tableau has fuelled political conflict and exacerbated governance problems that have impeded the process of economic reform.

This brief demographic and geographic description of the CARs demonstrates that initial conditions influence economic reform, a lesson that will surely resonate for Cuba and other transition countries. However, policies also matter, and a thorough analysis of these countries' transitions over the last decade must focus on both economic transformation and reconstruction of the state. This chapter will analyze the CARs' overall economic performance, and variations in this performance among the five countries, in light of the dual influence of *initial conditions* and *policies*. Specifically, it will assess the importance of geography, natural resource endowments, and institutional and historical legacies, balanced against the specific policies pursued to achieve economic reform.

Each of the Central Asian countries under consideration has followed a unique path to reform, determined by three key variables: initial conditions, policy options, and speed of implementation. While each republic worked with a different mix of initial conditions and policy options, the clearest distinction among them is the pace of reform, which provides a useful way to categorize the market transitions of the CARs. In this context, Kyrgyzstan and Kazakhstan are two countries that embraced reform fairly quickly, although the full effects of their transition processes are still unfolding. Uzbekistan has charted a mixed path, emerging from the Soviet bloc without the massive drop in output witnessed among its Central Asian neighbours. Although its relative success remains contentious, raising many questions about sustainability and cost, preliminary research suggests that the country has benefited from the gradualist pacing of reforms, protective social policy and its natural resource advantages. Tajikistan and Turkmenistan represent the slowest reformers and chronic economic underperformers, a result of the severe political dysfunctions that have plagued their transition to independent republics. Tajikistan descended into civil war following its separation from the Soviet Union, and has only recently reached a level of political stability necessary to consolidate new market-oriented economic policies. Turkmenistan's political system has gravitated in the opposite direction, towards absolute rule by an eccentric dictator whose reforms have made little progress away from a centrally planned economy.

As Cuba considers its economic future, the disparate experiences of the Central Asian Republics provide an objective lesson on the challenges facing transition economies in their struggle overcome the limitations of their initial conditions while moderating the potential for political chaos or misrule. However, the lessons of the CARs are not only cautionary in nature. By harnessing natural advantages and adapting policies to national goals, this region also demonstrates how Cuba may be able to benefit from the wisdom of their experience.

Trends in Central Asia's economic performance

A sharp initial fall in output was a defining feature of the transition in Eastern Europe and the former Soviet Union. What distinguishes the Central Asian states is the depth of this decline in output. As Table 5.2 reveals, compared to Central and Eastern Europe, and the Baltic states (CSB), the Commonwealth of Independent States (CIS) and the Central Asian countries suffered average output declines twice as prolonged and deep. While output for all the five countries has shown signs of recovery since 1998 (Figure 5.1), these countries are still below their output levels from a decade ago. However, this decline in output is not uniform throughout the Central Asian states. Uzbekistan, for example, has in general managed to avoid extreme fluctuations in growth that characterize the other four republics, and Kyrgyzstan has posted the strongest recovery over the past four years (barring Turkmenistan, whose data is highly suspect). Tajikistan posts output below half its total of ten years ago.

It should be noted here that problems with data imply that these output figures, which are all official government statistics, should be viewed with some degree of caution.[2] The statistics for Tajikistan, and particularly Turkmenistan, are known to be quite unreliable – for example, in 1992 official Turkmen statistics stated that the country grew by 36 per cent in 1992, a figure eventually revised by the government to report a decline of 15 per cent. These statistics also complicate conclusions about transition's effects on social welfare, since they do not take into account the size of the

Table 5.2 The transition recession in comparative perspective

Countries	*Consecutive Years of output decline*	*Cumulative output decline*	*Real GDP, 2000 (1990 = 100)*
Kazakhstan	6.0	41.0	90.0
Kyrgyzstan	6.0	50.0	66.0
Tajikistan	7.0	50.0	48.0
Turkmenistan	8.0	48.0	76.0
Uzbekistan	6	18	95
Average: Commonwealth of Independent States	6.5	50.5	62.7
Average: Baltic States	3.8	22.6	106.5

Source: World Bank, *Making Transition Work For Everyone* (Washington, DC: World Bank, 2001a).

Figure 5.1 GDP during the transition (annual % change)

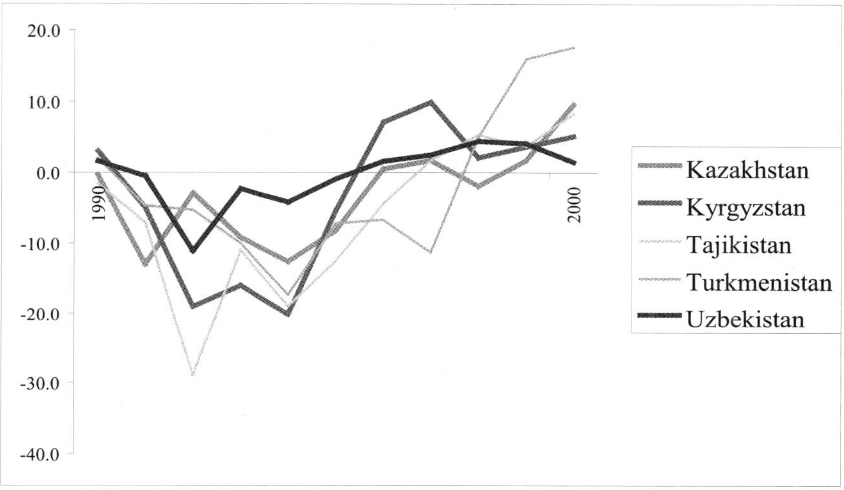

Source: World Bank, *Making Transition Work For Everyone* (Washington, DC: World Bank, 2001a).

informal sector that grew substantially. Once this growth of the unofficial economy is taken into account, as well as several other factors that falsely inflated output totals during the communist era, declines are somewhat less severe.[3]

Poverty rates have increased dramatically in the region. Using daily per capita income criteria, a World Bank study estimated that in 1998–99, 49 per cent of Kyrgyzstan lived below the poverty line – a figure that reached a staggering 68 per cent that same year in Tajikistan.[4] This increase in poverty resulted from the combined influence of falling output and rising inequality. As shown in Table 5.3, Gini coefficients, which measure the inequality of income distribution on a scale between 0 and 1, have risen sharply in all the countries for which data is available, and now approach those of the world's most unequal region, Latin America. Again, this trend is in contrast to that in Central and Southern Europe, and the Baltics (CSB), which have remained fairly egalitarian by global standards. The collapse of government revenues has also had a negative impact on social indicators, as families have been increasingly unable to afford the informal kickbacks that doctors and teachers have demanded to compensate for the reductions in their government salaries. For example, primary enrollment rates, which were more than

90 per cent for the region in 1989, have fallen by 10 or more percentage points in Turkmenistan and Tajikistan over the past decade.[5]

Why did Central Asia suffer such a severe downturn in comparison to Southeastern Europe and the Baltic States? At the start of transition, economists expected output to fall as a result of macroeconomic stabilization amid the reallocation of resources from unproductive to productive sectors of the economy. However, few expected the slump to be so severe. Empirical studies by the International Monetary Fund and the World Bank have analyzed this question by focusing on the effects of initial conditions – such as the level of economic development, natural resource endowments, geography, and history under communism – balanced against the policy choices pursued. The next section examines this dual influence of initial conditions and policy choices on economic performance in the CARs. In drawing lessons for Cuba, it is important to identify which of these initial conditions are relevant, and identify policies that successfully mitigated the pain of transition, particularly for the more vulnerable sections of the population.

Initial conditions and policy approaches

The Central Asian states started the transition process with demographic, economic and political disadvantages when compared with Eastern Europe. Beyond the Soviet legacy of weak and dysfunctional institutions, the CARs demonstrate that factors such as climate, terrain, and geographical location can have a profound impact on economic welfare.[6] For example, empirical studies have found that tropical regions are disadvantaged in development in comparison to temperate regions (primarily due to the greater prevalence of diseases), that coastal regions are more favoured in development

Table 5.3 CARs: trends in income inequality

	Gini coefficients of per capita income		
	1987–90	*1993–94*	*1996–98*
Kazakhstan	0.3	0.33	0.35
Kyrgyzstan	0.31	0.55	0.47
Tajikistan	0.28	—	0.47
Turkmenistan	0.28	0.36	0.45
Uzbekistan*	—	—	—
Average CIS	0.28	0.36	0.46
Average CSB	0.23	0.29	0.33

Note: *Uzbek data unavailable, est. in one district placed at 0.4.
Source: Johannes Linn, 'Central Asia: Ten Years of Transition' (talking points for The World Bank donor's consultation meeting, Berlin, March 2002).

than the hinterland, and that landlocked countries are particularly burdened due to their higher transportation costs. All five CARs are landlocked, and Uzbekistan claims distinction as the only 'double landlocked' country in the world.

While Kazakhstan, Uzbekistan and Turkmenistan have large energy resources, Kyrgyzstan and Tajikistan are remote and mountainous, endowed with very few natural resources, and highly dependent on unreliable energy imports. Deeper, structural problems tied to poor Soviet infrastructure also plague these countries, which were assigned specific production tasks in the Soviet economy's production chain.[7] This territorial division of labour was particularly pronounced in the Central Asian states, leaving them especially vulnerable to the economic disruptions caused by the break-up of the Soviet Union. Under Moscow's direction, the economic activity of the CARs was limited mainly to producing and processing raw materials, with few manufacturing capabilities outside those required by the Soviet-wide production chain. Large parts of the region, particularly Uzbekistan and Turkmenistan, were turned into cotton monocultures, which led to declining soil productivity due to lack of crop rotation. By the 1970s, the region produced 95 per cent of the Soviet Union's cotton and 15 per cent of its vegetable oil, yet Russia processed 70 per cent of the nation's cotton yarn.

The collapse of intra-regional trade among the countries of the former Soviet bloc, which accounted for 80 to 90 per cent of the total volume of trade in the CARs, hurt these nations considerably, as did the ending of the generous subsidies from Russia. According to one estimate, in 1989 Kyrgyzstan received budget transfers from the Soviet central government equivalent to 7.8 per cent of its GDP, Tajikistan received 8.2 per cent, Turkmenistan 9.0 per cent, Kazakhstan 9.3 per cent and Uzbekistan 11.3 per cent.[8] By 1994 these generous funds had disappeared with the adoption of national currencies, resulting in negative consequences for economic welfare, particularly for low-income groups. The breakdown of the Soviet welfare state and food subsidies has led to a considerable increase in malnutrition – Tajikistan for example, relied on the Soviet Union for 75 per cent of its food.[9]

In addition, the region's manufacturing and processing industries had been established without any regard to cost-benefit analysis. Mining was developed in Central Asia, but little attention was being paid to production costs or the quality of ore. Refining capacity was not adequately developed in Kazakhstan and Turkmenistan and instead the oil and gas from the region's vast reserves had to be transported to Russia for processing. Their limited capacity was not designed to handle local oil; instead, refineries in eastern Kazakhstan were built to process oil from Siberia. Similarly, Kyrgyzstan imported Cuban sugar cane (equal to about 3 per cent of GDP in the late 1980s) for refining and export within the USSR.

The Central Asian countries experienced inflation rates ranging from 650 per cent a year in Turkmenistan to 7,000 per cent in Tajikistan in the immediate aftermath of the Soviet collapse. Inflation exceeding 50 per cent is unambiguously bad for growth. The maintenance of the ruble zone until 1995, as part of the problematic common currency adopted by 15 post-Soviet states in 1991, was the primary culprit. The CARs favoured independent national currencies in principle, but feared that abandoning the ruble zone would disrupt the crucial flow of subsidized oil, grain, and other primary products from Russia. From 1991–1993, the CARs were constrained to follow the ruble and Russian price reforms, and their macroeconomic performance was determined exogenously.

The experiences of the CARs demonstrate that initial conditions matter, but are not the sole determinants of development. Economic policy plays a decisive role, and empirical literature has analyzed the impact of reform policies on the economic performance of transition countries.[10] As these studies underscore, the liberalization of prices and trade joined with structural reform and privatization offers the opportunity to rebuild and augment output as independent economies.

One prominent group of economists explicitly tested the importance of initial conditions versus policies in a sample of 28 transition economies.[11] The initial conditions included income levels, the degree of urbanization, the extent of industrial distortion, the richness of natural resources, geographical proximity to western market economies, the extent of repressed inflation, trade as a share of GDP, prior familiarity with market economics, and status as an independent economy prior to 1989. At first glance, the empirical results are not surprising. Countries that are richer, closer to western markets, with less repressed inflation, less industrial distortion, and a longer history of independence, perform better on average. However, the study also reveals that policies have the highest explanatory power among all sets of factors in the growth equations, accounting for 35 to 40 per cent of the variation in growth rates, as compared to 19 to 30 per cent for initial conditions.

This empirical literature also provides some interesting insights into the performance of the CARs, as well as the influence of certain initial conditions. These countries were disadvantaged vis-à-vis Eastern Europe by standards of development, geography, market memory, and dependence on the central Soviet government. However, two factors played to their advantage. First, the CARs were among the least over-industrialized of the transition economies, therefore claiming low levels of industrial distortion. Because they functioned as primary commodity producers in the Soviet hierarchy, the percentage of industrial production in GDP was lower, allowing for a fair representation of service industries such as banking and trade. Second, both Turkmenistan and Kazakhstan possessed reserves of oil and natural gas to ease the transition process by attracting large-scale foreign investment. Their initial conditions presented the dual policy challenges of overcoming weaknesses while properly harnessing economic strengths.

In the early 1990s, the Washington Consensus was the guiding economic policy framework for countries shedding socialist systems and entering the market economy. This policy package promoted short-run stabilization and liberalization of prices in order to remove economic distortions and improve distributive efficiency, and long-run structural reforms to put the economy on a path towards sustained growth. The Washington-based international financial institutions and many academics also favoured a 'Big Bang' approach, in which reforms would be pushed through as quickly as possible. The logic was primarily one of political economy – reforms would inevitably result in short-term dislocation and output losses, and the objective was to push through the reforms quickly before any sustained political opposition could develop against them. This followed the perception that the initial period following the break-up of the Soviet bloc was a period of 'extraordinary politics', a small window of opportunity that had to be quickly, and maximally, utilized. A gradualist reform programme risked encouraging rent-seeking behaviour, as the former communist elite could exploit the arbitrage opportunities of a partially reformed economy to enrich themselves and block further reform. This prediction was quite accurate in the case of the Central Asian Republics.

By contrast, advocates of gradualism pointed to the high costs of transition and the need to set up appropriate market institutions and welfare systems prior to introducing structural reforms. Institutional economists argue that the Washington Consensus underestimated the importance of informational problems and the perverse consequences of imperfect information.[12] This produces opportunistic behaviour by economic actors that harm society as a whole. In other words, Adam Smith's famous 'Invisible Hand' does not work under these circumstances, and rule-based institutions are essential to preventing these detrimental outcomes.

The concept of social capital is crucial to understanding the problems facing new market economies. Without efficient institutions, countries fail to accumulate social capital, the dense networks of interaction that develop trust and 'norms of generalized reciprocity'.[13] Social capital, like physical and human capital, is immensely productive for society and market economies. As the Nobel-Prize-winning economist Kenneth Arrow observed, 'virtually every commercial transaction has within itself an element of trust, certainly any transaction conducted over a period of time. It can plausibly be argued that much of the economic backwardness in the world can be explained by the lack of mutual confidence'.[14] Dense networks of civic engagement facilitate the transmission of information, create norms of reciprocity, and increase the costs of opportunism through social ostracism. These networks are also crucial in making democracies work better, because they lead to a more informed and politically aware citizenry that is better able to hold public officials accountable.

How social capital is influenced by rapid versus gradual reform should be kept in mind when analyzing the economic performance of the CARs. The experience of these countries reveals that the dangers of rent-seeking are inherent in a partial-reform strategy, and the commitment to liberalization and structural reform varied widely among these countries. Kazakhstan, and in particular Kyrgyzstan, liberalized prices quickly, implemented privatization and structural reform, and have made the greatest progress in reforming their economies. Uzbekistan has adopted a more gradualist approach, and has initiated a policy of import-substituting industrialization with the aim of diversifying its economy away from agriculture and towards industry. Turkmenistan has yet to embark on comprehensive liberalization and privatization, while the transition process in Tajikistan was delayed by civil war until 1997.

The European Bank for Reconstruction and Development (EBRD)'s transition indicators provide an important point of reference in judging the pace of economic reform, using the categories of markets and trade reform, enterprise reform, and financial institution reform. The indicators range from 1 to 4.3, with 1 representing little or no change from a planned economy, and 4.3 being equivalent to the standards in an industrialized market economy. Table 5.4 provides a quantitative snapshot of the cumulative achievements across these five countries as of 2000, while Figure 5.2 traces the yearly progress since 1990. Kyrgyzstan and Kazakhstan have reformed the most, although they lag behind other CIS countries and are far outpaced by Hungary, the Czech Republic, and Poland. Both of the leading CARs liberalized prices, enacted trade reform, and made substantial progress in small-scale privatization almost immediately after gaining independence, as indicated by the relatively high private sector share of GDP.

Large-scale privatization, however, has proceeded much more slowly, as has the more difficult task of creating a securities market and constructing an appropriate competition policy (Figure 5.3). By contrast, Uzbekistan, Tajikistan, and Turkmenistan remain the least reformed transition economies. Uzbekistan has reversed some of the initial gains made in trade reforms by reintroducing restrictive trade practices in 1997, while Turkmenistan is still very much a Soviet-era planned economy. Tajikistan, impeded by crushing poverty and unemployment and supported by massive international aid, has only just begun the reform process. The following analysis will detail the specific conditions and policy approaches of the two fastest reformers, Kyrgyzstan and Kazakhstan, followed by the gradualist reforms of Uzbekistan and concluding with the politically stillborn programmes of Tajikistan and Turkmenistan.

Table 5.4 Progress in transition in Central Asia

	Private sector share of GDP (%)	*Enterprise reform*	*Markets and trade reform*	*Financial institution reform*
Kazakhstan	60	3	2.8	2.3
Kyrgyzstan	60	3	3	2.2
Tajikistan	40	2.3	2.5	1
Turkmenistan	25	1.4	1.3	1
Uzbekistan	45	2.2	1.7	1.7

Source: *EBRD Transition Report 2001.*

Figure 5.2 Trends in transition in Central Asia

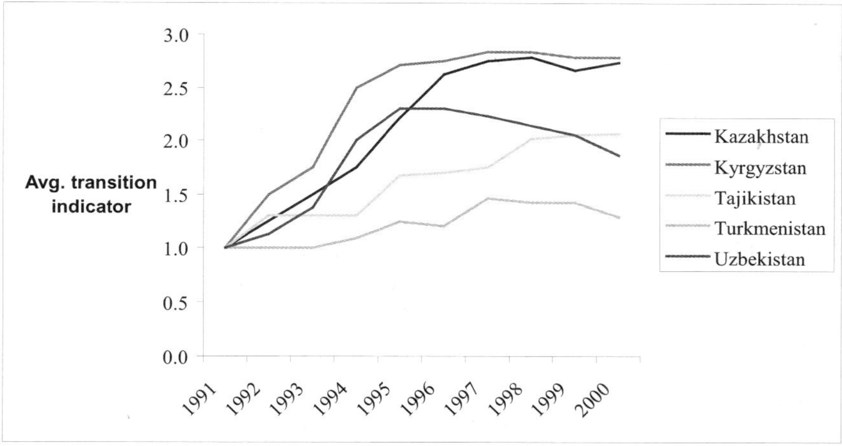

Source: *EBRD Transition Report 2001.*

Kyrgyzstan and Kazakhstan: fast reformers, mixed results

Despite their radically different starting points, Kyrgyzstan and Kazakhstan have emerged as the most rapid reformers among the five CARs. Resource-poor and sparsely populated Kyrgyzstan had few economic advantages to exploit, whereas the relatively well-endowed Kazakhstan, with three times the population, had a larger pool of labour and geographical advantages. Both countries clearly exhibited a greater degree of political willingness to

Figure 5.3 CARs: comparative transition indicators (1999)

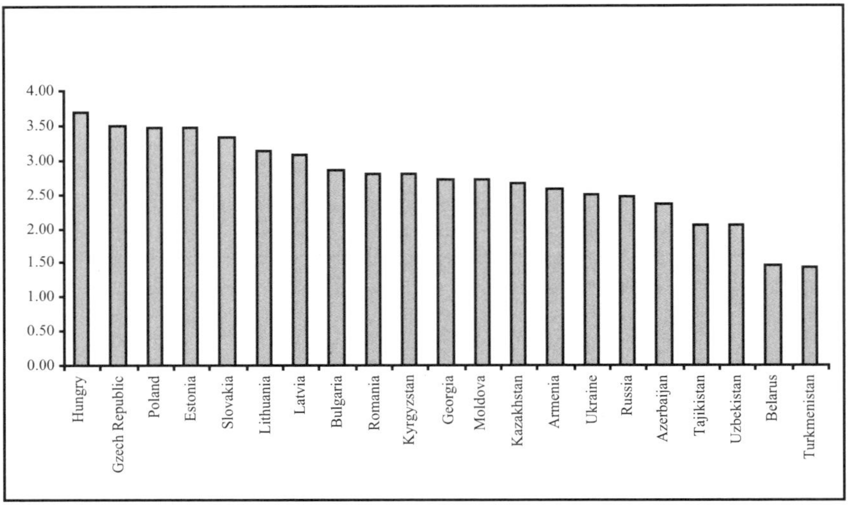

Source: *EBRD Transition Report 2001.*

embrace reform, although this motivation sprung from contrasting origins. With industrial production integrated into the Soviet complex, and without a true agricultural comparative advantage, Kyrgyzstan's accelerated response represented its only option for survival.[15] Kazakhstan, meanwhile, harnessed its strong resource base and diversified economy to enter the global markets.

Kyrgyzstan's path to reform was expedited in part because the communist party was unable to maintain its political domination following independence. The communist leadership was removed from power in the wake of ethnic riots between Uzbeks and Kyrgyz in 1990, and an outsider, Askar Akaev, a leading physicist and president of the Republic's Academy of Sciences, became president in 1991. Macroeconomic stabilization became the primary economic priority, beginning with an attack on the hyperinflation plaguing the former Soviet bloc countries. Price liberalization occurred by 1994, and soon thereafter the annual inflation rate was reined in to below 50 per cent. The controls on fiscal deficits and a tight monetary policy reduced inflation from 1,200 per cent in 1993 to 3.7 per cent in 2001. Price liberalization and the rehabilitation of state enterprise were other initial elements in the pursuit of Kyrgyz stability: small subsidies on basic foods, utility monopolies and agricultural producers remained, but these were phased out by 1997.

Additionally, the World Bank funded the diagnostic studies of 28 state-owned enterprises, freezing assets and employment until agreements were met to close five, retain four and reorganize the remaining 19 for eventual sale.[16] The rehabilitation programme was halted briefly in 1997 amid allegations of corruption, though by 2000, the State Property Fund was managing bidding for both Kyrgyz Telecom and the national airline. Two other state monopolies, KyrgyzEnergo and Kyrgyzgas, were also ready for privatization in 2000, and the state announced its intentions to sell its majority holdings in 50 smaller companies and minority holdings in 60 others. With these reforms and the complete privatization of small industry, the private sector accounted for 85 per cent of its GDP in 2000.[17] Though reform of state-owned enterprises proceeded more quickly, the later land reform programme has proven very successful. The importance of agricultural production within Kyrgyzstan is significant, and peasant farming now claims 90 per cent of the total agricultural production, despite controlling only 60 per cent of the arable land. On the other hand, farming co-operatives, which utilize 20 per cent of the total land, contributed only 8 per cent to production statistics.[18]

While private sector reforms have met with rapid success, reforming the small and under-utilized banking sector has proved difficult. New banking laws in 1991 initiated the process, though the 1996 passage of reform laws for the Central Bank marked a second starting point. Among the regulations to align the Central Bank with international standards, preparation began to develop non-bank financial institutions. These have played an increasingly important role in micro-finance lending for small enterprises and rural borrowers, and their strength reflects the lack of confidence in Kyrgyzstan's commercial banks, whose assets total only 7 per cent of GDP. Unfortunately, the transition of the financial system from commercial to non-bank institutions does not guarantee that reforms will continue successfully. Non-bank institutions such as the country's largest agricultural lender, the Kyrgyz Agricultural Finance Corporation, are state-owned. Seeking to become banks, they now reflect a profit margin buoyed by government subsidies. The constant shifts of reform mechanisms in the banking sector reflect a tenuous commitment, not the strength of regulatory improvements.

Kyrgyzstan also embraced a liberal trade regime, becoming the first former republic of the Soviet Union to join the World Trade Organization in 1998. President Akaev hoped that these reforms, combined with Kyrgyzstan's considerable natural beauty, would attract foreign investment and tourism, transforming the country into a 'Switzerland' of Central Asia. Unfortunately, multinational corporations have yet to respond with enthusiasm or the expected investment, in part because of the poor transportation infrastructure inevitable in a newly developing and mountainous, landlocked country. Foreign investors have likewise been dissuaded by the growth of Kyrgyzstan's external debt acquired during the initial reforms. Foreign exchange and domestic capital markets have yet to allocate efficiently, indicating both the effects of human capital flight and general inexperience with appropriate policy. Furthermore, low barriers to entry have led to a proliferation of commercial banks, which are unable to generate profit without substantial interest rates. Such conditions make the possibility of loan default much more likely. The Russian financial crisis in 1998 exacted a major toll on Kyrgyzstan, still dependent on Russia and the other CIS countries for trade, and reversed many of the initial gains of reform. With its scarcity of resources and high dependence on foreign aid, much of the Kyrgyz population finds the benefits of economic reform to be increasingly elusive.

While not a western-style democracy, Kyrgyzstan maintains a considerable degree of social pluralism. Civil society organizations have rapidly taken root since independence, numbering nearly 1,000 by 1997 and including political parties and movements, professional bodies, and national-cultural centres. Since the mid-1990s, Kyrgyzstan's political process has become less liberal than its economy. Until 1995, the country was the only CAR to hold free multi-party elections, but conflict between Akaev and the opposition, in part a product of the economic transition, has led to more repressive measures.[19] In 2004, intimidation of the media has increased and the proliferation of political parties has not prevented the leadership from manipulating elections and referenda, enabling Akaev to bypass the constitution and increase his personal power. He has been encouraged in these authoritarian actions by the leaders of Uzbekistan and Kazakhstan, for whom democracy poses a threat to their own repressive regimes. For example, in 1999 and again in 2000, Uzbekistan froze its gas supply to Kyrgyzstan to force Akaev to clamp down on the Islamic opposition in his country. Despite the early progress made in the 1990s, Kyrgyzstan is today experiencing declining political freedom amid intractable poverty. International dissatisfaction with President Akaev's manipulation of power may compound the situation by reducing the flow of foreign aid. The increasingly vocal opposition and the impending presidential elections in 2005 may limit the political capital and capacity necessary for the government to continue with reform.

Unlike Kyrgyzstan, neighbouring Kazakhstan was initially much better placed to take advantage of its entry into the world economy, due to abundant energy resources and a more diversified economic base. Furthermore, compared to the other CARs sandwiched between each other and countries such as Afghanistan and Iran, Kazakhstan's long borders with China and Russia represented a relative geographical advantage. Kazakhstan was also capable of attracting more substantial foreign direct investment than Uzbekistan: $5.6 billion compared to Uzbekistan's $533 million between 1989 and 1998. However, despite substantial commitment to reform, Kazakhstan was unable to translate these strengths into sustained economic performance, growing less than Uzbekistan during the same period.

Kazakhstan has suffered from macroeconomic distortions that have been widely documented in other energy-abundant economies.[20] The large inflows of capital into the country caused its real exchange rate to appreciate beyond its equilibrium level and trigger a recession. Moreover, in an effort to attract foreign investment, the Kazakh government offered overly generous tax breaks that contributed to a fiscal crisis in the late 1990s and a low rate of public investments, particularly in the social sectors.[21] To further complicate matters, the regime's liberalization measures were countered by Russia's control over the pipeline network and, therefore, over Kazakhstan's oil resources. Russia initially forbade Kazakhstan to build new pipelines, forcing them to use the existing network for its oil exports and thus ensuring control for Russia. However, with the construction of new pipeline projects and increased quotas through the Russian Federation's infrastructure, crude production and foreign investment have increased substantially.

Like Kyrgyzstan, the Kazakh government chose to prioritize stability in the post-independence period, focusing first on hyperinflation. Through fiscal discipline and floating exchange rates supported by the central bank, the government was forced to speed other structural reforms to stabilize gains and growth. The Kazakh currency, the *tenge*, was introduced in 1993, and monetary policy was tightened and prices liberalized in order to bring inflation to heel. Inflation remains precariously stable as Kazakhstan is increasingly dependent on exports of a single commodity, though its advanced stage of financial reform will allow the government to begin direct inflation targeting by monitoring changes in short-term interest rates. The central challenge of the government's programme for macroeconomic stability is the appropriate management of huge and increasing petroleum revenues.

Beginning with small enterprises, Kazakhstan completed the initial wave of privatization in 1993 before implementing the second phase, a voucher scheme to privatize medium-sized and large-scale enterprises.[22] Natural monopolies and infrastructure invested in large, state-owned enterprises represented the third and final phase of privatization, a process that was well underway in 1999. Kazakhstan has made the most progress of the CARs with a third phase of privatization, beginning with the initial restructuring of contracts and the sale of heat, railroad and telecommunications industries in 1997. Currently, large amounts of foreign direct investment have complemented the massive flow of petroleum wealth, and the government has expressed a desire to capitalize state-support for nascent technological and value-added industries.

Both private and public banks in Kazakhstan have undergone dramatic reform following independence, and recent financial sector reforms have led to a substantial increase in deposits and credits. Three pieces of legislation are credited with this jump in confidence: the assumption of international standards; depositor's insurance for household deposits; and banking secrecy and confidentiality provisions.[23] Fiscal management remains problematic, and tax collection throughout all sectors is the next step for resource-generating reform.

Banking reform took place in two stages, parallel to the initial stage of reform in Kyrgyzstan. Minimum capital requirements were established in both countries between 1993 and 1994, eliminating many small depository institutions and forcing the government to sell many of its own municipal holdings.[24] The second stage of reform, beginning in 1995, focused on the restructuring and deletion of bad, or non-performing, debt. A new central bank was introduced in 1996, though the success of Kazakhstan's reforms were not notable until sector-wide structural changes began in 2000. The commercial banking sector is the largest in the CIS states in relation to GDP, likely a product of high concentration and the significant legal and institutional regulatory reforms that have accompanied the continuing transition.[25]

Kazakhstan was the last of the CARs to declare independence from the Soviet bloc, and President Nursultan Nazarbayev has retained a firm grip on power with a declared commitment to 'democracy in doses'.[26] The constitution, written in 1995, affords him considerable executive power to issue decrees and ad hoc legislation without parliamentary oversight. After advancing the electoral contest by a year and outlawing the participation of his chief rival for attending a rally later declared illegal, Nazarbayev won re-election in 1999 with an alleged 78.3 per cent of the vote.[27] The leader has advocated development models following those of South Korea and Turkey, while focusing on external relations with the former Soviet allies. The system continues to lack transparency, and perhaps as a token of progress, in 2002 the Prime Minister informed Parliament of offshore accounts holding the proceeds of oilfield sales and foreign investment. Totalling approximately half a billion dollars, these accounts were drawn upon to balance budgets and finance the building of the new capital.[28] This revelation to the legislature can be viewed as a step towards transparency between branches of government, though the transfer of the remaining $321 million to the national savings and stabilization fund, the NFRK, was more likely a simple move to consolidate oil-sale profits.

Kyrgyzstan and Kazakhstan present interesting examples of the importance of speed in the economic reform of transition economies. Kyrgyzstan, inextricably tied to the Soviet infrastructure, had few options to sustain itself apart from the alluring promises of market-led development. Kazakhstan, by contrast, moved ahead with reform in order to capitalize on foreign interest in its natural resources. Yet the rapid reforms in Kyrgyzstan and Kazakhstan have produced mixed results. Kazakhstan had been dubbed the 'leader of the pack', as the most economically successful Central Asian state, posting GDP growth of 13.2 per cent in 2001.[29] Such success often garners dual benefits: committed, market-led reformers receive not only the potential benefits of the free market, but also the favourable attention of the international financial community. However, defenders of gradualist reforms argue that such success results from unnecessary concessions to foreign investors, associated under-taxation, incomplete reforms and poor policy implementation. Kazakhstan's natural endowments have led the market to focus upon economic development surrounding extractable oil, gas and mineral industries, neglecting diversification or the creation of light-industrial production. Not only have Kyrgyzstan's pre-existing underdevelopment and dependence on the Soviet trading bloc not been relieved by introduction to the global markets, but complications of corruption, distribution and efficiency have also been brought to the fore. The fast-track economic reforms of these countries have not absolved them of the initial conditions that dictated their market opportunity for implementing reform, but transparent markets have raised the accountability of these nations to the international community. It remains to be seen whether the benefits of such transparency translate to improved efficiency or resource distribution for their own citizens.

Uzbekistan: mixed reformer, good results

Uzbekistan's economic performance presents a dilemma to advocates of rapid reform. The country has grown more quickly than the high-paced reformers in Kazakhstan and Kyrgyzstan, defying standard economic predictions to such an extent that the IMF and World Bank have dubbed the phenomenon the 'Uzbek growth puzzle'.[30] The country has implemented reform gradually, and its halting steps towards macroeconomic stabilization have resulted in persistent high rates of inflation, limited liberalization and incomplete structural reforms. Yet Uzbekistan's growth has substantially outperformed what econometric models would predict for a resource-rich country with a mixed policy approach. This anomaly is most apparent with regard to the output index comparing the Baltics, Russia and former Soviet nations, in which Uzbekistan's net output index drops only 3 points between 1992 and 1997.[31] In comparison, the average index decline for the other four Central Asian Republics is 34 points.

Uzbek authorities attribute the country's relative economic success to import-substituting industrialization policies, while the international financial institutions point to unique initial conditions not captured in the general econometric framework. Uzbek President Islam Karimov has christened their experience 'an evolutionary model' of transition, with goals to privatize non-strategic state-owned industries, rationalize the financial sector and attempt to increase efficiency and knowledge with foreign investment – all with the state in a principal role.[32] In fact, the Uzbek case is not simply a growth puzzle, but a gradual reworking of various models and choices for development whereby neutral initial conditions have been met by realistic policy choices designed to minimize the impact of transition on social sectors.

The country's success stems from three central initial conditions: a low degree of initial industrialization, abundant cotton production, and self-sufficiency in energy.[33] Uzbekistan was the least industrialized of the post-Soviet transition economies and therefore its industrial sector did not suffer the same magnitude of shock when exposed to international competition. The country is also the second largest cotton producer in the world, a primary commodity that could easily be re-routed to western markets in contrast to oil and gas, both of which are constrained by lack of export transportation. Cotton exports and energy self-sufficiency mitigated the external financing constraints that other transition economies faced. These all represent favourable initial conditions somewhat unique to the Uzbek case. Thus, in the view of the IMF and advocates of rapid reform, Uzbekistan's performance was good *despite* the gradualist and import-substituting policies, and that growth would have been even higher if the favourable initial conditions had been augmented by liberal policies.

The incremental nature of Uzbekistan's market transition remains contentious, although macroeconomic indicators leave little room for debate. Inflation remains moderately high: an annual percentage increase of the money supply remains consistently in the twenties as a result of a loose monetary policy. Consistent with the inward focus on development, the Central Bank of Uzbekistan (CBU) has little control over liquidity, since the government continues to utilize state-owned banks to direct lending. The CBU is able to manage foreign exchange sales, however, and the loosening of credit following the Russian financial crisis has undermined any use of international reserves below the government quota.[34] In the absence of the tighter monetary policy implemented in 1999, inflation has remained high and the government-controlled Central Bank remains virtually powerless to combat it.

Privatization in Uzbekistan was designed to occur in three stages, proceeding from small enterprises to the largest industries. While roughly 90 per cent of the first stage transactions are complete, the second stage remains in progress and the third has yet to demonstrate results, despite World Bank support. The programme also included the option for workers to purchase stock in the enterprises, though size and diffusion of ownership is too limited to rival the continuing 25 per cent stake the state retains in many of the mid-size industries. Following the Russian financial crisis in 1998, the government launched a more aggressive privatization policy, the results of which have been stymied by attempts to avoid social disruption and business environment concerns on the part of foreign investors.[35] There is still a need for further state enterprise reform and re-scaling of state orders for cotton and agricultural products. Infamously slow banking reforms have been hastened in order to provide for corporate diversification and possibly to help fund investment in the state-led development of the chemical industry. No agency exists to oversee the restructuring, but the courts have declared 130 companies bankrupt, referring 70 for restructuring.[36] However, since Uzbekistan ranked near the bottom (along with Kazakhstan) of 100 countries in the 1999 corruption index produced by Transparency International, the functioning of the court system leaves much to be desired.

A 1998 presidential decree mandated the reduction of government ownership in commercial banks to 50 per cent, though no banks were able to meet the 1 July 1999 deadline. Despite this push for privatization in the banking sector, 60 per cent of all assets remain in the control of the National Bank of Uzbekistan. Of the 21 banks in the country, five specialized banks retain 95 per cent of the total investment. Recent liberalization remains closely tied to government policy, as the hastening of banking reforms are meant to provide corporate diversification and possibly fund investment in the state-led development of the chemical industry.

The economic indicators above demonstrate the gradualist and mixed approach to reform that has characterized the Uzbek transition. However, while Uzbekistan may have discovered a way to sustain output amid dramatic economic change, data indicates that the country has yet to harness the potential growth within its economy. In 2001, Uzbekistan claimed the lowest forecasted GDP growth rate, with a predicted total two-thirds the unweighted average of all seven CIS countries. The country is unlikely to deviate from its heavy-handed approach to state-led development, as the current president, Islam Karimov, maintains a tight grip on power. He has held two referenda to extend his rule by a total of 12 years, and is invested with power to overrule the parliament, judiciary and governors. Despite its socially conscious approach toward market economics, Karimov's administration exercises draconian repression upon its population of Islamic 'extremists', currently detaining more than 6,000 Muslim fundamentalists.

Tajikistan and Turkmenistan

Tajikistan and Turkmenistan provide two very different examples of how political externalities can impede the process of economic reform. Tajikistan, a poor mountainous country, emerged from the Soviet bloc only to descend into a devastating five-year civil war which ended when an armistice was reached in 1997. Turkmenistan suffers from corrupt, totalitarian leadership, and is the least free country of the CARs. As Cuba's political future remains uncertain, both countries provide relevant examples of how stalled or chaotic politics can undermine efforts to undertake economic reform.

Tajikistan is in the process of moving beyond its civil war. The conflict resulted from the volatile combination of ethnic and tribal rivalries, a rise in Islamic fundamentalism, economic collapse, and the political weakness of the Communist Party of Tajikistan (CPTJ). Following independence, several political opposition groups converged under the umbrella of the newly founded Islamic Renaissance Party (IRP). In 1992, the end of Soviet food subsidies provoked rioting in the capital that forced the Communist leadership to resign. The interim coalition government was led by the IRP but only survived a few months before their bloody overthrow by communist forces from the North, instigating the civil war. Over the next five years more than 50,000 people were killed in the fighting between communist forces and the IRP and its allies, as well as in the violence perpetrated by government militias against the civilian population. In 1997 the Peace Accord was signed between the communist and opposition forces. After another three years of intermittent fighting, its final implementation commenced with parliamentary elections in February 2000. The peace accords also enabled the government to initiate a reform programme. Inflation was brought under control, small-scale privatizations were completed by 1999, and a large-scale enterprise restructuring was initiated. These measures combined with the stable political environment facilitated cumulative economic growth of 20 per cent between 1997 and 2000.

Initially, Tajikistan attempted reforms by first targeting inflation (and temporarily succeeding) following currency reform and tight withdrawal restrictions in 1994. The jump in inflation the next year, largely as a result of a loosening in monetary policy, began a cycle of rising and falling inflation parallel to efforts to implement responsible monetary policy that were often derailed by the conflict. Price liberalization was also pursued throughout the period of the civil conflict, though it was halting and weak. Until 1995, the privatization of state-owned industries could only be initiated by company employees, a caveat that made for little progress. Since 1998, 1,100 small enterprises have been privatized, and the state has begun the second phase by selling or transferring shares in joint-stock companies to employees. The macroeconomic reforms have begun to overlap as farm privatizations are increasingly delayed due to the accumulation of external debt. More than half of the state and collective farms have been successfully dismantled, with 45 per cent of arable land now in private hands. The government is now attempting to write-off state-owned farm debts, in order to gain revenue from their sale.

The banking sector remains largely public, with 90 per cent of the country's credit situated in five main banks divided, de facto, by economic sectors. Unfortunately, Tajikistan's weak state infrastructure has left few means to enforce its liberal economic policies, as well as a desperately poor population and mounting multilateral debt left over from reconstruction. However, Tajikistan has now developed into a multi-party democracy and made considerable progress in liberalizing prices, eliminating trade restrictions, and initiating small-scale privatization.

The country still has a difficult road ahead in recouping the years of progress lost to the bloody internecine conflict, and its experience demonstrates how the collapse of central authority can lead to violence and chaos in highly polarized societies. Hopefully, this will not be the case in Cuba, but it is an important lesson to keep in mind.

While the Tajik government is making steps towards increased transparency and efficiency, Turkmenistan has made the least progress in economic reform among the CARs, and largely remains a closed nation as well as a Soviet-era, centrally planned economy. The government has yet to embark on any programme of liberalization or privatization, and as a result the IMF and other multilateral donors have not as yet engaged the country in any comprehensive lending programme. More than any other Central Asian state, policy choices in Turkmenistan have been determined by the whimsical preferences of its ruler, Suparmurad Niyazov. Niyazov has promulgated grandiose development plans with no regard for efficiency or the well-being of his country. His latest 11-year economic plan foresees cotton production increasing fourfold, gas exports increasing fivefold, and oil production increasing sevenfold.[37] His earlier 'ten years of prosperity' programme aimed to turn Turkmenistan into a 'new Kuwait'.

Niyazov has promoted a cult of personality best described as egotistic paranoia. Claiming the title of 'Turkmenbashi', or Father of the Turkmen, he has named buildings, streets, and entire cities after himself. He recently introduced a new spiritual code of conduct, based entirely on his own writings which he likens to the Bible and the Koran. Lavish amounts of the country's scarce resources have been spent on constructing shrines and monuments dedicated to the leader, leaving the capital city basking in ornate construction.[38]

Niyazov embraces an antiquated model of import-substituting industrialization. This model makes no attempt to appropriate resources accurately, using wealth generated from the export of raw cotton to fund inefficient, supposed vertical industries like the Turkmenbashi Jeans Factory rather than reaping the benefits of increased commodity production. Control of monetary policy resides with the president rather than the central bank, which exists mainly to finance the budget at his discretion. Perhaps as a result, Turkmenistan was the last CAR to embrace currency stabilization, posting an inflation rate seven times the next highest of the five countries in 1996.[39] Privatization of small enterprise has begun, resulting in the sale of approximately 2,000 companies – less than half the eligible industries. The privatization process in Turkmenistan has been hindered by a lack of government support, reflected in the failure to institutionalize channels to identify industries for sale or a legal framework by which to operate. In October 2000, while actively pursuing foreign development assistance in the oil and gas industries, the government announced that they would not be open for privatization for another ten to 15 years.[40]

The government has yet to liberalize the banking sector. Instead, restructuring and strengthening state control began with a December 1998 presidential decree. Joint-stock commercial banks were merged and shareholders bought out, creating a system of seven state-owned commercial banks around the still state-controlled Central Bank. These banks are assigned to different economic sectors, regressing to the Soviet-style division of labour. Though six other commercial banks remain in Turkmenistan without government majority ownership, they account for less than 5 per cent of the domestic loans. Government control increased again in March of 1999, when the Central Bank acquired oversight of all commercial bank loans to state-owned enterprises, as well as those to farmer and consumer associations.[41] Two issues cloud Turkmenistan's economic horizon still further: the extensive hard currency expenditures for the capital's Turkmenbashi idolatry, and the growing, non-transparent external debt.

Turkmenistan has made the least progress of any of the CARs, having actually returned to a centrally planned strategy. Abundant gas reserves have contributed to economic growth, foreign investment and high wealth indicators, though measures of allocation and reinvestment are poor. The country has the unfortunate distinction of being the most repressive and dictatorial regime in the region: Niyazov has banned political parties, controls all media outlets, and has forbidden public meetings. In 2000, the government ordered the monitoring of all foreign visitors, mail, and telephone calls, and also stripped Internet providers of their licenses. Turkmenistan has banned the teaching of English and other foreign languages in schools, and has forbidden students from taking scholarships abroad. These isolationist policies have deterred the foreign direct investment needed to develop the country's vast natural gas reserves and promote industrial economic growth.

Social policy in Central Asia

In the early 1990s, the Central Asian Republics were forced to contend simultaneously with the collapse of the Soviet Union, a rapidly changing political landscape, and the task of reorienting centrally planned economies to market mechanisms. Prior to 1990, social spending in Central Asia was a product of Soviet central planning based on three major government outflows: 'benefits in kind', namely housing, transportation, health and education; job provision and security; and cash transfers for household dependents. All three ended with the demise of the Soviet Union. According to one World Bank study,

> The drop in income and the development of a market economy knocked out the guaranteed job. The fiscal crisis... forced large cuts in [benefits] and [transfer payments]. As a result, households became at once poorer

> and more vulnerable. The vulnerability was exacerbated by the loss of financial savings, wiped out by the initial bout of hyperinflation and/or by subsequent banking system crises.[42]

Each of the Central Asian Republics has responded differently to the rapid depletion of social protection, taking strides to remedy social issues such as poverty, health and education. Like the economic liberalization programmes, each country has inevitably experienced different results based on the mixture of initial conditions and adopted policies.

Although Uzbekistan has largely failed to embrace economic liberalization, the country deserves considerable credit for its social policy during the transition. Unlike many of the others, the Uzbek government has given a high priority to investments in health and education, and to maintaining the Soviet legacy of social protection. While public expenditures in the social sectors have fallen from their Soviet-era levels, the decline has been less pronounced in Uzbekistan than in the other CARs. In 1998, public recurrent health expenditures were 3.3 per cent of GDP, while investments in education were a particularly impressive 7.2 per cent of GDP.

Uzbekistan's social policy is also distinguished by the use of *mahallas*, or neighbourhood committees, to provide targeted social assistance and child allowance to low-income groups.[43] *Mahallas* became the main vehicle for the government's new social policy following the loss of transfers from the central Soviet government in 1994, when Uzbekistan was forced to abandon the overall system of social protection and shift away from universal subsidies on basic food products and towards targeted interventions. Similarly, in 1997 child benefits were changed from a categorical benefit to a targeted benefit restricted to poor families with young children. *Mahallas* filled the gap by providing these traditional community institutions with social service capabilities. There are roughly 12,000 *mahallas* in the country, each ranging in size from 150 to 1500 households. Governed by local committees, these groups are given considerable license to distribute resources, and often do so even to needy families outside their collectives.

Evidence suggests that *mahallas* have been a particularly efficient means for helping poorer families. A 1995 survey revealed that around 20 per cent of households had received assistance from the system, although the numbers had decreased to 14.5 per cent in 1996 and 11.9 per cent in 1997. Over 80 per cent of households were aware of the existence of the scheme, and there was little social stigma associated with applying for assistance, which in part stemmed from the institutions' roots in local tradition. The system also harnessed community knowledge to target benefits towards the neediest; wealthier families were deterred from using a system based on neighbourhood committees. Essentially, the *mahallas* replaced the Soviet cash transfers, and in their essential decentralization, proved a more efficient means of distribution.

Uzbekistan's experience with the *mahallas* underlines the importance of using existing civil society and regulatory structures in the reform process. As Nobel-Prize-winner Joseph Stiglitz argues,

> one of the most difficult parts of a transformation, such as the transition from socialism to a market economy, is the transformation of the old 'implicit social contract' to a new one. If 'reformers' simply destroy the old norms and constraints in order to 'clean the slate' without allowing for the time-consuming process of reconstructing new norms, then the new legislated institutions may well not take hold.[44]

Neighbourhood institutions, cooperatives, labour unions, guilds, and clubs can be viewed as resources for developing the entrepreneurial skills and business networks so necessary for a successful market economy. Once social capital is destroyed it is very hard to recreate. Uzbekistan's successful use of traditional social institutions mitigated the shock of transition.

By contrast, Kazakhstan has not protected the social sectors from the disruptions caused by the speedy and rigid reform process adopted by the government. In 1998 Kazakhstan spent 3.4 per cent of its GDP on education, and 2.6 per cent on health – far below the spending levels in Uzbekistan. Starting from very similar levels at independence, male life expectancy in Kazakhstan had fallen to 59 years in 1998 as compared to 66 years for Uzbekistan, while educational participation has also been comparatively poor. The government's low prioritization of social welfare has led them to request that foreign investors pay pensions, wage arrears and supports for physical fitness, medical and educational facilities.[45] This relative lack of commitment to the social sectors raises the importance of the overall level of governance and its impact on growth. However, such decisions have led to the erosion of popular trust in government services.

Kyrgyzstan, the other early reformer, is slowly rebuilding its social expenditure as a share of GDP. Poverty still envelops 64 per cent of the population, including half of all urban citizens.[46] Unemployment is a chronic problem, and while the country claimed only 6.1 per cent in January 2000, the figure is estimated at closer to 20 per cent. The 'poverty shock' that followed the immediate market transition has also had a disproportionately heavy impact on women.[47] A disturbing reverse gender effect has also taken place in Kazakhstan, where the male suicide rate is more than four times that of comparably sized Uzbekistan.[48] As part of the Poverty Reduction Strategy Plan put forth by multilateral lenders, the previous focus on streamlining benefits and the payment transfers system among central planners has been supplemented by a push to better target social welfare programmes. This drive is typical of the second-wave reforms that emphasize institutional development, and Kyrgyzstan has seemingly prioritized one of its remaining public welfare systems: education. From March to August 2000, Kyrgyzstan spent approximately US$1.2 billion, or

20 per cent of its GDP, on the education system.[49] While this number is high, spending on education and health remains consistent with the international financial recommendations. However, in a country where the average monthly salary was US$800 and the cost of living US$1,200, the need for social safety nets may trump international long-term planning.[50]

Tajikistan's conflict slowed the necessary decentralization of the public infrastructure – in some instances, the process stopped altogether. Tajikistan now has the highest rate of poverty of the five CARs, and the country has yet to reform its state-owned health care system, which is largely unable to provide necessary services or medicines. This has led to a vibrant informal economy for medicines, an obvious problem for regulation and safety. Fortunately for Tajikistan, its population is young, leaving time for the recent international lending and construction of 300 new health clinics to better balance access.[51]

Turkmenistan remains wedded to Soviet-style social policy, including price controls and subsidies, guaranteed employment, pensions and family allowances. The government provides utilities (gas, water and energy) as well as a salt ration, with penalties for exceeding the allocated use. Some food is provided for free, though most is highly subsidized. Unfortunately, this attempted government buffer is often hamstrung by lack of supplies. Niyazov's recent attempts to cut spending have amounted to flat cuts across education and health. Downsizing in education has left 5,000 instructors unemployed, and by most accounts education is already poor. Recently, an estimated 10,000 public health employees were dismissed, and all rural clinics were closed as well, leaving many with long distances to travel for access to care.[52]

While social welfare in the Central Asian Republics was initially above the average for developing nations, these countries illustrate the difficulty of mitigating economic transition's impact on living standards and social services. Education and health care were not integrated into the Soviet system to the same degree as trade and production, but the social sectors relied on external support for these programmes. By harnessing local institutions, working cooperatively with international lenders, and prioritizing economic growth, the CARs are attempting to recover from steep declines in social conditions.

Conclusion: the relevance of the Central Asian Republics for Cuba

The Central Asian Republics have chosen markedly different approaches to the challenge of economic reform, ranging from the rapid liberalization of Kazakhstan and Kyrgyzstan to the continuation of Soviet-style central planning in Turkmenistan. Uzbekistan achieved some success using a mixed economic model accompanied by maintaining social welfare, while Tajikistan spent the first five years of independence locked in civil war and has only recently begun to pursue economic reform. The CARs remain among the poorest and least free of the successor states to the Soviet Union, and even those countries with abundant natural resources have failed to adequately harness their full capacity for economic development. Yet the experience of this region remains instructive, encapsulating many of the key problems of economic transition that Cuba will grapple with in the future.

The political dimensions of reform remain a central concern for the CARs. The case for radical reform argues that the political costs of economic transition will be unsustainable in the long term, and thus reforms must be pushed through as rapidly as possible in the small window of opportunity provided by the period of 'extraordinary' politics. Without aggressive reform, politicians would likely be ousted by citizens hurt by sharp reductions in output and social protection. Rapid reforms would also alienate powerful interest groups, such as public enterprise managers, while the future benefits would be diffuse. Democracy and economic transformation were therefore at odds – political power had to be concentrated in the hands of committed reformers insulated from popular opinion. Scholars advocating gradualism worried that the policies advocated by the Bretton Woods institutions would result in a breakdown of the newly emerging democratic process in these states.[53] However, progress in liberalization during the first year of transition was twice as high in countries where there was a turnover of the political authority than it was in countries, such as the CARs, where the former communist leadership continued in office.[54]

In fact, the greatest danger is for reforms to get stuck in partial-reform equilibrium. This enables the old guard, or the insiders, to exploit arbitrage opportunities and reap huge rewards for themselves at the expense of the public. This phenomenon has been most intensively studied in the case of Russia, where partial liberalization allowed managers of state companies to enrich themselves by buying commodities like metals and oil at low state-controlled prices in Russia, and selling them at world prices abroad.[55] Such scenarios are contrary to the tenets of rapid reform: with poor institutional checks and weak democratic structures, politicians may disproportionately benefit from aggressive privatization and contracts.

The mixed progress of the Central Asian states can be partially explained by the fact that the old communist elite has remained in power in these countries. In Kazakhstan, Turkmenistan, and Uzbekistan there was no grassroots democratization, and the former communist leaders – Nursultan Nazarbayev, Saparmurat Niyazov, and Islam Karimov, respectively – maintained an authoritarian rule with the help of old Nomenklatura networks.

Quality of governance is another important factor. Sustained economic growth depends on the degree to which the state is free from corruption, fulfills its necessary role in providing adequate law and order, and administers a transparent and fair tax and regulatory structure. Turkmenistan, subject to the extreme abuse of power by Niyazov, provides a clear example of how poor governance stymies growth. Empirical studies have demonstrated that there is a strong positive association between governance indicators – such as risk of appropriation, degree of law and order, and quality of bureaucracy – and economic growth, and a strong negative relation between corruption and growth.[56]

Corruption is a problem in all of the CARs, but not to the same degree. The World Bank and EBRD have conducted a systematic survey of the quality of governance in the transition economies by asking firms operating in these countries about the performance of the state along the relevant dimensions. Among the three CARs surveyed, Uzbekistan had the highest score, followed by Kazakhstan and Kyrgyzstan.[57] In fact, Uzbekistan was one of the best-performing countries of all the transition economies, while Kyrgyzstan was the second worst. Nearly three-quarters of the firms surveyed in Kyrgyzstan were insecure about their property rights, as compared to a quarter in Uzbekistan. Nearly a quarter of the firms believed government policy in Kyrgyzstan was being unduly influenced by a narrow set of interest groups, as opposed to 20 per cent in Kazakhstan and less than 10 per cent in Uzbekistan. Rapid reforms increase the opportunity for state capture by elites. Without sufficient political liberalization to provide a check on the main economic powers, transition will become mired in a partial-reform equilibrium that enriches a small subsection of society at the expense of the whole. This is largely what has happened in the Central Asian Republics.[58] Uzbekistan has not liberalized sufficiently to create the demand for state capture that exists in Kyrgyzstan. Furthermore, Kyrgyzstan also has the highest levels of inequality in the region (Table 5.3), again suggesting the presence of concentrated wealth that is characteristic of partial reformers.

Cuba will have to guard against the partial-reform equilibrium that has been holding the Central Asian economies hostage for much of the past decade. In many ways, Cuba is more favourably positioned for economic reform than were the Central Asian Republics at the time of the Soviet Union's collapse. Cuba has a more diversified economy, is close to the United States, and is an island with easy transit routes to neighbouring countries in the Caribbean basin. By contrast, the CARs were landlocked states integrated into the Soviet production system, and resistant to economic cooperation in the aftermath of their newfound independence. Yet the experience of the CARs also demonstrates some of the key challenges facing Cuba.

Three major lessons for Cuba's future emerge from the study of economic transition in Central Asia. First, the recent infusion of international support and attention to the CARs following the war in Afghanistan proves that politics, both domestic and global, matter. Tajikistan and Turkmenistan exemplify the primacy of politics in transition and the importance of moderate stability for successful economic reform. Good governance therefore emerges as a first priority for states in transition, and in fact matters more than the speed of reform packages. Kyrgyzstan and Kazakhstan demonstrate the more precarious dangers of market-led development amid corruption and inefficiency, while Uzbekistan, far from an ideal type of socialist transition, imparts the potential benefits of conscientious state-led reform. The importance of governance and institutional structures trumps the pace at which reforms are enacted, regardless of whether a country claims to be a democracy or not.

Secondly, Cuba must avoid partial-reform equilibrium, a vital lesson from the Central Asian transitions. Rapid reform programmes are often accompanied by significant favouritism for international lending and foreign investment – a definite perk for transition economies in desperate need of capital, but a potential threat to citizen-consumers without established regulatory recourse. Incomplete economic and political reforms can become stuck in these partial-reform scenarios, controlled by anachronistic power players or the early foreign investors who maximize their individual gains. Moreover, such maximization can often prolong the hold on political and economic power by domestic elites without the democratic accountability necessary for change. Avoiding partial-reform equilibrium requires good governance and government, the burden for which falls not simply on the leadership but also on the institutional and regulatory structures to provide independent oversight.

Cuba can also study the exception of Uzbekistan, which demonstrates that the welfare costs of transition can be mitigated by the protection of social sectors from the fiscal crunch of 'market shock'. Foresight and good governance are components of such action, and can help prevent the collapse in social indicators experienced by many of the CARs. However, advocating social safety nets during the process of market transition should not be confused with protectionism, a line that often falls prey to state-led development programmes. Such reluctance to reform can jeopardize not only medium- to-long term output and growth, but also the retention of human capital, and increase the likelihood of partial-reform complications.

While no single case can provide a model for Cuba's economic path, these three central conclusions can contribute to successful market reform in Cuba. Important lessons for Cuba's future can indeed be derived from the distant countries of Central Asia. Inevitably, Cuba will have to balance its own unique combination of initial conditions and policy options stemming from its political and economic realities at the time of transition. However, as the Central Asian experience has shown, those realities must be incorporated into the decisions made throughout the transition, relying on good governance and existing social infrastructure to successfully reduce the pain of market development. Cuba is well positioned to outperform the Central Asian Republics, but only if it avoids the policy paralysis that continues to cast a shadow over economic performance in this region of the world.

Notes

1 Johannes Linn, 'Central Asia: Ten Years of Transition' (talking points for The World Bank donor's consultation meeting, Berlin, March 2002).
2 Asad Alam and Arup Banerji, 'Uzbekistan and Kazakhstan: a Tale of Two Transition Paths?', *World Bank Working Paper*, no. 2472 (2000).
3 Anders Åslund, 'Lessons of the Post-Communist Transition', *Carnegie Endowment Institute for Peace Policy Brief*, no. 10 (2001).
4 World Bank, *Making Transition Work For Everyone* (Washington, DC: World Bank, 2001a). In general a $1 per day criterion is used to estimate poverty in developing countries. A $2 criterion (or, more precisely, $2.15 criterion) is used for the transition economies to account for the added heating and clothing expenses due to the colder climate.
5 Ibid.
6 See Jared Diamond, *Guns, Germs, and Steel* (New York: W.W. Norton, 1999) and John Luke Gallup, Jeffrey Sachs, and Andrew Mellinger, 'Geography and Economic Development', *Centre for International Development Working Paper*, no. 1 (1999).
7 This discussion on the structural difficulties facing the CARs and the environmental degradation relies heavily on Richard Pomfret, *The Economies of Central Asia* (Princeton: Princeton University Press, 1995).
8 As quoted in Åslund, 'Lessons of the Post-Communist Transition'.
9 World Bank, *Prospects for Improving Nutrition in Eastern Europe and Central Asia* (Washington, DC: World Bank, 2001b).
10 The main works include Martha De Melo, Cavdet Denizer, Alan Gelb, and Stoyan Tenev, 'Circumstances and Choice; the Role of Initial Conditions and Policies in Transition Economies', *World Bank Economic Review*, 15 (2001); and Stanley Fischer and Ratna Sahay, 'The Transition Economies After Ten Years', *National Bureau of Economic Research Working Paper*, no. 7664 (2000).
11 De Melo *et al.*, 'Circumstances and Choice'.
12 See Joseph Stiglitz, 'Whither Reform?' (Annual World Bank Conference on Development Economics, 1999) for a detailed critique of the neoclassical perspective.
13 Robert Putnam, *Making Democracy Work* (Princeton, NJ: Princeton University Press, 1993).
14 As quoted in Ibid.
15 Richard Pomfret, *Economic Diversification of the New Independent Central Asian Countries* (Adelaide: University of Adelaide, 2001).
16 Emine Gurgen et al., 'Economic Reforms in Kazakhstan, Kyrgyz Republic, Tajikistan, Turkmenistan, and Uzbekistan', *International Monetary Fund Occasisional Paper Series*, no. 18, (1999).
17 World Information Business Intelligence Report, *Kyrgyzstan* (Essex: WIBIR Press, 2002).
18 Tapio Saavalainen *et al.*, *Kyrgyz Republic: Selected Issues and Statistical Appendix* (Washington, DC: International Monetary Fund, 2003).
19 Ibid.

20 Richard Auty, 'Mineral Wealth and the Economic Transition: Kazakstan', *Resource Policy*, no. 24 (1998).
21 Alam and Banerji, 'Uzbekistan and Kazakhstan: a Tale of Two Transition Paths?'
22 Emine Gurgen *et al.*, 'Economic Reforms in Kazakhstan, Kyrgyz Republic, Tajikistan, Turkmenistan, and Uzbekistan'.
23 Asian Development Bank, *Kazakhstan: Country Economic Review Update* (Manila: Asian Development Bank, 2000).
24 Gurgen *et al.*, 'Economic Reforms in Kazakhstan, Kyrgyz Republic, Tajikistan, Turkmenistan, and Uzbekistan'.
25 Peter Keller *et al., Kazakhstan: Selected Issues and Statistical Appendix* (Washington, DC: International Monetary Fund, 2003).
26 World Information Business Intelligence Report, *Kazakhstan* (Essex: WIBIR Press, 2000).
27 Ibid.
28 International Monetary Fund, *Republic of Kazkahstan: Staff Report for the Article IV Consultation,* Country Report, no. 03/210 (Washington, DC: International Monetary Fund, 2003).
29 World Information Business Intelligence Report, *Tajikistan* (Essex: WIBIR Press, 2002).
30 See, for example, Jaromin Zettelmeyer, 'The Uzbek Growth Puzzle', *IMF Staff Papers* No. 46 (1999); and Alam and Banerji, 'Uzbekistan and Kazakhstan: a Tale of Two Transition Paths?'
31 Zettelmeyer, 'The Uzbek Growth Puzzle'.
32 Leif Hansen *et al., Republic of Uzbekistan: Recent Economic Developments,* Country Report, no. 00/36 (Washington, DC: International Monetary Fund, 2000).
33 Zettelmeyer, 'The Uzbek Growth Puzzle'.
34 Hansen *et al., Republic of Uzbekistan: Recent Economic Developments.*
35 Ibid.
36 Gurgen *et al.*, 'Economic Reforms in Kazakhstan, Kyrgyz Republic, Tajikistan, Turkmenistan, and Uzbekistan'.
37 Turkmenistan, 'Dream On', *The Economist,* 8 January 2000.
38 Ibid.
39 Gurgen *et al.*, 'Economic Reforms in Kazakhstan, Kyrgyz Republic, Tajikistan, Turkmenistan, and Uzbekistan'.
40 World Information Business Intelligence Report, *Turkmenistan* (Essex: WIBIR Press, 2000).
41 Gonzalo Pastor *et al., Turkmenistan: Recent Economic Developments,* Country Reports, no. 99/140 (Washington, DC: International Monetary Fund, 1999).
42 Louise Fox, *Safety Nets in Transition Economies: a Primer* (Washington, DC: World Bank, 2003).
43 This discussion of *mahallas* is based on Aline Coudouel, Sheila Marnie and John Micklewright, 'Targeting Social Assistance in a Transition Economy: the Mahallas in Uzbekistan', *Centre for Economic Policy Research Discussion Paper,* no. 2064 (London: CEPR, 1999).
44 Stiglitz, 'Whither Reform?' (1999), 8–9.
45 Jim Nichol, *Central Asia's Security: Issues and Implications for US Interests* (Washington, DC: Congressional Research Service, 1999).
46 Fox, *Safety Nets in Transition Economies: a Primer.*
47 For more information, see Kathleen Kuehnast, 'Poverty Shock: The Impact of Rapid Economic Change on the Women of the Kyrgyz Republic', in Nora

Dudwick *et al.* (eds), *When Things Fall Apart: Qualitative Studies of Poverty in the Former Soviet Union,* (Washington, DC: World Bank, 2002).

48 Alam and Banerji, 'Uzbekistan and Kazakhstan: a Tale of Two Transition Paths?'

49 World Information Business Intelligence Report, *Kyrgyzstan.*

50 Ibid.

51 World Information Business Intelligence Report, *Tajikistan.*

52 Ibid.

53 Adam Przeworski, *Democracy and the Market* (Cambridge: Cambridge University Press, 2000).

54 European Bank for Reconstruction and Development, *Transition Report 1999: Ten Years of Transition* (London: EBRD, 1999).

55 Åslund, 'Lessons of the Post-Communist Transition'.

56 For example, see Stephen Knack and Phillip Keefer, 'Institutions and Economic Performance: Cross-country Tests Using Alternative Institutional Measures', *Economics and Politics,* vol. 7, no. 3 (1995); Paulo Mauro, 'Corruption and Growth', *Quarterly Journal of Economics,* 110 (1995).

57 European Bank for Reconstruction and Development, *Transition Report 1999: Ten years of Transition.*

58 Joel Hellman *et al.*, 'Measuring Governance, Corruption, and State Capture', *World Bank Policy Research Working Paper,* no. 2312 (2000).

Part III

The Gradualist Approach

6
China: The New Global Giant

Shahid Javed Burki

Introduction

In a little more than half a century, China has left behind mass poverty, extreme backwardness, and economic and political isolation to march onto the global stage as a major player – an economic and military giant. Chinese presence is now felt in all areas of international financial discourse, including how the value of its currency impacts upon East Asia and the entire global economy, its contribution in keeping inflationary pressures in check around the globe, and its role in the World Trade Organization. China is also a major player in global politics. The United States and Europe sought its counsel during the build up to the 2003 war in Iraq, and China continues to play an important role in the global effort to denuclearize the Korean Peninsula.

Why has China become such a large economic and political player on the global stage? The reasons for this development include the size of its population and economy, its high rates of economic growth, the country's emergence as a large trading nation, the accumulation of large foreign exchange reserves, its increasing desirability as a focus for foreign direct investment, and China's attractiveness as a tourist destination. Above all, it is the country's perceived potential that draws so much attention.

China's remarkable performance raises a number of questions that will be addressed in this essay, including whether China can serve as a model for a country such as Cuba – one of the few nations that continues to manage its economy along strict Marxist lines and has yet to integrate its economy into the global system. However, any comparison of China to Cuba must first examine why China has been the only communist country to have succeeded in making such remarkable progress over a short period of time, surpassing even its closest competitor, Vietnam. The essay focuses on two central sets of questions regarding both the economic reform process, and the relationship between the evolution of the Chinese economy and the political system.

RUSSIA
KAZAKHSTAN
MONGOLIA
KGZ
Harbin
Changchun
Shenyang
Kashgar
XINJIANG PROVINCE
NORTH KOREA
Beijing
SOUTH KOREA
Shijiazhuang
Xining
Qingdao
Zhengzhou
CHINA
Xian
Hefei
Nanjing
Shanghai
Wuhan
Hangzhou
NEPAL
Lhasa
Chengdu
Chongqing
Nanchang
INDIA
BHUTAN
Guiyang
Taipei
Kunming
Xiamen
GUANGDONG PROVINCE
TAIWAN ISLAND
Guangzhou
Foshan
Shenzhen
Guizhou
Hong Kong
N
MYANMAR
VIETNAM
Zhuhai
BANGLADESH
Pearl River Delta
LAOS
Haikou
HAINAIN ISLAND
0 500 Kilometers
0 500 Miles
THAILAND
PHILIPPINES

Map 5 China

First, how much of China's progress can be attributed to the implementation of a carefully designed strategy for bringing about change? And, conversely, to what degree does China's economic development and modernization represent a highly pragmatic response on the part of its leadership to the rapidly changing situation within the country and the world outside? Secondly, how important was the stability brought by a highly centralized political system to China's economic success? Should China have attempted a serious restructuring of its political system alongside the development of its economy, in essence following the path taken by Russia and other communist countries of Eastern Europe at the end of the Cold War? In a related vein, as the world's second largest economy, how have China's relations with the world's largest economy and its only superpower, the United States, evolved?

In order to address these questions, and to explore the relevance of the Chinese experience for Cuba, this essay tells the story of China from several different perspectives. An assessment of basic information about the country reveals those characteristics – mostly economic – that have enabled China to emerge as such an important global player as it progressed from a socialist and centrally planned economy to one where market forces play a much greater role.

China's interplay between politics and economics suggests that a highly centralized political structure helped, rather than hindered, the country's impressive social and economic development. China, as is its wont, may have begun to change its political structure in a very deliberate and cautious way. The new generation of leaders – inducted into the Communist Party of China in November 2002, followed by their assumption of various government positions in May 2003 – is opening the political system to greater representation of the citizenry. This is likely to involve some experimentation – that is how all change has occurred in the country in the past. At the same time, China's relations with the United States have become increasingly significant for both countries, and to some extent China's future progress will depend on how the relationship between these two global giants evolves over the next few years and decades.

The evolution of the Chinese economy since the Communists took control of the country in October 1949 demonstrates that two approaches adopted by the Chinese leadership helped the country's transformation. First, leaders have shown the ability to carefully draw up reform programmes and test them as pilots before applying them to the entire country. This has created space for economic innovation while minimizing the political risks that make the Chinese reticent to embrace far-reaching or dramatic reforms without sufficient understanding of the consequences. Second, the leadership groups have exhibited impressive pragmatism and flexibility in their economic strategy, accommodating new demands set forth by the external operating environment.

This approach in particular offers a view on how the Chinese experience can be of help to Cuba, one of the few countries that continues to use central planning for economic management. There are a number of parallels we can see between the Cuban situation today and China's situation a quarter century ago when the latter country launched its programme of reform. As Cubans reflect upon their own future, they should take good measure of the Chinese experience, reflecting on the similar conditions prevailing in the two countries at the start of the reform period.

China: some telling facts

China is the most populous country in the world, with a population of 1.285 billion at the beginning of the twenty-first century. It is likely to retain that position for at least the next couple of decades, with a projected population of close to 1.4 billion by 2015 (see Table 6.1). China today draws a great deal of strength from its large population, with almost as many people as the combined population of the third to the tenth most populous countries, which together amount to 1.364 billion. India, its closest rival with a population estimated at 1.105 billion in 2002, is growing much more rapidly than China – by an estimated 1.3 per cent each year against China's 0.7 per cent. By 2015, India's population, at 1.2 billion, will still be shy of China's by 200 million, but if these trends continue, India could overtake China sometime in the next 40 to 50 years. However, there is no question that China's massive population will continue to contribute to its global strength over the next century.

Table 6.1 World's ten largest countries by population

Country	*Population 2002 (million)*	*Average annual growth (%)*	*Population 2015*	*Growth Rate 2000–2015*
China	1,285	0.9	1,395	0.7
India	1,105	1.7	1,228	1.3
United States	287	1.2	318	0.8
Indonesia	217	1.6	251	1.6
Brazil	175	1.4	201	1.1
Pakistan	145	2.5	193	2.2
Russia	144	–0.2	135	–0.5
Bangladesh	136	1.8	168	1.6
Nigeria	133	2.7	169	1.9
Japan	127	0.3	125	–0.1

Sources: World Bank, *World Development Report 2003*, 2002, Table 1, pp. 234–5; World Bank, *World Development Indicators 2002*, Table 2.1, pp. 48–50.

China also derives economic strength from a very significant urban population, which is much larger than the population of the European Union even following the admission of ten new members in 2004, and more than one and a half times the size of the total population of the United States. In fact, China would have many more people residing in its towns and cities had it not deliberately introduced policies to constrain rural to urban migration. A country with a rapidly growing economy but with a large rural sector, a large population residing in the countryside, and an increase in the rural–urban income differential should expect to see significant rural to urban migration. However, China's communist state was powerful enough to prevent rural people from leaving the countryside in search for jobs, higher incomes and the better quality of life found in the large and rapidly modernizing cities, particularly on the country's east coast. A welter of regulations institutionalized discrimination against migrant workers, whose numbers are estimated at 100 million. These regulations kept the population residing in the cities to below 38 per cent of the total between 1997 and 2002, the period that saw a rapid growth in the urban economy (see Table 6.2).

The strict limits on rural migration may change. On 5 January 2003, China's state council issued a cabinet-level directive declaring that 'rural migrants have a "legal right" to work in cities. It prohibits job discrimination based on residency, potentially opening all jobs to rural migrants, and orders police to promptly provide residency documents to any migrant who finds employment. The directive heralds an end to a system that attempted to lock rural Chinese out of the cities, with the better schools and medical care.'[1] China's urban population is set to boom further in the coming years.

But China's significance is not limited to population alone; the Chinese economy, already large, grew by an average of 10 per cent per annum in the last 12 years, most recently increasing by 8.1 per cent in 2002. The current growth rate is more than three times the average increase for the global

Table 6.2 China's urban population as a percentage of total population

	Total population	*Urban population*		*Growth (%*
		(million)	*(%)*	*per annum)*
1997	1,230	407	33.1	
1998	1,242	422	34.0	2.43
1999	1,254	437	34.9	2.36
2000	1,263	452	35.8	2.4
2001	1,272	467	36.7	2.44
2002	1,281	487	38.0	4.3

Source: World Bank, *World Development Indicators*, selected years.

economy. In purchasing power parity terms, it is already the second largest economy in the world (see Table 6.3).

In conventional terms, China's economy ($1.13 trillion) is not very large; it is smaller in size than that of Japan ($4.57 trillion), Germany ($1.95 trillion), U.K. ($1.45 trillion), and France ($1.38 trillion) and only slightly larger than that of Italy ($1.12 trillion). But in purchasing power parity (PPP) terms – as shown in Table 6.3 – it is equivalent to 43 per cent of the US economy. Comparison with the United States provides an interesting window into China's current economic situation. In terms of unadjusted per capita income, Chinese income is only 2.6 per cent that of the United States, but adjusted for purchasing power parity, it represents 12.2 per cent of US GNP. China has also begun to outperform the US in growth rates. Over the last dozen years, its gross domestic product has increased at a rate nearly three times that of the United States, and in 2000–01, Chinese per capita income increased at a rate 22 times higher than the United States'.

What makes China stand apart from a developed economy is the proportion of income that goes into capital formation – 39 per cent for China versus 15 per cent for the United States. This, no doubt, accounts for China's much larger economic expansion, with almost the entire difference accounted for by a much smaller share of household consumption in China compared to that in the United States.

Not surprisingly, China exhibits the characteristics of a middle-income country still dependent on agriculture for more than one sixth of its total GDP. By contrast, the US long ago arrived at what is sometimes described as the post-industrial phase, with agriculture contributing only one per cent to its GDP. Table 6.4 summarizes some basic data on the economies of China and the United States. While China clearly has a long way to go, its

Table 6.3 The world's largest economies, 2001

	Population (millions)	*Per capita income (US$)*	*GNP (billions US$)*
1. USA	284	34,870	9,901
2. China	1272	4,260	5,415
3. Japan	127	27,430	3,487
4. India	1033	2,450	2,450
5. Germany	82	25,530	2,098
6. France	59	25,280	1,495
7. UK	60	24,460	1,446
8. Italy	58	24,340	1,404
9. Brazil	173	7,450	1,286
10. Russia	145	8,660	1,225

Source: The World Bank, *World Development Indicators 2002,* Table 1, p. 235.

Table 6.4 Chinese and US economies, 2001

		China	*United States*	*China as % of the US*
Gross national income (US$ billion)		1,131	9,901	11.4
Gross national income (PPP, billions)		4,260	9,902	43.0
Per capita GNI		890	34,870	2.6
Per capita GNI (PPP)		4,260	34,870	12.2
Average annual GNP growth(%): 1990–2001		10.0	3.5	286
GNP per capita, 2000–2001 (%)		6.5	0.3	2,166
Value added as % of GDP	Agriculture	15	1	71.4
	Industry	52	24	216
	Services	33	75	12
Household final consumption expenditure (% of GDP)		48	68	70.6
General government final expenditure (% of GDP)		12	14	85.7
Gross capital formation (% of GDP)		39	15	260

Source: World Bank, *World Development Indicators 2003* (Washington, DC: The World Bank).

economy shows signs of further narrowing the gap with the US over the next several decades.

International trade statistics tell another important part of the story. Large countries normally do not have a significant trade to GDP ratio, but China is an exception, in part because it has relied heavily on trade to reform and modernize its economy. Brazil, India and the United States, all continental economies, have trade flows equivalent to about one-fifth of their gross domestic product. Trade's share in GDP is more than twice as large in China (see Table 6.5). The other distinguishing feature of the Chinese trade pattern is the high proportion of manufactures in its merchandise trade compared to other large developing countries. China's share of manufactures is even larger than that of the United States. By comparison, India, which in recent years has groomed the IT sector to be a major contributor to its exports, still exports a much smaller share of high technology items than China.

One consequence of the rapid increase in exports from China is that it has been able to build a comfortable level of foreign exchange reserves,

Table 6.5 Brazil, China, India and the United States: trade

	Trade as % of GDP	*Merchandise trade*		*Manufactured exports as % of total merchandise exports*	*High technology exports as % of manufacture of exports*
		Exports (US$ billion)	*Imports (US$ billion)*		
Brazil	22.0	58	58	59	19
China	45.0	266	243	88	19
India	20.0	44	51	79	4
United States	19.3	730	1180	83	34

Source: The World Bank, *World Development Indicators 2002*, table 4, pp. 240–1.

which reached $270 billion at the end of 2002. It has been running large trade surpluses now for several years, which may be one cause of friction with the United States in the years to come.

Similarly, China is now a major destination of foreign direct investment. Initial foreign corporate interest in investing in China was based on the expectation that a large population with a rapid rise in per capita income would eventually provide a very lucrative market for all kinds of consumer goods. 'What if each Chinese citizen consumed one bottle of Coca Cola every day, every year?' is a version of a question that was asked by many in the corporate headquarters of large transnational corporations (TNCs). This was a tantalizing prospect. The possibility of 365 billion Coca Cola bottles being consumed every year was enough of an incentive to draw a large number of western corporations into the country in the 1980s. Jim Mann's seminal work, *Beijing Jeep: A Case Study of Western Business in China,*[2] exploded a good part of this myth. It became painfully apparent to many corporations who ventured into China that, in spite of its large population and increasing affluence, the country's market was not quite ready for western products – not in the 1980s, not even in the early 1990s. As already noted, the household savings remained high and, correspondingly, the levels of consumption low. The Chinese masses were not yet quite ready to spend on consumer products.

While China may not have offered an attractive market for consumer goods, its low wages, a reasonably well-educated and disciplined workforce, and the government's willingness to invest large amounts of resources in physical infrastructure turned the country into a workshop for the rest of the world. 'The best thing about China is the workers', says the chief of quality control at Guangzhou Honda Automobile who had served in the same capacity in his company's plant at Longbridge in the UK. 'They are much better than the workers in the UK.'[3] In the 1990s, foreign direct investment was mostly directed to produce exports back to the countries of origin of the TNCs.

A recent article from the *Financial Times* captured the prevailing sentiment about China's fortunes as a magnet for FDI:

> The $52.7 billion in foreign direct investment that China attracted last year is an impressive sum. Barring unforeseen disasters, this flow will continue and increase. Manufacturing operations are expanding their presence. Intel, for example, plans to raise its current $200 million commitment to $500 million by the end of 2003. And China's entry to the World Trade Organization in 2001 is allowing foreign business to buy significant stakes in large companies in sectors previously closed to them – hence HSBC Insurance's announcement in October that it was spending $600 million on a ten per cent stake in Ping An Insurance, China's second largest life insurance [company]. With many more such deals in the pipeline, talk of China's annual FDI inflows rising to $100 billion is anything but fanciful.[4]

But there are those who have begun to question the belief in China's unparalleled potential. Some commentors believe that it has taken on the order of obsession. During the 1990s, China attracted over US$300 billion in foreign investment, but much of it will not produce anywhere near the hoped-for results. It is not only the expected return on investments that may not materialize. The concentration of FDI in a few coastal provinces – 50 per cent of all FDI went to just three locations, Guangdong province next to Hong Kong, the city of Shanghai, and its neighbour Jiangsu – may be creating enormous disparities in geographical income distribution.

Inland areas, particularly the poorer provinces, are receiving little foreign investment. According to one observer, 'the map of the Pearl River delta shows large swathes of green in between the cities of Guangzhou, Shenzhen, Foshan and Zhuhai. But, traveling by car between these pulsating new centres, it quickly becomes apparent that maps made just a few years ago are woefully out of date. New industrial estates have eaten up most of the farmland that, until recently, lay between the cities.'[5] By contrast, in 2001, Guizhou, China's poorest province and home to nearly 40 million people, attracted less than $30 million in foreign investment. FDI will help China maintain the 7–8 per cent annual growth in gross domestic product that its leadership deems necessary to keep the country's economy ahead of its fast-growing labour force. But it will do so by having growth rates of 10 per cent or above along the coast, and dropping those inland to 5 per cent or perhaps below. This raises an important question: does China have enough strength in its political system to absorb the tensions that will be created by the growing disparity in income at both individual and regional levels? According to the latest estimates provided by the World Bank, China has a Gini coefficient of 40.3, indicating a fair amount of income inequality. India has a Gini coefficient of 37.8, Pakistan 31.2, the United States 40.8.[6] This will clearly be a central challenge for the country's political leaders in the coming period.

Furthermore, China's economy is facing a second transformation. Setting aside the known scepticism regarding projections about future growth, if China is able to grow at 6.5 per cent a year in the next three decades while the US economy expands at an estimated 3.2 per cent, it will become the world's largest economy by the year 2035. If that happens – or when that happens – China would be an economy twice transformed. Both times, China went through a metamorphosis by using its vast human resources. The first time a well-educated workforce that was also healthy and disciplined turned China into the world's workshop. By the opening years of the twenty-first century any TNC of significance had production facilities working in China. Now, another change has begun to take place: China is using its large population to attract not only transnational corporations that manufacture, but also companies that need highly skilled workers to provide various kinds of services. For example, according to one report,

> General Electric company employs some 6,000 scientists and engineers in foreign countries. GE Medical Services integrates magnets, flat-panel, and diagnostic imaging technologies from labs in China, Israel, Hungary, and India in everything from its new x-ray devices to $1 million CT scanners. 'The real advantage is that we can tap the world's best talent, says GE Medical Global Supply Chain Vice-President, Dee Miller.'[7]

A lot of the talent the TNCs are looking for can be found in China, which is ready to meet the demand for skilled workers of an increasingly globalized economy with a large workforce and a reasonably good educational system.

As shown in Table 6.6, China's size has helped it to produce a large pool of workers with advanced skills. In the ten-year period between 1989 and 1999, the number of people earning BAs increased by 154 per cent, compared to an increase of 52 per cent for India and a paltry 12 per cent for the United States. Over the same period the Chinese saw an increase of 116 per cent in MAs and PhDs, compared to a decline of 6 per cent for India.

Conscious of the fact that China must have a world-class educational system in order to promote this second transformation of the economy, the leadership has begun to turn its attention towards reforms in this sector. A survey conducted by the Education Ministry in the late 1990s found more than 80 per cent of students disliked school. Drop-out rates

Table 6.6 Global pool of skilled workers (number of natural science and engineering college graduates)

	BAs			*MAs and PhDs*		
	1989	*1999*	*Growth 1989–99 (%)*	*1989*	*1999*	*Growth 1989–99 (%)*
China	127,000	322,000	153.5	19,000	41,000	115.8
India	165,000	251,000	52.1	64,000	63,000	–5.9
Philippines	40,000	66,000	50.0	255	937	267.5
United States	196,000	220,000	12.2	61,000	77,000	26.3

Source: National Science Foundation.

have been rising in rural areas – partly for economic reasons, but also because of the stultifying atmosphere of their classrooms. To deal with this situation, the country has set ambitious targets to ensure that the country's more than ten million primary- and secondary-school teachers acquire the skills and determination to change the habits of a lifetime. 'The reforms started in September 2001 with about 420,000 primary- and junior-school students (out of a national total of more than 215 million) taking part in 38 experimental zones around the country. In September of this year, participation increased to 9.1 million pupils in 572 zones.'[8]

In conclusion, China differs from other large nations in many ways. It is the world's most populous country, and its economy has grown more rapidly and over a far longer period than any other major world economy in the last 150 years. Notwithstanding the size of the economy, especially when measured in PPP terms, China remains a relatively poor country with pockets of extreme poverty. If it becomes the world's largest economy in the next couple of decades, it will do so with average per capita incomes much lower than that of other large economies. As such, its economic priorities may be very different from those of other large countries. To take one example: China may be less willing to sacrifice economic growth in return for preserving its physical environment or in return for joining the international effort to save such 'global commons' as the atmosphere and the oceans. Conflict over such issues could become serious. For these and other reasons, it is important to understand not only what China is today but also to develop a good idea of how it made the transition from a poor country to a global economic, political and military power.

China's stability: the role of political authoritarianism

The contribution made by China's political system to its economic development is an understandably controversial subject. The strong authoritarian character of the Chinese political structure channelled through the Communist Party goes against the liberal instincts of much of the West. People in the West – even those who know the country well – would have liked to see China adopt a liberal political system as it began to open its economy. The Chinese, on the other hand, were convinced that their effort to modernize the economy would have been inhibited by any easing of the Party's hold on politics. This view had other adherents in Asia as well. Several influential leaders – in particular Lee Kuan Yew of Singapore and Muhammad Muhatir of Malaysia – believed that 'Asian values' have contributed significantly to the rapid economic development of their countries. While the focus on these values diminished somewhat after the severe economic downturn sparked by the financial crisis of 1997, many Asian leaders continue to believe that they need to guide the political system with a firm hand without which politics could become disruptive and inhibit economic progress. China is not unique in this regard. However, China's relationship between economic reform and political centralization is particularly pertinent to the conclusions relating to Cuba later in the essay.

The Communist Party of China has governed without being seriously challenged by any group or organization. In staking his claim for political dominance, Mao Zedong, the founder of modern China, went back a couple of millennia into Chinese history, to the reign of Qin Shihuang. Qin exercised fearsome power some 2,200 years ago. He was a military adventurer who unified China for the first time by subsuming six warring states and sought to keep foreigners out by building the Great Wall. Ruthless, he imposed absolute order by executing those suspected of disloyalty including a would-be assassin who, with a split second to spare, decided not to kill the emperor. The historical Emperor Qin left little evidence of his compassion. His ruthlessness left him few admirers until Mao, the Communist leader, praised the emperor in a 1973 poem supporting his suppression of Confucian Orthodoxy.

Mao was not only a Marxist. Being a careful student of Chinese history he learnt a great deal from the way in which Emperor Qin had unified China, consolidated his own power, and isolated the country he ruled from all types of foreign influences. The Communist Party – like the court of Emperor Qin – was to be Mao's instrument for governing China. Over time, the party became a formidable apparatus, dominating all other institutions, including the armed forces, the bureaucracy, the industrial structure, financial institutions and agricultural production. For the last activity – agriculture – Mao used the system of communes, with its own tightly knit bureaucratic system, to bring the Communist Party to the doorstep of the Chinese farmer.

Watching Change in China: The Tragedy of the Communes

Over the past forty-five years, I have personally worked with China in a number of different positions at various points in that country's remarkable history. I first went to China in the summer of 1965 to study the system of communes, as part of a three-person delegation from Pakistan sent in response to a request from Prime Minister Zhou Enlai of China to President Ayub Khan of Pakistan. At the time of that assignment, I was directing the Rural Works Programme in what was then the province of West Pakistan and had some knowledge of rural development. The Chinese were mindful that their experiment to 'communize' agriculture by having the state acquire all assets – not only land, but also houses and implements owned by the farming community – had not won much favourable comment in the world outside. They were interested in a review by a group of outsiders, and Pakistan was invited to send such a group.

Criticism of the Chinese programme increased considerably when it was learned that the country had herded the rural population into male and female dormitories. While this part of the communization effort was abandoned quickly, the Chinese authorities were taken to task for using draconian measures to bring about structural change in the rural sector of their economy and society. Stung by that criticism, the Chinese requested the government of Pakistan to produce an independent assessment of their experiment.

The Pakistani team visited thirteen communes in nine provinces of China, and spent six weeks in the country during which a great deal of data on various aspects of the production process was collected. In those days, China published few statistics on agriculture. It had taken that step following the government's own embarrassing admission that the 1958 grain harvest had been grossly overestimated. The world was to learn later that hundreds of thousands of people were dying of starvation when the Chinese authorities were claiming that they had produced a bumper harvest.

We collected information through interviews with village leaders and officials in order to produce a report for the governments of Pakistan and China in which the Pakistani team questioned two basic assumptions behind the communization programme: that it had resulted in increasing grain and agricultural output and that it had reduced income inequality, particularly among different regions of the country.

Our report found that land and worker productivity was much higher on the small parcels of land the peasants had been allowed to cultivate on their own compared to the bulk of the land that was tilled by highly organized production teams and brigades. We also found that instead of narrowing the income gap among different parts of rural China, the system of communes had, in fact, widened it. The official Chinese reaction to our report was exceptionally cold and we heard nothing of it. It was obviously shelved since it did not serve the purpose for which the Chinese had invited the team from Pakistan in the first place.[9] – *S.J.B.*

Mao also followed Qin in attacking Confucius and China's old culture in the ill-fated Cultural Revolution that lasted for 13 years, from 1965 to 1978. There was a clear purpose behind what appeared from the outside to be madness. Mao would brook no opposition to the Communist Party he led with an iron will. He recognized that China's addiction to its past, to its culture and, in particular, to Confucianism, could dilute the loyalty to the Party that he demanded of all citizens. He also felt that he had to clear the Chinese ground of all historical debris before building a new country with a new political structure. This helps to explain the attack on the country's history and its culture during the waning days of Mao's rule over China.

The Chinese identify the passage of power from one group of leaders to another as a transfer between generations. Mao Zedong and his associates, including Zhou Enlai, Liu Shaoqi, Lin Pao, Chu Teh, and Chen Yuan, belonged to the first generation. Some – such as President Liu Shaoqi and Vice President Lin Pao – shared power with Mao only to be disgraced later. The latter actually died in a plane crash attempting to flee China, while others survived Mao and wielded some power once he passed from the scene. Since totalitarian systems inevitably fail to prepare for the transfer power from those who rule to those who should succeed, Mao's death in 1976 left a gaping hole. This resulted in a great deal of chaos and confusion. It took Deng Xiaoping, once a close associate of Mao but never a designated successor, to remove the challengers to his ascent – including the Gang of Four assembled around Mao's wife – before he could be identified as the country's supreme leader. That happened in 1979. Deng is identified as the leader of the second generation.

In 1979, Deng made the decision to open China's economy to the outside world and allow the gradual loosening of state control over economic institutions and policy making. In the decades following Deng's initiative, China began to witness exceptional economic growth accompanied by an equally remarkable change in the economy's structure. While accepting the need for economic change and modernization, Deng was not prepared to do the same in the area of politics. The Communist Party of China was to retain supreme authority, and it was not prepared to have any competitors.

The most serious challenge presented to Deng's political orthodoxy came in 1989, in the context of what started as a movement by students in Beijing. The students – later joined by the urban employed – took control of Tiananmen Square, virtually imprisoning the country's senior leaders. Deng, who had moved out of the Zhongnanhai having surrendered all formal levers of power, worked from his house outside the official compound to mobilize the support of the armed forces. On 4 June, Deng Xiaoping used his authority as the supreme leader of China to persuade the country's senior leaders to declare martial law and remove the protestors from Tiananmen Square. According to the Chinese authorities, the army's action resulted in the deaths of hundreds of people. The western governments and media estimated the number of dead at more than one thousand. A world shocked by the pictures it saw on CNN decided to act against Beijing. At the annual meeting of the G-7 group of countries held in Houston, Texas, the western nations and Japan ordered all multilateral institutions, including the World Bank, to suspend their operations and contacts with China. The legacy of this tragic conflict is what the Chinese allude to as the Tiananmen Square incident and what the West calls the Tiananmen Square massacre.

The events in Tiananmen Square had a profound impact on China's political development. They were provoked to some extent by the death of Hu Yaobang, a popular leader of the Communist Party who had worked to open the political system. Deng Xiaoping's decision to force the protestors from Tiananmen Square resulted in the political demise of Zhao Ziyang, another party moderate. Zhao was the secretary general of the party in June 1989 and wanted to work out some kind of a compromise with the 'agitators' who had occupied Tiananmen. His efforts were thwarted by the hardliners in the government, in particular Prime Minister Li Peng. Had the June 1989 confrontation not occurred, there is every possibility that with Zhao Ziyang at the helm of political affairs, the Communist Party might have been more willing to accept some competition. Zhao may have also opened the National People's Congress – China's legislature – to the expression of dissenting views and to the development of its role as an overseer of the authority exercised by the executive. But history had different plans in mind.

Deng Xiaoping removed Zhao Ziyang from the leadership of the party. He was replaced by Jiang Zemin, a close associate of Deng with no particular following of his own. Jiang was to become an effective leader of the third generation, defying predictions that he would not be able to stay in power for very long. He steadily consolidated his authority by aligning himself closely with the powerful military establishment, the generals of the People's Liberation Army. He also benefited from the steady growth in the economy and increasing prosperity of most of the citizenry. The economy was placed under the charge of Prime Minister Zhu Rongji, who was a capable administrator but was not an ideologue. Zhu did not have a close relationship with Jiang and, at times, the two leaders seemed on the verge of clashing openly. The most serious rift occurred in 1999 when Zhu, on a visit to the United States, promised economic reforms that went beyond those acceptable to the more orthodox wing of the Communist Party. He took that step in order to gain American support for China's entry into the World Trade Organization. Most of the promised reforms were not carried out within the time promised by Zhu. But, in the end, the two leaders – Jiang and Zhu – and other members of the third generation ruled China for a dozen years without taking the country into a major crisis. In that respect, their stewardship differed from that of Mao Zedong and Deng Xiaoping, the leaders respectively of the first and second generations.

Deng Xiaoping not only orchestrated the change in party leadership; he also set in motion a succession plan that was to materialize a dozen years later – the passing of the mantle from the third to the fourth generation. He had obviously realized the importance of introducing some process to manage change in leadership, aware of the fact that each time one generation of leaders passed on power to a successor generation, China had to go through a period of intense chaos and confusion. This had happened in 1976 after the death of Mao Zedong and was beginning to occur once again as his own demise neared. Deng was determined not to let the process of economic development and modernization that he had set in motion to be interrupted by political turmoil. In retrospect, Deng was surprisingly successful in achieving that objective.

The matter of succession appears to have been resolved for China's immediate future. In the fall of 2002, the Communist Party managed to bring about a transfer of power from one set of leaders to another according to its constitution and at the promised time. Party Secretary General Jiang Zemin stepped down along with six other members of the Standing Committee of the Politburo. The 21-member Politburo was also re-elected. Hu Jintao, 60, became the secretary general at the head of a new politburo and a new seven-member Standing Committee. There was considerable speculation in the western press about the intense backroom politics that preceded the formal decisions taken by the 16th Party Congress. Apparently, Jiang Zemin made an effort to retain some power but, in the end, he was persuaded to surrender the party leadership to Hu Jintao. Nonetheless, he was permitted to retain the chairmanship of the Party's Military Commission. He also managed to secure seven seats on the expanded nine-seat Standing Committee of the politburo. Zeng Qinzhong, a close Jiang associate, joined the Standing Committee and was also given the chairmanship of the Communist Party's Central Party School, a think tank that helps the leaders formulate ideas on political reform and development.

In keeping with China's constitution, Jiang Zemin stepped down as the country's president in March 2003 following the meeting of the National People's Congress. At this time then he had served the two terms to which the president is entitled. He was succeeded by Hu Jintao, who now held two of the three jobs for which his predecessor, Jiang, was responsible. The Military Commission's chairmanship remained with Jiang, a position he relinquished in mid-2004. Prime Minister Zhu Rongji also gave up his post and was succeeded by Wen Jiabao, one of his vice premiers. By March 2003, China had transferred political and administrative power to the leaders of the fourth generation in a peaceful and constitutional manner. This was the first time such a passing of the baton occurred in a communist country.

Will the new leadership succeed in setting a new policy line? Even before Hu Jintao became China's leader, he had displayed the skills necessary not only to hold the job in which he had been placed but also to build a solid backing for himself in the 60 million-strong Chinese Communist Party he now headed. The son of a tea merchant, Hu had proved himself willing to tackle entrenched interests. In the early 1980s, while still in his early forties, he had used his position as the leading official of the party's youth wing to mount counter-attacks on politically influenced loyalists criticizing the introduction into the Chinese society of western ideas. According to one observer,

> While many in his generation made their careers in charting China's course to free markets, Mr. Hu has used his job overseeing the party to lead change in the party itself. He has sponsored programmes to bring greater transparency to the party and government bureaucracies whose inefficiency has become a millstone for governing China's dynamic economy. Under his guidance, the once dogmatically Marxist Central Party School has been transformed into a hothouse of ideas, studying how European socialist parties made the transition to the democratic mainstream and how state monopolies compete in market economies. Chief among his pet projects is a programme to build a more professional civil service. Requiring competitive examinations for some posts and detailing qualifications for promotion, the regulations were first tested seven years ago, revised, and then implemented in July. The rules strike at the prerogatives of political privilege – the nepotism, cronyism and patronage that allow individuals to build personal power.[10]

Within a couple of months of assuming control of the country, Hu Jintao began to signal a major change in the position of the Communist Party in the country's political structure. According to one observer, 'the real message behind Mr. Hu's first two months in office is at once more subtle and more bold. Subtle because it requires interpretation; bold because a new vision for China's development has begun to emerge.' He has indicated that China's constitution was of supreme importance and that no individual or organization could operate above it. 'Although he did not spell it out, the sense of this remark is that the Communist Party – which currently operates "above everything" – will have to obey the constitution.'[11]

A number of other changes followed. At the 16th Party Congress held in November 2002, the outgoing Secretary General of the Party had already begun the task of broadening the base of the Party by extending membership beyond peasants and workers to include the owners of capital. 'The fundamental interests of the people of the whole country should be protected', he told the party gathering. Not only should the owners of capital and property be brought in, 'all legitimate income, from work or not, should be protected'. Commenting in an editorial on the immensity of the doctrinal change that was made, *The New York Times* wrote that

> China's communists are trying to do something remarkable... The [Party] Congress will make a visible effort to attract the loyalty of a rising entrepreneurial class. New membership rules permit billionaire businessmen to become card carrying communists. Some of these will now be elevated to party officers. The Congress will also sanctify the 'three represents' formula associated with its outgoing leader, Jiang Zemin. The doctrine stands Marxism on its head by proclaiming the Communist Party's duty to represent not only workers and peasants but also the capitalist class.[12]

As party secretary general and later president, Hu began to build on this changed foundation once he assumed these two offices. He opened the lower echelons of China's vast administrative system to electoral competition. Non-members were allowed to participate in the elections. Systematic work was begun on changing the constitution by permitting greater protection to individual rights. The Party's high command also showed the willingness to correct itself in public when it was shown that some of its senior functionaries had not managed well the spread of SARS (Severe and Acute Respiratory Syndrome) in the Beijing area.

It appears, therefore, that China's fourth-generation leaders are now taking steps – admittedly tentative ones – to reform and modernize the political system. They are conscious that a wide gap must not be allowed to develop between the degree of popular participation in the country's economic and political systems. The economy is now wide open; the political structure cannot stay shut for too long into the future. China appears to be 'mimicking capitalist-oriented authoritarian regimes, like the old South Korea, Taiwan and Chile. The fact that those countries have long since become democracies does not disturb party officials. They argue that the transition took 30 years in South Korea and Taiwan. China has just begun.'[13] If Hu succeeds in making this change, he would have brought about a significant political change from the days when Mao, Deng and Jiang were prepared to go to extreme lengths to preserve the supremacy of the Communist Party in China.

The US–China relationship

The United States' association with China goes back more than 150 years. In the nineteenth century, the United States relied heavily on cheap labour from China to construct the vast railway network in their country. The labourers brought in for that purpose remained and founded the numerous 'China towns' that are now a familiar feature of America's urban landscape.

Christian missionaries from the United States were active for decades bringing their religion to China. The United States also developed strong commercial interests in China and, like so many other western powers, laid claim to some sections in the country's cities, in particular in the port city of Tianjin. In the Second World War, the United States received considerable help from both the Communist Party and its rival, the Kuomintang, to repel the Japanese occupation of the city.

The advent of Communist rule in China in October 1948 cooled relations between Washington and Beijing. For more than two decades, in particular during the Vietnam War, the United States regarded China in the same light as the Soviet Union – a country determined to spread its ideology at the cost of American influence in several parts of the world. This changed in the early 1970s. For the next three decades, China and the United States sought to reconcile their differences – and these, at times, were quite severe – mostly through negotiations. On occasions, as we will see below, China provoked enough resentment in Washington for the latter to use its considerable economic muscle to get the former to correct its ways.

China's relations with the US evolved rapidly after the secret visit by Henry Kissinger, National Security Advisor to US President Richard Nixon, to Beijing in 1971, followed by a visit by the President himself to Shanghai in 1972.[14] The relationship was initially grounded on mutual interest; both countries wished to contain the influence of the Soviet Union in Northeast Asia. As China opened its economy and American corporations sought to enter the large Chinese market, Sino–US relations developed a strong economic underpinning which served China well during the frequent periods of tension in the relations between the two countries. The most stressful period came after the Tiananmen Square incident, and the World Bank played an important part in restoring economic ties between the US and China.

The interruption in the relationship caused by the Tiananmen crisis, while short-lived, led to the highlighting of human rights as an issue in the relations between the two countries. No US president before George W. Bush could ignore the strong domestic lobby that held out China's indifferent human rights record as a reason for being firm with the Beijing regime. This firmness was to be displayed in a number of areas, in particular in trade with the United States on which China depended to a great extent. A succession of administrations in Washington kept Beijing's leaders on edge as China's most favoured nation status came up for annual renewal before the US Congress. The United States only dispensed with these annual renewals after agreeing to support China's entry into the WTO. However, as part of backing China's membership in the trade organization, Washington sought economic concessions rather than significant movement on political reform or improved guarantees in the area of human rights.

Relations between the United States and China went through a dramatic transformation after September 11. The harsh rhetoric and tense encounters of the first year of President George W. Bush's administration gave way to growing signs of cooperation. The presidents of the two countries met an unprecedented three times following the terrorist attacks on New York and Washington. They reportedly established a smooth working relationship and agreed to downplay their most potentially volatile differences to address common problems, especially the struggle against global terrorism. According to one analyst, 'China's decision to greatly reduce the level of friction with Washington and to cooperate in the war on terror and in other important areas such as nonproliferation greatly facilitated the shift in Washington's stance. The Chinese policy change began well before September 11 but received enormous impetus from that day's tragedies. It was motivated by many factors, both tactical and strategic.'[15]

The Chinese leadership quickly realized that the basic post-September 11 reorientation of US strategy presented major opportunities for their country. In the US-led struggle against terrorism, China was well positioned to provide help at a low cost to itself. Beijing's political and diplomatic support in the United Nations and its provision of important intelligence on terrorist activities earned it credit in Washington.

China's leaders had also come to the conclusion that many political, economic, and perhaps even military trends regarding Taiwan – the most volatile issue between Washington and Beijing – favoured Beijing in the long run. China was prepared to put the Taiwan issue on the back burner, convinced that time was on its side. As the country increased its economic and military strength, it could more easily negotiate Taiwan's merger with the mainland. Beijing was of the view that there was not much to be gained by forcing the issue at a time when it was itself in a state of considerable economic and political flux.

The shift in United States–China relations was confirmed on the US side by the Bush administration's National Security Strategy of September 2002, which identified global terrorism – not a rising China – as the nation's primary strategic threat and clearly asserted the need for Washington to work closely with China and the other major powers to combat it. On the Chinese side, Beijing offered significant levels of assistance to Washington in the war against terror and, since the fall of 2002, greatly strengthened its formal mechanisms for enforcing internal controls on the export of items related to weapons of mass destruction or that have dual uses. As a result of both countries' heightened commitment to greater cooperation, hardliners in Beijing and Washington have been quieted, at least for the present.

China's growing regional and global political and economic influence has diminished its long-standing international insecurities. Chinese leaders are more confident in their interactions with other powers and feel they can exercise more subtle leverage against potential American pressure from the US. This change has made Beijing less inclined to confront the United States openly over a variety of issues.

Finally, Russian president Vladimir Putin's post-September 11 decision to align more closely with the United States greatly undermined China's nascent efforts to develop a close China–Russia partnership, which had been infused with anti-Americanism. Beijing was thus left with the option of either standing alone against US unilateralism or adopting a more cooperative stance.

Figure 6.1 US–Sino relations from 1989 to the present

April 1989	Massive demonstrations in Tiananmen Square by Chinese students calling for democratic reform. In June the government cracks down on the protesters with tear gas and tanks.
December 1991	Candidate Bill Clinton accuses Bush administration of 'coddling China' and promises he will pursue a tougher policy if elected.
January 1992	Premier Li Peng travels to US to meet President Bush at the UN in New York. During the summer, Bush approves the sale of 150 F-16 fighters to Taiwan, a major policy reversal signaling stronger US support for the Island.
May 1993	Clinton signs executive order linking 'Most Favored Nation' status for China with improvements in human rights over the following year.
August 1993	Clinton administration imposes sanctions on China for sale of missile parts to Pakistan. One month later the administration calls for policy of 'constructive engagement' with China.
February–March 1994	Dissident Wei Jingsheng meets in Beijing with US assistant secretary of state for human rights John Shattuck; China begins roundup of dissidents, including Wei, on the day US Secretary of State Warren Christopher leaves DC for a visit to Beijing. In May, Clinton announces end of policy to link MFN with China to human rights.
May–June 1995	After resolutions of support from both houses of Congress, Clinton administration reverses a 15-year-old policy and allows Taiwan president Lee Teng-Hui to make a private visit to his alma mater, Cornell University. China recalls its ambassador in protest.
February–March 1996	China conducts military exercises and missile tests in the Taiwan Strait during the run-up to Taiwan's presidential election; US dispatches aircraft carriers Independence and Nimitz to the seas around Taiwan.
October 1997	President Jiang Zemin visits the United States.
June–July 1998	Clinton becomes first US president to visit China since Tiananmen; he affirms 'three Nos' policy toward Taiwan: no US support for Taiwan's Independence, no support for a 'two Chinas' or a 'one China, one Taiwan' formula, and no support for Taiwan's membership in international organizations that require statehood.
May 1999	NATO warplanes mistakenly bomb Chinese embassy during raid on Belgrade, killing four Chinese nationals; violent demonstrations in Beijing, US Consulate in Chengdu burnt by mob; World Trade Organization negotiations suspended. Also, the Cox Committee of the US House of Representatives releases report accusing China of plotting to steal US nuclear secrets.
September–November 1999	WTO negotiations resume, US and China agree on terms for China's entry. Candidate George W. Bush states that China should be viewed as a 'strategic competitor' rather than a 'strategic partner.'
April 2001	Emergency landing by US EP-3 spy plane on Hainan Island after a mid-air collision with a Chinese fighter jet. Crew taken into custody by the Chinese, released only after President Bush says he is 'very sorry' that the Chinese pilot was killed; Bush announces increased weapons sales to Taiwan.
October 2001	Bush and Jiang meet for first time at APEC conference in Shanghai. Jiang affirms support for US war on terror.
November 2001	China joints the WTO.
February 2002	Bush visits China.
August 2002	In Beijing, US deputy secretary of state Richard Armitage announces that US has agreed to classify separatist group East Turkestan Islamic Movement, based in Xinjiang Province, as a terrorist organization.

Source: Kynge and Harding, 2003.

The transformation of the Chinese economy[16]

In addition to revamping its relationship with the United States, China has clearly succeeded in changing the structure of its economy. The rate of GDP growth began to pick up in the 1980s following the institution of reforms in 1978. Over the last decade, it has averaged about 9 per cent a year (see Table 6.7). The growth rate in 2002 was estimated at 8 per cent, exceeding the official 7 per cent forecast for the year. Exports grew by 21 per cent and the value of trade reached $600 billion – from $500 billion in the preceding year, implying a growth rate of 20 per cent. Foreign direct investment grew to a record $57 billion in 2002 up from $48.6 billion in 2001 – a growth rate of 16 per cent.

Such high levels of investment and growth have exacerbated some of China's structural problems, particularly oversupply and deflation. Ex-factory prices of manufactured goods fell in the last two months of 2002. According to official estimates, oversupply rose to 86 per cent. In other words, China has begun to exhibit some of the characteristics of a developed economy. China's performance in the last few years and its development into a relatively modern economy raises an important question: how did China achieve so much over such a short period of time? Since 1949, China has undertaken a number of policies that have radically reformed its centrally planned economy.

For analytical purposes, it is useful to identify four phases in China's economic transformation. The first lasted for 30 years – beginning with the Communist Party's takeover of Beijing in October 1949 and ending with the 'second coming' of Deng Xiaoping. By 1979 Deng and his colleagues

Table 6.7 China's real GDP growth

Year	*% change*
1992	14.2
1993	13.5
1994	12.6
1995	10.5
1996	9.6
1997	8.8
1998	7.8
1999	7.1
2000	8.0
2001	7.5
2002	8.0
2003	9.1

Source: *Economist Intelligence Unit*: www/eiu.com.

had finally established their control over the Communist Party and over China. In the 30 years before Deng became China's supreme leader, the country had gone through a social revolution of unprecedented proportions. The Chinese government had succeeded in bringing education and health to the masses. When measured in terms of gains in indices such as infant mortality, maternal mortality, life expectancy at birth, school enrolment for boys and girls, and adult literacy, China made extraordinary gains. Such a transformation of the quality of life for so many people in such a short period was without precedent in human history.

This transformation was not without cost. In bringing it about China's leaders made many mistakes. Two episodes in particular – the Great Leap Forward of the late 1950s and the Cultural Revolution launched in 1965 – took a very heavy toll. Nobody knows the exact human cost of these ill-advised moves, both ordered by Mao Zedong, the Great Helmsman. There is little doubt that scores of millions of Chinese died of starvation during these two periods. Indeed, it is not an exaggeration to suggest that the Chinese sacrificed a generation or two to build a better future for the generations to come.

Could the Chinese have brought about the unprecedented social revolution of 1949–79 without these upheavals? The answer to this question is an obvious yes, but the more interesting question is where would China be today had Mao and his colleagues not launched the Great Leap Forward and the Cultural Revolution?

China, still a poor country in 1980 with a per capita income estimated by the World Bank of only $290 (in 1980 dollars), had by then reached a level of social development comparable to that of the middle-income countries. Its population was estimated at 978 million, the adult literacy rate was 66 per cent and life expectancy was 64 years. Total fertility rate had declined to 2.9 per woman, the birth rate to 21 per thousand persons and the death rate to 8 per thousand persons. In the 20 years between 1960 and 1980, the Chinese had succeeded in reducing both the birth and death rates by nearly one half – from 40 to 21 per thousand persons for the birth rate, and from 14 to 8 for the death rate.[17] Comparable information for India and the middle-income countries is presented in Table 6.8.

Having achieved this level of human development, China launched another revolution in the late 1970s, this time in the agriculture sector. It carried out the privatization of agriculture by handing over the ownership of land to the families that were cultivating it. This could be done quickly, as the Chinese, unlike the Soviet Union, had not fully collectivized agricultural land. Family farms had been preserved – although under the ownership of the state.[18] This ownership was transferred back to the families living and working on the farms. Thus began the second phase of the transformation of the Chinese economy.

Table 6.8 China's social transformation

		China	*India*	*Middle-income Countries*
Population	1980 (millions)	978	673	1139
Rate of population increase	1960–70 1970–80	1.9 1.8	2.3 2.1	2.5 2.4
GNP per capita	1980 (1980 dollars)	290	240	1,400
Life expectancy at birth (years)		64	52	60
Adult literacy, 1977 (%)		66	36	65
Crude birth rate) (per 1,000 persons	1960 1980	40 21	44 36	43 35
Crude death rate (per 1,000 persons)	1960 1980	14 8	22 14	17 11
Total Fertility Rate	1980	2.9	4.9	4.8

Source: The World Bank, Tables 1, 17 and 18, pp. 110, 142 and 144; World Bank, *World Development Indicators*, 2002

Many of the key questions facing China were revealed when the country moved to rejoin the important international financial institutions. In 1979, China decided to renew its membership in the International Monetary Fund and the World Bank, and the process was completed in 1980. China was a founding member of the Bretton Woods institutions in 1944. However, after the Communist Party took control of China in October 1949, it decided to walk away from Bretton Woods institutions, leaving its seat to be occupied by the Kuomintang nationalists with whom it had fought for control of China. The Kuomintang fled from China and established themselves in Taiwan. It took thirty years for China to change its mind and reclaim its place in the Bretton Woods institutions.

A great deal had to be learnt by both sides. China had to learn a new language in order to begin to think of managing its economy not simply by the dictate of central authorities. It also wished to incorporate the notion of incentives based on some kind of price signals, and to begin to move away from what the economist Janos Karnai had called the 'soft' budgetary constraint under which most state institutions in communist countries operated.[19] There were other issues as well. For instance, how should the Chinese people, with surpluses to save, actually save? How should the banking system use ordinary people's savings? Could banks in the public sector – the only banks allowed to operate in China at that time – be allowed to undertake some due diligence of their own or should they act as simple conduits for financing the projects and activities sponsored by the state? What should be the role of the central bank in a socialist economy in which the financial system was restricted to a small number of very large public sector banks and in which capital markets did not exist?

There were many other questions to be asked and for which answers had to be provided. Some of these were unique to China, not because it was a socialist country but because of its long – and often very turbulent – history. China had a peculiar fiscal system in which taxes were collected by the provinces and then remitted to the centre. However, this was not carried out according to an established formula but was accomplished through negotiations between the central and provincial authorities. To ensure that the provinces did not assume so much power that they would overwhelm the centre, the Chinese Communist Party rotated senior officials, who had to be its members, around the country. A vice-minister in the central government could not expect to be promoted to the higher level unless he or she had held a senior position in one of the provinces, and provincial authorities were obliged to spend some time working in the central government.

In 1980, when China decided to reassume its seat in the IMF and the World Bank, it was not a large trading nation. External trade was concentrated in the hands of a few state organizations that procured goods to be exported from the state-owned enterprises (SOEs) at the prices that would produce profit for them. Since the trading organizations could not dictate prices to foreign purchasers they operated by laying down prices to the SOEs instead. In other words, the incentive structure under which the state-controlled enterprises operated was completely different from those that guided enterprises in the capitalist system. Once the initial steps to incorporate market mechanisms were taken, China embarked on a path towards market socialism that remains unmatched.

The Chinese peasantry, who had made significant strides towards better health and improved education, responded with palpable enthusiasm to the stimulus of privatization. Between 1970 and 1988, value added in agriculture increased nearly fourfold – from US$36 billion to US$121 billion (both in current dollars), and consumption of fertilizer increased nearly sixfold, from 41 kilograms per hectare of arable land to 236 kg. In the period 1987–88, when Chinese farmers were applying more than a quarter of a ton of fertilizer per hectare of arable land, their counterparts in India – the other major Asian agricultural economy – were using only 52 kg. From 1979–81, the period during which this revolution in agriculture took hold in the Chinese countryside, to 1986–88, the index of food production per capita of the population increased by 32 per cent. During the same period the Indian index increased by only 5 per cent. From 1980–88, agricultural

China and the World Bank: A Personal Note

Almost two decades after my first visit to China in the 1960s, I began to work intensively with the country as a staff member at the World Bank. Since I had some knowledge of China, I was inducted into a task force organized in the spring of 1980 to facilitate China's entry into the institution. Our China Task Force developed detailed terms of reference for the first World Bank report on the Chinese economy, a major undertaking that involved more than two dozen staff and many visits to the country.

In 1982, I was invited to speak at a workshop organized by the London-based South Institute, which was treated as an important event by the Chinese authorities since they had taken the decision to open their economy to the outside world. The gathering enabled the Chinese to engage in a learning process and investigate the way the rest of the developing world functioned in the global economic and financial system.

From May 1987 to January 1994, I was the Director of the World Bank's China Department, with a staff of more than one hundred professionals.[20] But perhaps the biggest challenge emerged in 1989, when the violent events of Tiananmen Square prompted a sudden interruption of the Bank's relations with China. On June 14, I was dispatched to China following a conversation between President George Bush of the US and President Barber Conable of the World Bank, in order to ascertain whether China met the three conditions necessary for the Bank to continue its operations in any country: creditworthiness to borrow and service the loans provided by the institution; a generally acceptable economic policy programme; and demonstration that the projects and programmes financed by the Bank were being reasonably well implemented.

I spent a week in China[21] and returned to Washington with the conclusion that since the three conditions were being met, there was no reason for the World Bank to suspend its operations. This finding notwithstanding, the Bank was not able to resume its operations for several more months. Lending to China could only resume after some of the European countries began to realize that by staying out of the country they were likely to miss some very attractive commercial opportunities. France was the first G-7 nation to break the impasse; it was soon joined by Japan, which had, all along, been a reluctant participant in the sanctions placed on China. Even though the sentiment on the part of some G-7 countries had begun to soften, it still needed a face-saving excuse for them to allow the World Bank to lend again to China. This my department provided by quickly putting together an earthquake relief project to address the damage caused by a mild tremor in a northwestern part of the country. Under ordinary circumstances, the World Bank would not have gotten involved in providing assistance to China for a relatively minor natural disaster, but the earthquake in 1990 provided us with a good opportunity for international organizations to return to China. This episode clearly demonstrates that, irrespective of what is said in the charters of the international financial organizations, it is the will of the major shareholders that ultimately prevails.

During my tenure at the World Bank, China received $14.7 billion worth of assistance for 102 projects. The Bank also wrote 82 reports covering various aspects of the Chinese economy. – *S.J.B* output in China increased at the annual rate of 6.8 per cent compared to only 2.8 per cent per year in the 15-year period between 1965 and 1980. The comparable figures for India were 2.3 per cent and 2.5 per cent per year respectively.[22]

In a few years, the Chinese farmers saw an enormous increase in their earnings. As the Chinese save a significant proportion of their income – the World Bank's estimate for 1988 was 37 per cent[23] – the Chinese peasantry was flush with liquidity. Once again, the response of the Chinese leadership was highly pragmatic. The peasants were to be allowed to use their accumulated savings and invest them in small enterprises in commerce, small-scale manufacturing and transport. With this decision – a momentous development, as it turned out – the Chinese process of economic transition entered its third phase.

During this phase, China developed an economy in the non-agricultural sectors that was parallel to the one operated by the state. It was during this period that the town and village enterprises (TVEs) began to grow rapidly. From 1985 to 1995, the output of this sector of the economy increased by an astounding 20 per cent a year, doubling every three and a half years. In addition, employment increased by 15 per cent, picking up the slack in the growth of the state sector.

China's TVEs were a unique institution in the communist world. The TVEs were not strictly privately owned; they were collectives with many different forms of ownership. They started out from the base that had already been created by the commune system, which allowed small-scale enterprises to process their agricultural output, repair the equipment they owned and provide employment to women in activities such as textile and handicrafts production. But the sector was to expand rapidly once the peasantry was allowed to invest its savings in non-agricultural activities.

The TVEs were distinctive because they were not obliged to work within the complex planning and regulatory environment that encumbered enterprises owned by the state. The state-owned enterprises were obliged to keep their workers employed irrespective of demand for their output. They were also required to provide the workers with health and recreational facilities and pensions when they reached mandatory retirement age, to run facilities for educating the children of workers, and to provide workers with housing and transport from their home to their place of work. The state-owned enterprises were central to China's intensive social security system.

By the mid-1990s, the non-state sector – mostly the TVEs – employed about the same number of people as the state sector, 100 million each. The non-state sector was creating 15 million jobs a year, which provided some space for the reorganization of state enterprises. It was possible for some to close down, and for their workers to move over to the TVEs. Although this process of adjustment was slow, it was not disruptive.

China has now entered the fourth phase of the effort to reform and modernize its economy and integrate it with the global economic, financial, and trading system. This phase involves reforms in a number of areas, in particular the state enterprises. During this period, China also successfully negotiated its admission to the World Trade Organization, the only international body from which it was still excluded. The country became a formal member of the WTO on 1 January 2002. In 2001, China also succeeded in getting the International Olympic Committee to agree to stage the 2008 Olympics in Beijing. China's effort to hold the 2000 games in its capital was unsuccessful in 1993 on the grounds that it had a record of suppressing human rights. Such a record did not conform to the system of values promoted by the Olympic movement. Eight years later, the qualms of the IOC on that score had obviously been mitigated.

What lies in China's economic future? This question has often been asked and has led to much speculation.[24] It is within the realm of possibilities to imagine China becoming the world's largest economy by 2025, if its gross domestic product is measured in terms of purchasing power parity (PPP). According to the World Bank's estimates, in 2001 there were nine economies with GNP valued at more than US$1 trillion in PPP terms (see Table 6.9).

Our projections, based on guess-estimates of growth rates for the nine countries listed in Table 6.9, suggest some significant realignments in their ranking by 2025. China, by overtaking the United States, is likely to become the world's largest economy. If that happens, its share in global output will increase from 11.1 per cent in 2001 to 20.2 per cent in 2025. On the other hand, the United States, now in second place, will see its share decline from

Table 6.9 The world's largest economies

	PPP Gross national income 2001 ($ billion)	*Growth per annum 2001–2025*	*Estimated PPP gross national income 2025*
United States	9,781	3.0	19,883
China	5,027	6.0	20,353
Japan	3,246	1.6	4,751
India	2,913	5.0	9,395
Germany	2,078	2.2	3,503
U.K.	1,431	2.4	2,528
France	1,425	2.4	2,518
Italy	1,422	1.9	2,234
Brazil	1,219	3.2	2,596
Subtotal	27,119	3.8	66,542
World total	45,183	3.4	100,801

Notes: Author's estimates for 2025. Estimates for 2001 are from the World Bank, *World Development Report 2003*.

21.6 per cent in 2001 to 19.8 per cent in 2025. The other significant change is likely to be in the case of India, which may displace Japan and become the world's third largest economy. Its share in global income is projected to increase from 6.5 per cent to 9.3 per cent in the period between 2001 and 2025. Taken together, the two Asian giants may well account for nearly 30 per cent of the global income estimated for 2025. While these estimates are highly speculative, they are provided here to underscore the important point that China is well on the way to becoming an economic giant. Its influence on the global economy, already considerable, will only increase with time.

Is the Chinese model relevant for Cuba?

There is significant debate about how China could be treated as a model for other countries in transition, and this debate has also encompassed the situation in Cuba, the way it is evolving and also the way in which it should evolve. Could Cuba follow the Chinese reform model? Or – posing the same question from a different perspective – is it in the interest of the international community to attempt to persuade the Cuban authorities to take the Chinese route?[25]

The United States government has clearly answered this question in the negative, as evidenced by the high degree of emphasis placed on democratic transition in Cuba above all other policy considerations towards the island. Most US policy makers will argue that in reforming itself, Cuba should follow the route taken by the former communist republics of Eastern Europe. This is similar to the argument advanced by a number of people about China in the late 1980s – that it was much more important to focus on the democratization of the political system. With democracy would come the right set of economic policies, as happened in most countries of Eastern Europe.

However, a review of the Chinese experience raises some doubts about the relevance of the Eastern European model, since in the latter case communism was imposed from the outside and did not put down deep roots in the political, social, and economic soils of the region. By contrast, Chinese communism was the result of a reaction against centuries of exploitation of the masses by those who had political and social power and economic wealth. In retrospect, it would have been naïve to argue that the demise of communism in Eastern Europe in the late 1980s and 1990s would induce a similar move in China. It did not happen then, and even today it remains unlikely that we will see a rapid loosening of the grip the Chinese Communist Party has on China.

Is the same true for Cuba? While the future remains uncertain, there is significant evidence that the Cubans will not easily forsake the Communist Party either. Those who hold that in post-Castro Cuba – whenever that period arrives – the country will be ready to transform its political system may be seriously deluding themselves. The revolution in Cuba was also the consequence of a reaction against decades of exploitation.

If this parallel is correct, then the Chinese experience could prove to be quite relevant to the task of bringing about economic change in Cuba. While the adoption of the Chinese model would not result in the immediate democratization of Cuba, it would be less disruptive. Cuba could comfortably draw many lessons from the Chinese experience, not just in developing its economy, but also in rejoining the global economic system including the Bretton Woods institutions and the World Trade Organization, and establishing good relations with the United States. It could also draw some lessons from the way China has handled the question of succession within the one-party system and the way it has conducted its relations with the United States.

As shown in Table 6.10, Cuba has achieved impressive successes in human development. In terms of various health indices and in terms of life expectancy at birth, Cuba's record is now better than countries with per capita incomes three times as high. If it comes out with a lower Human Development Index (HDI) rank, this is because the HDI is a composite index that includes political freedom as one of its components. In the area of human development, Cuba's record exceeds China's with respect to the advances made by women. Women's share of income in Cuba is about a third of the total, compared to slightly over one-fifth for Argentina and China, two countries that are considerably richer than Cuba.

It appears that the stage is set for Cuba to provide the kinds of incentives to agricultural producers that revolutionized China's agriculture in the 1980s. In fact, Cuba could compress China's second and third phase of reforms into one phase. Instead of waiting for the peasants to accumulate savings, it could open up the small-scale manufacturing, commerce and transport sectors immediately for private and collective investment. Very quickly, Cuba, drawing upon the experience of China, could leapfrog to the point where it could undertake the important but difficult task of reforming the large and inefficient state sector.

As Cuba opens up and begins to integrate itself into the global economy, its economy will develop a strong service sector. In that way it would be very different from China, where light manufacturing led the way. In Cuba, tourism and telecommunications may provide the lead. This is likely to happen, given the proximity of the United States. It will also be facilitated by the better economic and social situation of Cuban women, who could provide valuable human resources for the growth and development of these sectors.

All this would be possible if Cuba were to open its economy to private initiative and to facilitate the flow of foreign direct investment, much as China began to do in the early 1970s. Following China, it could begin to

Table 6.10 Human development in Cuba and other Latin American countries

	Argentina	*Cuba*	*Chile*	*Dominican Republic*
Population (millions)	36	11	15	8
GDP per capita (dollars)	8,500	3,100	9,930	3,900
HDI rank	36	85	31	88
Life expectancy	73	76	75	70
Adult literacy	96	96	95	82
Enrolment rate	79	66	73	73
Gender related HDI	48	85	46	88
Life expectancy:				
male	69	74	72	72
female	76	78	78	68
Adult literacy rate:				
male	96	82		
female	95	82		
Share of earned income:				
male	78	68	78	76
female	22	32	22	24
Gender empowerment measure (rank)	—	25	61	58

Notes: [1] Human Development Index
Source: United Nations Development Programme, *Human Development Report 1988*.

promote private enterprise in small-scale agriculture, as well as small-scale manufacturing, small-scale commerce and small-scale transport. Going beyond China's early reform period, Cuba could allow greater private (including foreign) participation in the service sector, particularly tourism.

It would also be instructive if the aging Cuban leadership studied the way in which power was effectively and efficiently transferred between generations in China. Communist systems typically do not have well-established ways of doing this. China is an exception to this phenomenon. It achieved such a transfer over a four-month period between November 2002 and March 2003 when power was handed over by the 'third generation' led by President Jiang Zemin and Prime Minister Zhu Rongji to the fourth generation under the command of President Hu Jintao. The transfer was first achieved in the party and then in the government with the third generation still keeping some control over the military – the People's Liberation Army. Fidel Castro has in principle designated his brother Raúl Castro, head of Cuba's armed forces, as the immediate successor. Yet, in reality, Cuban succession remains a guessing game for those on the outside, and also, one suspects, for members of the current government as well.

Finally, the Chinese leadership has shown both sophistication and pragmatism in developing its relations with the United States. It adopted a long-term view of the way it wished to work with Washington, ignoring the problems created as power was transferred from one US administration to another. The Chinese kept their attention focused on their long-term objectives, which included rapid economic development and the ultimate reunification of Taiwan with the Mainland. While the Cuban government appears to relish its ongoing confrontation with the United States, this approach has yielded little in the way of results. If Cuba wanted to learn a thing or two about getting along with the world's dominant superpower in a way that encourages trade and growth, it could do worse than to examine how China has managed its relations with the United States to help engineer its remarkable economic rise. China's market reforms, emphasis on integration, and pragmatic attitude towards the United States have created a precedent that could benefit Cuba when and if the island decides to open further to the global economy.

Notes

1 Charles Hutzler, 'Hu's cautious political strategy aided ascent to top China post', *The Wall Street Journal,* 18 November 2002.
2 Jim Mann, *Beijing Jeep: A Case Study of Western Business in China* (New York: Simon and Schuster, 2002).
3 James Kynge, 'China: An industrial powerhouse emerges by the waterfront', *Financial Times: The World – 2003,* 23 January 2003.
4 Simon Cartledge, 'The other side of China's success story', *Financial Times,* 20 January 2003.
5 James Kynge, 'China: an industrial powerhouse emerges by the waterfront.'
6 The World Bank, *World Development Indicators, 2002* (Washington, DC: World Bank, 2002).
7 Peter Engardio, Aaron Bernstein and Manjur Kripalani, 'Is your job next?', *Business Week,* 3 February 2003.
8 'Roll over Confucius', *The Economist,* 25 January 2003.
9 Two years after making the trip to China I went to Harvard University for graduate studies. Using the data and information I had gathered during the 1965 visit to China, I wrote a short monograph on the Chinese communes as a doctoral student in economics. The monograph was published by Harvard University Press in 1969.
10 Charles Hutzler and Susan V. Lawrence, 'China acts to lower obstacles to urban migration', *The Wall Street Journal,* 22 January 2003, A12.
11 James Kynge, 'Profile: Hu Jintao', *Financial Times: The World-2003,* 23 January 2003.
12 'China's Chameleon Communists', *The New York Times,* 10 November 2002, 12.
13 Kahn, 'China's Congress of Crony Capitalists', *The New York Times,* 10 November 2002, 12.
14 Henry Kissinger, *Diplomacy* (New York: Touchstone, 1994) and Richard Nixon, *Memoirs of Richard Nixon* (New York: Grosset and Dunlap, 1978).
15 Michael Swaine, 'Reverse course? The fragile turnaround in US-China relations', *Carnegie Endowment Policy Brief,* No. 22 (2003).

16 This section draws heavily upon an essay written by the author in 1999. The essay was based on a talk given at a lunch organized by the Inter American Dialogue on 8 May 1999, at its headquarters in Washington, DC (see Shahid Javed Burki, *Changing Perceptions and Altered Realities: Emerging Economies in the 1990s* [Washington, DC: The World Bank, 1999], 187–94).

17 The World Bank, *World Development Report, 1982* (New York: Oxford University Press, 1982).

18 Shahid Javed Burki, *A Study of Chinese Communes* (Cambridge, MA: Harvard University Press, 1969).

19 Janos Karnai, *The Socialist System: the Political Economy of Communism* (Princeton: Princeton University, 1992).

20 Of this contingent, economists constituted a group that numbered nearly three dozen. This was the largest group of economists working on China full time in any institution outside China.

21 One condition of my visit to China was that I would not meet with Prime Minister Li Peng, the man who had imposed martial law in Beijing and ordered the army to vacate Tiananmen Square. I met, instead, with the three vice premiers as well as Mayor Zhu Rongji of Shanghai. Zhu was later to become China's Prime Minister and the main architect of the country's further opening in the latter part of the 1990s.

22 The World Bank, *World Development Report, 1990: Poverty* (New York: Oxford University Press, 1990).

23 Ibid.

24 Shahid Javed Burki, 'An Asian Stampede'. *Financial Times*, 11 June 2001.

25 This question was asked of me at a lunch meeting organized by the Inter-American Dialogue in May 1999. Bernard Aronson, former Assistant Secretary of State in the administration of George H.W. Bush, was the other speaker at the meeting. He expressed the common view of the United States that Cuba should embrace the path taken by Eastern Europe. Based on my personal experience in China, I offered the different view that the Chinese model may indeed be more appropriate for Cuba.

7

Vietnam and Cuba: Yin and Yang?

David Dapice

Introduction

Vietnam is a poor, rural country that anticipated the break-up of the Soviet Union, its major trade partner, aid donor, and political-military ally. During the mid-1980s, when the country faced inflation rates of over 10 per cent per month, sporadic food shortages and isolation from most western donors, the Vietnamese leadership crafted a policy of *Doi Moi*. This policy, often translated as 'renovation', dismantled cooperatives, permitted the creation of family farms, liberalized prices for most goods, and introduced gradual macroeconomic stability. Although Vietnam's progress was slowed by the financial crisis in East Asia in the late 1990s, growth in output and exports took off, and real GDP has never grown more slowly than 5 per cent annually for any extended period. It grew nearly 9 per cent per annum between 1991 and 1997.

Vietnam's current official estimates and targets are for 7 per cent annual growth. Official realized FDI is approximately US$2 billion per year, with an equal or greater amount in remittances, some of which double as investments. By most estimates, poverty has been cut in half, food output has risen sharply, and social indicators have exceeded the levels reached under central planning. Throughout this period, the Communist Party has kept strict control over political activity. The government now allocates 50–60 per cent of total investment, up from approximately 40 per cent in 1995, though the private sector accounts for a growing share of total output and nearly 90 per cent of all employment. The Vietnamese label this 'market socialism'.

In contrast, Cuba – admittedly more reliant on Soviet aid and less rural – has fared much worse, following an economic pattern more like that of the Soviet Union. Income per capita declined by roughly one-third between 1989 and 1994. What followed was an uneven and partial recovery marked by rising inequalities and inefficiencies caused by a dual-currency system. Debt arrears have risen, FDI (except in nickel and

Map 6 Vietnam

tourism) is miniscule, and major industries such as sugar have collapsed. Were it not for the estimated US$500–$750 million each year in remittances, these economic pressures might have forced more substantial reforms. However, gifts and tourism have allowed policy paralysis that further endangers the social advances that have been achieved. Havana permits even less debate than Hanoi, and small-scale private activity, unlike in Vietnam, faces harassment from officials. Cuba has not allowed as much of a 'socialist market economy' to emerge from the ruins of subsidized central planning and the result is an economic slump aggravated by a demographic structure that will cause workforce stagnation and growing pension burdens over the next two decades.

The obvious conclusion is that Vietnam has been shrewdly pragmatic and managed to jump from the sinking boat of central planning to a more seaworthy craft powered by market economics, albeit still socialist in some respects. Cuba, by contrast, is seen to be trapped in politically inspired contradictions at the cost of its economic self-interest. However, this broad analysis fails to capture some important nuances. Without contesting the significant differences in Cuban and Vietnamese outcomes, this chapter argues that future progress in Vietnam is less secure than many now believe, while the size, circumstances and educational levels of Cuba would allow faster economic transformation than its leaders' anti-market rhetoric would suggest.

The numbers

A snapshot of key figures for both Vietnam and Cuba clearly establishes the differences in their performances. Variables including GDP per capita, exports, FDI, agricultural output, and child mortality demonstrate a general pattern of advances for Vietnam and economic (if not social) declines for Cuba.

Table 7.1 illustrates that the 1990s were a period of rapid expansion in Vietnam, with healthy FDI, brisk GDP and agricultural growth, and exploding export levels. In contrast, Cuba experienced shrinking GDP per capita, collapsing agricultural output, modest FDI, and sharp export declines. The immense disparity in economic performance is underlined by the fact that Vietnam's exports increased from one-half of Cuba's in 1991 to *twelve times* Cuba's in 2003. However, Cuba improved on its already low child mortality rate, while Vietnam reduced its child mortality rate by 40 per cent, reaching a level similar to that of Cuba 25 years ago and that of China today.

The levels of GDP per capita tell a different story than the overall growth patterns. Given Cuba's fragmented pricing system, it is difficult to estimate its GDP per capita with any precision. It is normally said to be 'lower middle income' with gross national income in 2002 between $750 and $3,000 per capita (not in PPP terms). Vietnam is said to have $400 to $500

Table 7.1 Vietnam and Cuba since 1989

	GDP per capita (1989 = 100)	*Food output (1989 = 100)*	*Exports (goods only) (US$ billion)*		*Under-five mortality (per 1,000 births)*		*Cumulative FDI (US$ billions)*
	2003	*2002*	*1991*	*2003*	*1990*	*2001*	*1995–2000*
Cuba	85	87	3	1.6	14	9	0.1 to 1.0
Vietnam	215	200	1.6	20	65	38	8.5 to 12.0

Sources: Please see statistical annex for a discussion of sources.

per capita income, so a reasonable guess is that average income in Vietnam is one-fifth to one-half that of Cuba.[1] Vietnam's electricity consumption per capita in 2000 was only about one-quarter of Cuba's, but was growing at 15 per cent per year, versus 3 per cent for Cuba.[2] Food consumption was nearly equal: 2,500 daily calories per capita in Vietnam and 2,600 in Cuba in 2000 – and again, Cuba's intake has been falling while Vietnam's is rising.[3] Overall, it is quite possible that by 2004 the food intakes will be equal while the gap in electricity use will have shrunk considerably. This might suggest that the real per capita income of the two nations is much closer than official data suggest.

Education is another ready area of comparison, measured by enrollment and graduation rates. Except among isolated minorities, Vietnam has reached virtually universal primary net enrollments of 95 per cent overall, while Cuba's rate is 97 per cent. For secondary education, Vietnam's net enrollment rate is 62 per cent while Cuba's is 82 per cent.[4] In the course of ten years, Vietnam has doubled its secondary enrollment while Cuba has raised its rate by one-fifth. One-eighth of Cuba's labour force has a college or university education; in Vietnam that figure is only 4 per cent, though again the figure is falling in Cuba and sharply rising in Vietnam.[5] Educational quality is another matter and one that is hard to estimate without more data. In terms of telecommunications, the rapid increase in telephone and Internet use may actually give Vietnam an edge over Cuba. Vietnam's current user rates are slightly higher than Cuba's and they are growing much faster. While concerned about certain content, the Vietnamese authorities allow their population much wider access to global information than their Cuban counterparts, whose control of the Internet approaches that of Myanmar.

Comparing the economic performance of Cuba and Vietnam does have some limitations. Cuba is a small island nation with a 75 per cent urban population and a large rural proletariat (on sugar plantations) with moderate per capita income, while Vietnam is a large, poor, rural country with 60 per cent of its population working as peasant farmers.[6] Another important difference is that 75 to 80 per cent of Cuba's labour force is employed in the public sector, compared to only 10 per cent in Vietnam.[7] Even more, after winning the war against the Americans, getting bogged down in Cambodia and observing reforms by Gorbachev in the former USSR, the Vietnamese realized they needed normal relations with the United States. as well as a market economy. In contrast, the Cuban government often seems to want neither. Friendly relations between Cuba and the United States would rid the Cuban leadership of its scapegoat for manifest economic failures. Opening to foreign direct investment and establishing a market economy could potentially result in an inflow of Miami Cubans who are hostile to the regime. Thus, both the objective circumstances and the constraints facing each government are sufficiently different that a solution for one may be anathema for the other. Yet Vietnam's communist political structure, experience with centrally planned economics, and difficult historical relationship with the United States and the broader international community do make the country an illuminating counterpoint to Cuba. Vietnam's development trajectory over the last two decades suggests interesting possibilities for Cuba's economic future.

Vietnam starts *doi moi*: 1987–92

The roots of Vietnam's homegrown set of reforms emerged after the 'American War,' as they call the war that ended in 1975. The victory was followed by an attempt to impose collective agriculture and central planning on the peasant economy of the South and the cooperative farm economy of the North. Basically, this failed, as food output grew more slowly than population from 1976 to 1980. Farmers in the Mekong Delta[8] had benefited from land reform prior to the end of the war and had become accustomed to a market economy. They passively resisted the collectivization and output stagnated or fell. When Vietnam invaded Cambodia and was in turn invaded by China, there was a need for pragmatism and some reforms were introduced. These worked, but the reforms were weakened as external threats diminished. As long as Soviet aid was available, the Vietnamese government continued to push for central planning and collective farming. Only when Gorbachev's reforms indicated that the Soviet Union itself might fundamentally change or even collapse did the Vietnamese leadership begin to earnestly reconsider its economic strategy.

In 1985–86, prices were quadrupling every year and there was an acute dependence on Soviet aid. Exports were less than $500 million per year, while imports were more than twice that figure. Barring hyperinflation, prices meant little since socialist pricing was divorced from scarcity. There was an emphasis on heavy industry and an effective de-emphasis on food production. The collective structure of agriculture itself resulted in distorted incentives, much waste, and some corruption. Food imports were needed in 1987. Without outside support, such a system would collapse. It was clear that Soviet support was not likely to last, so some serious decisions needed to be made.

Beginning with a Party Congress in 1986 and continuing over the next several years, Vietnam was transformed by the process of *Doi Moi*. The aim of the policy was to preserve the socialist system by allowing markets and private economic activity to strengthen the economy. Immediate steps were taken to de-collectivize agriculture and allow family farming, along with a liberalization of most prices. Longer-term land use rights were assigned, but not land ownership. Food output jumped sharply from 281kg per capita in 1987 to 346kg in 1992. Real agricultural GDP rose 25 per cent in that same period, or 4.5 per cent annually. Rice, which had been imported in 1987, reached export levels of 1.86 million tons in 1992.[9]

Vietnam brought inflation under control in stages. Prices rose 500 per cent in 1988, 70 per cent in 1989 and 40 per cent in 1990.[10] Exchange rates in 1989 were set at market levels, which were many times higher than the old official rates. In any case, the old rates were largely notional since all trade had been managed by the state. The floating market exchange rate, aided by an increase in oil exports, allowed for a quadrupling of the dollar value of exports from 1987 to 1992. From 1990 until western aid and FDI began to grow in 1993 and 1994, exports and imports were nearly equal, and at import levels 50 to 100 per cent higher than in 1987.[11] Trade was progressively allocated away from monopoly state trading companies to many more firms. Fiscal deficits were reduced. The monobank typical of socialist economies was broken up into a central bank and four state-owned commercial banks with sectoral lending responsibilities. Interest rates were allowed to exceed inflation by the mid-1990s, though many private firms borrowed from informal lenders with higher rates.

Public enterprises also went through a partial restructuring. The oft-cited decline in number of enterprises from 12,000 to 6,000 is correct but somewhat misleading. Most of the entities closed or privatized were local enterprises with few employees and a limited role in the central planning system. Even so, this shrinkage combined with the decline of cooperatives created some space in which small-scale private activities could and did flourish. It was much easier to make a living, and even to move to another place and open a shop or restaurant when capital was available. However, it was still dangerous for enterprises to grow very large, and in most cases, the state banks were unwilling to lend to private borrowers. The non-farm private sector was allowed to exist but hardly to thrive in this first round of economic reform – but the crisis had passed. Despite the collapse of the Soviet Union, a healthier agricultural sector, increasing trade, and an expansion of petty services established a degree of stability and even modest prosperity.

The bubble years: 1993–97

At the end of 1992 a Vietnamese official could reflect on a good past five years. GDP growth had averaged 6.7 per cent, and had reached over 8 per cent in 1992. However, the next five years were to make the previous five look like a sluggish transition phase rather than a golden age. Every important indicator grew at rates more typical of China than anything Vietnam had known previously. Real GDP growth averaged nearly 9 per cent per year. Between 1992 and 1997, exports leapt from US$2.5 billion to US$9.2 billion, while imports exploded from US$2.5 billion to US$11.6 billion. The exchange rate was essentially stable in nominal terms, while inflation rates fell to about one per cent per month during this period.

Several things conspired to produce such a favourable set of results. Aid had been modest in 1992, but began to rise following normalization of diplomatic relations with the United States in 1995. By 1997, aid loan disbursements had risen to US$550 million, in addition to US$175 million in grants and another US$457 million in commercial loans. Thus, these foreign resources more than doubled in five years. But it was the foreign direct investment that provided the largest lift. FDI registered at only US$250 million in 1992 but rose to over US$2 billion by 1997. Much of this FDI was in real estate or high-cost, import-substituting enterprises with partial state ownership. Even so, it gave the economy an immediate lift and helped drive the import boom. In an economy of only US$26 billion, these inflows accounted for 12 per cent of GDP. Oil exports added another 5 per cent of GDP. [12]

In most rapidly growing economies, the share of state production in output tends to fall as exports lead growth. Usually, manufacturing exports come from FDI or domestic private firms and these grow much faster than state enterprises that tend to be stronger in services. In Vietnam, exports rose from 25 per cent of GDP in 1992 to 43 per cent in 1997. Yet the state share of GDP rose from 36 per cent to over 40 per cent, even though employment in state jobs rose less than ten per cent and grew more slowly than in the private sector.[13] The early stages of dualism began to appear here, as the state sector absorbed most capital and little labour. However, the picture changes a bit when looking at non-farm output. The farm sector tends to grow more slowly than overall output and in Vietnam farms were largely private. If only non-farm output is considered, then the state's share of output was roughly unchanged over this period.

An interesting observation on the dynamics of Vietnamese reform comes from *Assessing Aid*, a 1998 World Bank study of aid effectiveness.[14] On page 107, a graph shows an index of reform in Vietnam rising sharply when the Aid/GDP ratio was low, and then flattening out when aid rose sharply, beginning in 1991. While normalization of diplomatic relations with the United States certainly helped Vietnam attract more export-oriented investment, the primary economic impact of renewed US support was the resumption of normal lending to Vietnam by the International Monetary Fund and World Bank. These flows then attracted investments in import-substituting industries that could not earn foreign exchange, but were encouraged so that profits could be kept within the country.

In the early 1990s, Vietnam's investment averaged 28 per cent of GDP and the *effective* capital stock was probably growing rapidly (estimates suggest 11–12 per cent per year from 1991–95 for the *total* capital stock), since much of the Soviet-era equipment was not economically useful. The labour force was growing at 2–2.5 per cent per year and improving in quality. Per capita output was growing at 6 per cent per year. If the share of capital is assumed to be 50 per cent, it is likely that most of the growth was 'explained' by input growth rather than productivity.[15] Most poor nations have a capital share closer to one-half. Total factor productivity growth outside of agriculture was probably rather low, given the high state enterprise and import-substitution investments. However, estimates of factor productivity are difficult to make with poor data.

Vietnam was growing fast, but largely due to high capital and remittance inflows, oil revenues and rapid labour force growth. At the same time, the financial sector was directing more credit to the private sector, though it amounted to only 10 per cent of GDP and was largely for working capital. Thus, domestic private businesses were small in scale and quite weak, though numerous. Loans to state enterprises increasingly replaced subsidies as a way to keep loss-generating firms afloat, but the loans could not be recovered. Of course, this meant the banking system was insolvent. Official data on loan losses were initially classified, and the data eventually released[16] was said by many observers to be overly optimistic. Probably, the actual situation is similar to China with non-performing loans equal to one-third to two-fifths of total credit outstanding.

Vietnam's total factor productivity was not growing very rapidly, and the stability of the nominal exchange rate[17] was creating a problem as domestic prices nearly doubled between 1992 and 1997. In a way, the capital flows created a kind of 'Dutch Disease' in which plentiful foreign exchange allowed the exchange rate to remain stable while prices rose. Export revenue grew remarkably from US$2.5 to US$9.2 billion, a compounded growth of 30 per cent per year. The explosion was composed largely of raw materials exports, though labour-intensive exports, helped by US diplomatic recognition, also soared.[18] On the other hand, imports grew by 35 per cent per year to US$11.6 billion, creating a trade deficit equivalent to 9 per cent of GDP. This led to various quantitative controls and ad hoc measures to control imports. These measures succeeded in keeping imports between US$11 and US$12 billion from 1996 to 1999. Part of this can be attributed to import substitution, but a good deal is due to the use of administrative measures. [19]

The Asian crisis and its aftermath, 1997–2000

The collapse of several Asian economies coupled with China's stability led Vietnamese economic and political authorities to conclude at first that more socialism was needed, not less. They saw that open capital flows, speculation, and uncontrolled markets could cause problems for economies with certain underlying imbalances – and even for some without such problems. The speculative attacks on Hong Kong, for example, required its government to intervene in stock markets and buy back shares. Thus, there was a tendency to increase controls and regulation and boost the relative share of state-directed investment, which had fallen below 40 per cent in the mid-1990s. If Indonesia and Thailand were not invulnerable to capital flight, even with good diplomatic relations with the United States and Japan, then what would happen to Vietnam if it fell into difficulties?

Thus, the state extended its control over financial flows and its share of total investment approached 60 per cent. 'Equitization' (a kind of limited privatization) of state enterprises proceeded at a glacial pace. Foreign investors were required to deposit foreign exchange earnings in official banks and then had to apply to use their own funds. Import-substituting industries had to earn their profit remittances in hard currency, unless they had gotten prior permission to exchange *dong* for dollars. FDI, which had averaged over US$2 billion in annual inflows from 1995 to 1997, began a long slide to an average of US$1.3 billion between 1999 and 2001.[20] This was a decline of nearly 40 per cent, signalling rising investor disenchantment with Vietnam and its policies.

On the other hand, there were some countervailing tendencies. A decision was reached in 1996 to join the ASEAN Free Trade Area (AFTA) and commitments were made to lower tariffs within eight to ten years. Inflation dropped to single digits, but the exchange rate was devalued to 14,000 *dong* per dollar by the start of 2000. This resulted in a real depreciation that helped offset the devaluations of neighboring countries. Exports continued to grow rapidly – except in 1998, when oil prices and the Asian Crisis held export growth to 2 per cent.[21] However, on the whole, it was a period of lower GDP growth.

The growth of tourism was another bright spot during this period. Arrivals had already jumped from 250,000 in 1990 to 1,350,000 in 1995, and were to continue growing through the Asian Crisis, reaching 2.6 million in 2002.[22] While the emergence of a new respiratory infection, known as SARS, hurt tourism in 2003, Vietnam's good record in security, high number of international quality hotels, and improved marketing make it likely that this sector will continue to grow. However, spending per tourist is not as high as in some other nations, and gross revenues in 2002 were only US$1.5 billion, contributing less than 10 per cent of total export earnings. One estimate puts tourism-related jobs at 150,000, a small fraction of the 40 million-person labor force. While Vietnam's tourism revenue is of roughly the same magnitude as Cuba's, the relative importance of tourism in Vietnam is much less than in Cuba, where gross tourist receipts are about equal to total export revenue.[23]

Vietnam's policy towards remittances also changed during this period. There had been an attempt to tax the gifts that overseas Vietnamese sent to their relatives in 1996. This caused 'official' remittances to fall to below US$1 billion, though informal money transfer mechanisms allowed actual giving to continue above that level. Recognizing that it was better to facilitate these flows from 2.5 million émigrés in the United States, Europe, and Australia, the government abolished the remittance tax in 1999. Recorded remittances grew quickly and are now estimated at US$2 to US$3 billion per year, and may be higher. It is not clear how much of these transfers are simple gifts and how much are really investments in real estate or small businesses. Some even suggest Taiwanese and Hong Kong investors use relatives to start more sizeable businesses in the South. There are about 100,000 Vietnamese who are 'guestworkers' overseas in construction, merchant marine, and domestic activities who also send money back and their funds are included in the total figure, which is about 20 per cent of exports. Remittances clearly play an important role in financing consumption, investment, and imports.

Vietnam's actual GDP growth rate is a matter of some dispute. The IMF and the Asian Development Bank make independent estimates of growth and they both concluded that actual growth was lower than the official figures. The official GDP growth estimate from 1997 to 2000 was 5.8 per cent, but the ADB estimate was 5.1 per cent, and the IMF's was 4.4 per cent. All of these estimates indicate a considerable slowdown from the nearly 9 per cent average growth during the preceding five years. Since Vietnam, like China, lacks open capital markets, it had very little difficulty with short-term capital flows. Nevertheless, Vietnam's economy remained stuck in a lower gear well after most other crisis-struck economies had begun to recover. This was in spite of export growth that, after pausing in 1998, resumed at 20–5 per cent in both 1999 and 2000. Imports grew more slowly, so the trade deficit (taking imports in CIF terms) contracted from US$2.4 billion in 1997 to US$1.2 billion in 2000.[24] This smaller deficit, combined with growing infusions of aid and remittances, and the lower level of FDI, improved the balance of payments. Inflation also remained in the low single digits. There was no macroeconomic crisis, but the sluggish growth was a concern.

Vietnam was approaching an inflection point in its labour force. The growth of those who said they were mainly farmers was slowing sharply and would soon turn negative. Many young agricultural workers with some secondary education were leaving their meager prospects in the rural zone behind for the chance of a better life in the cities. Since most new workers had at least some secondary education, they knew of urban opportunities and average – if not marginal – incomes three or four times higher than in the rural areas. These income differences were not only large but were also growing every year. The rapid flow of rural migrants into the cities outpaced the growth of formal employment there, posing new challenges for the Vietnamese government. Rising levels of unemployment and underemployment, overcrowding, poor sanitation, crime, and drug use threatened to grow into real discontent.

However, the public sector was not a prolific generator of jobs. It was unable to employ as much as 10 per cent of the total workforce on average, and had trouble absorbing as many as 100,000 per year when over one million jobs per year were needed for new, displaced, and underemployed workers.[25] Many state enterprises were overstaffed and in need of downsizing. Those lacking protection, monopoly power, or other advantages in securing contracts, land, and loans had trouble competing on a 'level playing field,' which many donors and few Vietnamese talked about. Although the threat was more diffuse than when the Soviet Union was disintegrating, it was also more insidious. Trouble with demonstrations in Thai Binh province,[26] in which government and Party members were arrested and their offices or houses burned down, were a reminder that corruption combined with slow growth in jobs and incomes was a political threat.

The threat of disorder helps to concentrate the mind. The reaction to these internal tensions was a bold step: the Enterprise Law. Enacted in January 2000, it greatly eased the regulatory steps in registering a domestic private business. A 'private business' in Vietnam is one step up from a household firm, which could always be registered at the local level with little difficulty. The private firms had more capital and employees, a different legal and tax status, and could extend up to joint-stock corporations. In the past, provincial officials had to grant a license to do business and this was a de facto barrier to entry. To enter a similar but distinct line of business required more permissions, and often delays and expenses. Even expansion of the same line sometimes required a new license of one sort or another. The shift from licensing to a system of registration with few formalities or delays made establishing a private business much easier. This change was fiercely resisted by many bureaucrats and state enterprise officials, but was supported by Vietnam's top leadership. The private sector was the only possible hope for generating decent jobs and its leash was lengthened.

Vietnam's slowdown in FDI also caused worries. If direct job creation was less than in domestic firms, it was still true that a lot of management, marketing and technical know-how was added by foreign investors – an assessment that led to a new law on foreign investment and an easing of restrictions on the use of foreign exchange. Decisions were also made to allow some big FDI infrastructure projects in gas and electricity. In spite of Vietnam's rather poor ratings (near the 20th percentile) in various international indices such as Transparency International's corruption ratings or the World Economic Forum's competitiveness ratings, FDI did respond to these new conditions and began to pick up after 2000.

For several reasons, foreign investment clustered primarily in and around Ho Chi Minh City (abbreviated HCMC; formerly known as Saigon). First, it is the economic center of Vietnam and the largest single market. Second, some of the provinces around HCMC adopted a business-friendly approach even before the enterprise law or new foreign investment law, by developing industrial zones, infrastructure, and simple regulation that appealed to both domestic and foreign investors. Third, many of the skills and services that foreign investors required were more readily available there. The area in and around Hanoi, though its infrastructure is rapidly improving and in some ways superior, has tended to attract a different kind of foreign investor. While FDI in the South was especially concentrated in export-based manufacturing, investments in the North have typically supported production for the domestic market and services such as real estate. Even today, the North still has a reputation for being a more difficult business climate. Some indication of the different regional reputations can be gleaned from the *Guidebook for European Investors in Vietnam*, which is excerpted below.[27]

In 2002, the Binh Duong province, just outside of HCMC, received US$340 in FDI inflows per capita, while the capital of Hanoi had only $14 and Haiphong – the chief northern port for the entire Red River Delta, with an excellent industrial zone – had $23. Bac Ninh is among the most business-friendly Northern provinces and has considerably improved its road system, but even it reached only US$38 in per capita FDI. The historical cumulative FDI data are more equal; the South has about 2.3 times the

The Guidebook for European Investors in Vietnam

In a Guidebook written by Asia Invest of the Europe Aid Investment Office, the question of where to locate a business in Vietnam is addressed. Their summary table is as follows:

Positives	*Negatives*
South	
Business Friendly Environment	Far from Political Decision Centers
'Can Do' Attitude with Foreign Investors	Higher Competition
Better Infrastructure	
Major Concentration of Existing FDI	
Largest Domestic Market	
Good for Expatriate Living	
Center	
Lowest Costs for Labor and Land	Poor Infrastructure
Access to Specific Commodities	Limited Existing FDI and 'Clusters'
Low Competition	Higher Regulatory Uncertainties
	Limited Local Markets
North	
Close to Political Decision Centers	Stronger Bureaucratic Hindrances
Most HQ of State Enterprises	Still 'Defiance' to Foreign Investors
Most Efficient for 'Special'* Projects	Uncertainties on 'Inside Political Issues'
Satisfactory Infrastructure	
Large Local Market	
Access to Mineral Inputs	[* 'special' = needing influence]

cumulative FDI of the North. However, the cumulative numbers include some real estate and import substituting projects not likely to be repeated, especially in the North.[28] Clearly, foreign investors perceive the North and South as remarkably different investment atmospheres.

Foreign investors are not the only ones to notice these differences. Though domestic investors spread their activity much more widely than do foreigners, as shown in Table 7.2, they still favour the South. The data in the table shows private domestic investment for 2001 only, but it is likely that this pattern will persist unless new policy changes are introduced. As the European Investor's Guide said, many Northern (and Central) provinces still regard large private investors as somehow undesirable, even if necessary. These attitudes are changing slowly in some places.

If it is indeed true that state investment is relatively inefficient and provides few jobs, the above pattern of investment has obvious dangers. Many regions rely almost entirely on state investments. Even in the area around and including Hanoi (the Red River Delta) three-quarters of total investment flows from the state. If the South continues to attract a greater share of investment and more effective investment, it will grow in influence and attract ever more migration. This would cause tremendous social and political tensions, and many regions would lobby national authorities for infrastructure investments to enhance their own competitiveness vis-à-vis the North. The South would argue that its own economic and demographic growth demands new infrastructural investment more urgently. Building political consensus for market-oriented reforms in Vietnam requires getting more regions to see their future in non-state investment and market-driven growth. Only this can avert long-distance and disruptive population movements, maintain inter-regional harmony, and provoke a wider and more

Table 7.2 Regional trends in per capita state, foreign, and private domestic investments[29]

Region	*State (%)*	*Foreign ($)*	*DPI ($)*	*Total ($)*
South East (HCMC)	113 (37)	117	75	304
Red River Delta	104 (74)	6	29	140
South Central Coast	69 (60)	33	14	115
Mekong Delta	50 (63)	23	8	80
North East & West	62 (79)	4	12	78
Central Highlands	60 (86)	3	6	70
North Central Coast	56 (89)	1	6	63
All Vietnam	**74 (60)**	**26**	**22**	**123**

Notes:
State investment is for 2000; foreign investment is realized FDI in 2002; DPI is enterprise law investment for 2001. Data in parentheses are share of state in total regional investment.

even geographical distribution of investment. Otherwise regional tensions are likely to increase in the coming years.

Current developments and problems

The period since 2000 has been marked by a number of conflicting trends. On the plus side, FDI and Enterprise Law domestic investment has risen. Exports have continued to grow. It seems likely that commitments under AFTA (ASEAN Free Trade Area) and the more recent BTA (Bilateral Trade Agreement with the United States) will be broadly followed and it is at least possible that Vietnam will accede to the WTO by 2005.[30] On the other hand, Vietnam's transparency and investment ratings in many international tables remain in the bottom fifth of countries. The amount of investment needed to create one per cent of growth is rising, along with reports of increasing corruption in public contracts and alleged misallocation of public investments. Most parts of the country seem unable to attract much non-state investment. Reforms in both state enterprises and the financial system proceed very slowly. Perhaps most crucially, Vietnam is not yet developing large, efficient domestic firms capable of competing with those in China and other ASEAN economies. It is not likely that FDI alone will provide the stimulus and momentum needed to overcome the strong tendencies towards slow and unequal growth created by conservative interests.

Growth in GDP since 2000 has picked up and is currently estimated as between 6 and 7 per cent. Investment is about one-third of GDP and rising towards 40 per cent. It used to take $3 of investment to create $1 of growth, but that ratio is drifting up to $5 or even $6. This suggests that the quality of investment is poor, and the public investment project list indeed looks problematic. There is a US$4 billion 'Ho Chi Minh Highway' connecting remote villages to each other but not to Highway 1, the main North–South coastal highway, with its ports and markets. Connecting the villages to Highway 1 would involve cheap and short roads in valleys rather than long, expensive ones over mountains.[31] There are two refinery projects, costing over $3 billion. Both fall in a typhoon-prone region far from either sources of raw materials or major markets. There is a high dam that will cost US$3 billion and put Hanoi under ten metres of water if it ruptures or is attacked – in addition to its dubious economic potential and the population displacement it requires.[32] The list goes on and on. It is difficult to imagine that economic considerations played even a minor role in making these choices.

The choice of public projects is influenced by the same regional politics that influences the regional distribution of investment. Vietnamese informally say that money on poor project selection is 'burned', meaning wasted. In addition, there are reportedly significant diversions of public investment amounting up to perhaps 30 per cent of the nominal amount.

While the exact amount siphoned from public construction is uncertain,[33] the extremely high land prices in Hanoi and Ho Chi Minh City are indicative of considerable skimming. Prices for land are said to be as high as in Hong Kong or Tokyo, even though Vietnam's per capita GDP is only 2 per cent of Hong Kong's. Real estate purchases are one place where 'extra' income is stored by officials.

As farms are consolidated and new jobs are created, it is all but certain that many Vietnamese will have to move to cities in the next two decades. Yet with land prices far beyond the purchasing power of ordinary urban workers (most earning only $40 to $80 a month), the prospects for new city-dwellers are little better than for those who remain in the countryside. There, the government decided to spread land use rights – and this increasingly means effective ownership – widely and equally among peasants. In the cities, land ownership is much more concentrated, and the re-zoning of agricultural land for residential or commercial use has resulted in a booming real estate industry. Typically, a buyer will purchase agricultural land for just above its value, make modest improvements, and then secure permission to re-zone – increasing the land value by a factor of ten as it is sold to the highest bidder. Even with the help of remittances, most urban Vietnamese are excluded.

If this trend continues, Vietnam risks becoming a 'high-cost economy' unable to compete with other countries that have more sensible policies. As these urban moneyed interests consolidate their wealth and, consequently, political influence, unstable policies and poor investor reviews will drive high quality investment elsewhere. As result, real tension has emerged between policy makers seeking economic growth and social stability, and entrepreneurs aiming to profiteer off the current situation to accumulate wealth on a large scale.

Vietnamese authorities and some international donors, like the World Bank, have expressed scepticism about this critique. According to one World Bank economist based in Hanoi, 'Corruption is not a serious problem in Vietnam.' He cites as proof the $2 to $3 billion in formal FDI inflows and a similar amount in remittances, accepting official growth figures despite doubts voiced by the IMF. This official cited the reductions in poverty and improvements in exports and social indicators Another World Bank expatriate resident said, 'There can't be much corruption because the cost of roads comes in for less than we estimate they should cost.'[34]

Of course, Vietnam has certainly proven competitive for foreign direct investment, with FDI inflows of US$2 to US$2.5 billion representing 6 to 7 per cent of GDP. In many provinces, setting up an export-oriented foreign firm is not particularly difficult, and the approval of a few major gas and electric projects has helped to raise the total FDI level.[35] Remittances from overseas Vietnamese also total more than US$2 billion, and these flows likely include a large amount of de facto investment, often in real estate. Crude oil supplies another US$3 billion per year in net revenues and aid another US$1.5 billion – all in a US$36 billion economy. Taken together, these inflows comprise at least 25 per cent of GDP – an amount that would make almost any country look healthy. Indeed, the trade deficit in 2003 will be more than 12 per cent of GDP, reflecting the availability of so much outside finance.[36] Many doubt, however, that such flows can be maintained for very long or that they are aimed at efficiently earning or saving foreign exchange.

Exports reached US$20 billion in 2003, implying 10 per cent annual export growth since 2000. Much of the gains were due to the bilateral trade agreement with the United States, opening American markets to Vietnamese products. In 2002, higher exports to the United States. accounted for over 90 per cent of total export growth, and over half of export growth in 2002-3 will be in the United States market.[37] Yet the domestic value-added component of many manufactured exports is low, and supplier industries have been slow to take form. Commodities such as seafood have also boosted recent growth, but are probably not nearly so promising for the future. It is extremely uncertain if Vietnam is positioning itself well to compete for future FDI, or if it can increase the value-added component of manufactured exports and expand their variety. Certainly, in spite of the Enterprise Law, private firms in Vietnam face many more barriers than elsewhere, even China.

In addition to land and capital, private firms lack access to reliable market and technical information. In Taiwan, a country with many small and medium-sized private firms, business associations are able to provide such information. In Vietnam, all associations must be affiliated with the government and they do not function nearly so well. A recent initiative to allow independent business associations was quashed for fear that the precedent might allow other groups (social, political, religious) to form independently and in opposition to the government. Indeed, some fear that even smaller private firms might grow too powerful and create a middle class that opposes rule by the Communist Party. This sequence is called 'peaceful evolution' and is sometimes put forward as a capitalist or US plot, although most simply see it as an independent phenomenon. Of course, many Vietnamese would like to have 'a nation of laws' and have less corruption and uncertainty, and it is not at all clear that the results would be negative for the Communist Party. Indeed, such a development – a stable and progressive society getting steadily richer with widely shared benefits – is likely to prolong rather than shorten the political status quo.

Vietnam's handling of trade policy will be crucial. The level of smuggling is already considerable, depressing prices of many highly protected goods from electronics to sugar. Chinese motorcycles have penetrated the local market, bringing the price of locally assembled Hondas down from

US$2,400 to about US$1,000. (The Chinese motorcycles, while not equal in quality, cost only US$400 to US$500.) If trade barriers really are lowered, it will be increasingly difficult for protected industries to function and there will be immense pressure to accommodate efficient firms rather than subsidize state enterprises with high costs.

However, many argue that Vietnam should either cut corners and use creative administrative measures to curtail particular imports, or even reject low tariffs outright and opt instead for some form of industrial policy.[38] Certainly, many of the investment decisions now being made are not consistent with a low tariff future. Official rhetoric continues to advocate self-sufficiency, promote the need for heavy industry, and warn about the dangers of depending on others for sugar, cement, steel, plastics, petroleum products, fertilizer, and other important products. The Vietnamese authorities may not decide for an entirely open or closed economy, but Vietnam's economic future will depend on whether the rhetoric of self-sufficiency determines economic policy making. Most public industrial and infrastructural investments are of shockingly low productivity and employment intensity. They seem to be increasing with few restraints on their growth.

Job creation will suffer if the private sector is kept small and weak. As a result of the Enterprise Law in 2000, 55,000 new enterprises were created and output has grown at 18 per cent per year, albeit from a low base. Most new firms are in services, food processing, wood products, garments, and construction materials. At the end of 2002, the entire formal domestic sector accounted for only 4 per cent of GDP and 3 per cent of employment. FDI-generated jobs comprised only 1 per cent of the total labour force.[39] These firms need to achieve strong and sustained growth, but it is not clear that the private sector will be allowed to strengthen its toehold in the near future, even with its growing share of output. Faster growth in this sector is inhibited by a weak legal system, an inadequate financial system that is slow to change, and an unfriendly and unhelpful institutional environment.

Policies relating to the Internet and telecommunications provide one example of the adverse institutional environment. While it is true that Vietnam is much more liberal with these technologies than is Cuba, the main question is how fast can it move? Compared to China, another planned economy, Vietnam's policies toward these technologies are restrictive. Low-cost international telephone calls cost 85 cents a minute from Vietnam and 13 cents from China. (However, both countries are beginning to offer very cheap calls over the Internet.) T-1 data lines, used by many software and information-intensive firms, cost $5,000 a month in Vietnam and $1,000 in China. In an 'e-readiness' report by the Economist and IBM, Vietnam ranked 13 out of 14 Asian countries and 56 out of 60 nations rated.[40] None of this is fatal for Vietnamese businesses, but neither is it supportive.

Likewise, income taxes in Vietnam rise to 50 per cent on income above $800 a month.[41] In practice, taxes apply mostly to private sector salaries, since the income of government officials is often not fully declared or is treated as a fringe benefit. Because of these tax rates – the highest in ASEAN – many foreign firms actually find it cheaper to hire skilled foreign workers, as they pay lower income taxes. This tends to drive skilled Vietnamese out of the country, further slowing the growth of private firms.

The educational system provides another example of what might be called institutional failure. Despite rapid expansion, salaries are low and in many cases it is difficult to do well without 'tutoring' – and some of this will include giving exercises similar to later tests. Many people seem to acquire degrees rather than earn them by gaining relevant knowledge.[42] Still, there is a fairly pervasive sense that most Vietnamese education is of poor quality, even if it is good at the very top, as in the school for gifted children[43] or a very few private schools.

These observations can be combined in a 'SWOT' analysis. This is a business technique that looks at **S**trengths, **W**eaknesses, **O**pportunities, and **T**hreats in order to provide a concise overview of the strategic situation. A 'SWOT' analysis for Vietnam would be as follows:

Strengths:	**Weaknesses:**
Moderate GDP Growth, 1998–2002	Weak Financial Sector
Rapid Export, Industrial Growth	FDI Disappointing
Explosive Private Firm Formation	Rising Investment to Growth Ratios
Good Poverty Reduction to 1997/8	Poor Public Investment, Corruption
Macroeconomic Stability	Poor Industrial Investments
Good Social Indicators	Growing Rural-Urban, Regional Split
Opportunities:	**Threats:**
Better Provincial Policies	Overemphasis on Directed Investments
Sustain Private Firm Growth	Poor Education Quality (Likely)
Attract More/Better FDI	Minimal IT Progress (Quality/Use)
Funds Available for Efficient Use	Rising Regional and Urban/Rural Inequality
Small Size of State Sector	Possible Delay of WTO Entry

Conclusions

Vietnam's economic future depends on the country's ability to create jobs and sustain growth in a highly competitive environment. An optimist would point to the progress made thus far and treat the corruption, resource misallocation, and durable institutional obstacles as teething problems. A pessimist would fear that those benefiting from the current system have become so entrenched and powerful that they will frustrate attempts to create a more efficient economy where low-cost firms can emerge and grow to significant size. Certainly, the presence of large amounts of oil revenues, foreign aid and remittances reduces the pressure for hard choices. Many current choices appear to be driven by politics and bureaucratic convenience rather than economics and professionalism. Vietnam is not the first or only nation to indulge its preferences for growth-slowing behaviour when the economy seems to be good enough.

It may be that another shock or threat is needed to concentrate the minds of the decision makers and improve policy again. It is not clear what would provide such a shock, nor how much time or how many opportunities will be lost if the perception is that moderate growth (even if driven by unsustainable inflows) is good enough and structural changes are not needed. The pessimist's prediction would be that institutional failures will be significant and slow to change, creating inequality, social tensions, instability, capital flight, and more corruption. The optimist would point to the period since *Doi Moi* started as proof that further mid-course corrections will be made when needed. As Vietnamese national politics are shaped by local and regional needs, much depends on what happens at the provincial level. Even now, the central government *allows* but does not *require* provinces to choose a low-cost and efficient path.

This analysis of Vietnam's economy raises the following question: if reform benefits so many, why not move forward with stronger and more rapid reform? The answer lies in the Vietnamese government's need to balance a complicated system of interests while keeping the general population satisfied and sufficiently supportive. In fact, one recent survey by the Pew Research Center found that people in Vietnam were more optimistic than in any of the other 44 countries surveyed.[44] This suggests a widespread confidence that state economic management will benefit the greater population, and that the current path of reform has been perceived as means to improve the quality of life, rather than a bitter medicine imposed by foreign lenders.

In contrast, Cuba today faces very different circumstances from those that prompted Vietnam's reform process in the 1980s. First, despite very difficult conditions, Cuba faces neither hyperinflation nor economic emergency. Unlike Vietnam, Cuba's agricultural base is a decapitalized rural proletariat engaged mainly in sugar cultivation – not a potentially productive peasantry – so agricultural reform will not necessarily spur major increases in productivity. In any case, agriculture accounts for a small share of GDP (7 per cent),[45] and inefficient state industry accounts for a much greater share of GDP than in pre-reform Vietnam. Cuba has neither cheap and energetic labour, nor low total operating costs compared to countries like Mexico with its lower transport costs and ease of trading with the US. Small enterprise could be expanded in Cuba, but it has already been allowed, albeit with severe restrictions. The Dominican Republic, with similar labor costs, is also less politically risky, though its educational levels trail Cuba's. If Cuba moved to market pricing, this would be seen by many as a kind of admission of error on the part of Cuban President Fidel Castro, and its benefits would be limited without legal and administrative reform, an overhaul of the financial system, and large injections of technical and managerial talent. Finally, as has been argued, normalization with the United States is unlikely so long as Castro retains power.[46]

Real change is likely to come to Cuba only when Fidel Castro finally moves on. Even his handpicked successors are likely to be more flexible, as they will have less personal authority and will face rising expectations. The current situation, with its radical inequalities caused by the peso–dollar dual economy, cannot be compared to the stern equality of poverty, even with some Soviet aid, for almost everyone in Vietnam in the 1980s. Rather, it is a temporary and transitional state. If, after Castro, the Cuban exile bloc in Miami removes or loses its veto on normalizing relations with the island, then US policy is apt to shift more rapidly than it did with Vietnam, where a long and costly war had been lost.

In this sense, Cuba's economic future will depend on the ability of Cubans to adjust to new conditions after so many years in which little has been permitted. One possibility is that, as happens elsewhere in the Caribbean, the ambitious will migrate to the industrialized world and the others will remain, relying primarily on natural resource exports, remittances and tourism. Perhaps the Miami Cubans will return, if allowed, with their capital and skills and rejuvenate the economy. Forging a political agreement between those in power and new investors from the diaspora will be a delicate and difficult task, but need not be impossible. The economic pie could be much bigger and power could be balanced so that neither group immediately gained the upper hand.

Without agreement between the Cuban leadership and the exile community based in the United States, Cuba is unlikely to recover very quickly, though presumably tourism and perhaps biotechnology would prove lucrative. Still, these industries alone may not support a high share of the workforce. Other foreign investors are unlikely to be attracted en masse to an island with uncertain work habits, an aging labour force, relatively high labour costs, and virtually no domestic private sector to lobby for enterprise-friendly legislation. However, if Cuba's high levels of education are reflected in workforce quality and discipline, then there will be opportunities for growth, if not 'dragon' rates of expansion that can be sustained over many years.

It was Yogi Berra who said that predictions were hard, especially about the future. Projections of the future based solely on past performance tend to fail in economics. If Cuba faces a shock that can break up old interest groups and allow a more productive alignment of labour, capital, and technology, it is likely to improve on its recent economic performance.[47] If

Vietnam fails to see where inflexible policies might lead, it could join the ranks of nations, among them many neighbours in Southeast Asia, that briefly grew rapidly but then stagnated. Cuba's ascendance is no more certain Vietnam's deterioration – but both are possible. In the meantime, the future of both countries will depend on the intelligence and cohesion of their leadership. It remains to be seen whether the governments of Cuba and Vietnam will be able to plan a plausible and desirable future for their citizens – or create an environment where the citizens have greater freedom to plan for themselves.

Statistical Annex

Reliable data are often not easy to come by in transition economies. Cuba has been left blank or excluded altogether from many standard World Bank tables, while GDP in Vietnam has differences among official, IMF and Asian Development Bank estimates. In Table 7.1, I used GDP from Carmelo Mesa-Lago's 2003 paper 'The Slowdown of the Cuban Economy in 2001–3: External Causes or Domestic Malaise?' augmented by a Reuters online story about 2003 GDP growth of 2.6 per cent, as officially reported. For Vietnam, I used official data as printed in World Bank sources. The World Bank has decided to accept these rather than IMF or ADB estimates, but the cumulative difference is less than 10 per cent over the decade. The food data come from the FAO website (www.fao.org) and its database, FAOSTAT. The export data for Cuba come from Professor Ritter's 2003 paper 'An Overview of Cuba's Economy in the 2000's: Recuperation or Relapse?', p.6, augmented by the same Reuters online story. For Vietnam, the data are reliable and readily available in World Bank reports or online subscription services such as Intellasia (www.intellasia.com). The under-five mortality rates were taken from the 1993 *Human Development Report*, Table 11 (UNDP) for 1990 and the 2003 *World Development Report*, Table 2.20 (World Bank) for 2001. They are likely to be fairly reliable. Finally, the FDI data are quite unreliable for both nations. The Economic Commission for Latin America has a 2002 report on *Foreign Investment in Latin America and the Caribbean* in which Cuba is estimated to have under $100 million of cumulative realized FDI from 1990 to 2002 (page 25, table 1.2) This presumably deducts profit remittances. Ritter estimates about $1.5 billion for roughly the same period. For Vietnam, the differences between official and IMF estimates are less but still not small. The differences for 1997–2002 can be found in the December 2003 statistical annex, available at www.imf.org, and these amount to $5.5 vs $12.3 billion for just five years. Earlier estimates of inflows differ by less and can be found in World Bank reports. It may be that reinvestments are not fully covered in the IMF data. Even with these large differences, it is clear that investment in Vietnam has been many times that in Cuba. Foreign investment in recent years in Cuba has been very low while it is surely well over $1 billion and perhaps over $2 billion per year now in Vietnam. Vietnam has clearly decided to join the international economic system, while Cuba remains reluctant. Table 7.1 shows, whatever the statistical fog, that Vietnam has done very well and Cuba has not, aside from similar percentage reductions in child mortality rates.

Notes

1 These data are from The World Bank, *World Development Indicators, 2003* (Washington, DC: World Bank, 2003), Table 1.1. Here after this is referred to as *WDI*.
2 Electricity often grows faster than GDP, so the 4:1 ratio is likely to be higher than the real income difference.
3 Food intake data are found in the FAO statistical database at www.fao.org. It is called FAOSTAT.
4 Enrollment data are found in *WDI*, Table 2.12 for 2000.
5 Data for Cuba are in Chapter 7 of Pedro Monreal (ed), *Development Prospects in Cuba*. Vietnamese data are found in various annual Labour and Employment Surveys, especially *2002 Statistical Data of Labour-Employment in Vietnam*, Table 62. (Hereafter this is referred to as Labour Survey 2002.)
6 Urban population is found in *WDI*, Table 3.10. Farm employment data are in the Labour Survey 2002, Table 17.
7 The Cuban figure is found in Monreal, Development Prospects, 123; the Vietnam figure in Labour Survey 2002, Table 115.
8 The Mekong Delta provides most of the surplus food in Vietnam. In 1985, it produced more than twice as much food as the Red River Delta, which had nearly the same population.
9 Data are found in Sinh Cuc Nguyen, *Agriculture of Vietnam, 1945–1995*, Table 14 and World Bank, *Vietnam: Economic Report on Industrialization and Industrial Policy*, No. 14645-VN, 1995, Tables 2.2 and 3.2 (hereafter, World Bank 1995).
10 These data refer to the GDP deflator, but consumer price index figures tell a similar story in terms of trends. See World Bank 1995, Appendix Table 2.3
11 These data are found in appendix tables of World Bank 1995.
12 See World Bank, *Vietnam: Delivering on its Promises* (December 2002), Tables 2.1 and 3.1 (hereafter, World Bank 2002).
13 World Bank 2002, Tables 1.3 and 2.2.
14 World Bank, *Assessing Aid* (Washington, DC: World Bank, 1998).
15 Official estimates put the labour share slightly over 60 per cent, but this classifies proprietor's incomes and some other items as wages. A paper by James Ridel and Suiwah Leung, *The Role of the State in Vietnam's Economic Transition*, cites another study that shows labour growing at 1.3 per cent and capital at 10.6 per cent per year from 1988–94. Even with a labour share of 0.6, that would suggest that 4.2 per cent growth came from capital stock increases and 0.8 per cent from labour, while total growth was 6.1 per cent in that period. Later periods, i.e. 1995–2000, are covered in a preliminary PhD thesis by Khuong Vu (Harvard University). He finds 2.2 per cent out of 6.7 per cent growth was due to TFP. However, if IMF figures are used for GDP growth, the TFP growth contribution falls to 1.5 per cent per year. In 1998–2002 with IMF data, the TFP rate falls to 0.2 per cent per year. This suggests a decreasing efficiency of capital investment and use.
16 The IMF has official data showing 8–12 per cent non-performance rates from 1995 to 1998. This is certainly too low.
17 The exchange rate averaged 11,150 against the dollar in 1992 and 11,683 in 1997– a depreciation of 5 per cent. The GDP deflator grew 86 per cent in the same period. There are various estimates of TFP growth, around 1–2 per cent.
18 To be clear, diplomatic recognition did not allow 'most favoured nation' trade status, but did encourage many investors to enter in expectation that Vietnam would receive MFN status. Vietnam did not receive MFN status until 2001.

19 Trade data can be found in World Bank 1995 and 2002: Table 3.3.
20 World Bank 2002: Table 3.1.
21 Ibid.
22 *2002 Statistical Yearbook*, Table 210.
23 Mesa-Lago (2003:10) puts Cuban tourist revenues at US$1.8 billion, just above goods exports, in 2002. While Vietnam attracts over 2.5 million visitors, the amount spent is only about US$600 per person. This implies US$1.5 billion in tourist gross income compared to $20 billion in exports in 2003.
24 World Bank 2002: Table 3.1
25 Ibid., Table 1.3.
26 Thai Binh province is in the North, near Hanoi. It has provided a large number of soldiers and revolutionaries and it was these organized groups, fed up with corruption, that organized the takeover of the local government. The Army was not used to suppress these groups, but many of the demonstrators were later punished.
27 The Guidebook can be found online at www.europa.eu.int/comm/europeaid/-projects/asia-invest. It was produced in 2002 by Asia Invest in the EuropeAid cooperation office and the table is found on page 61.
28 Data are from the appendix of David Dapice, *Vietnam:Success Story or Weird Dualism* (UNDP, 2003).
29 Ibid.
30 If Vietnam accedes to the WTO after 2005, negotiations will be more difficult and membership will come with more conditions. Vietnam has yet to put forward a serious negotiating proposal.
31 This was initially supposed to cost US$1 billion, but the costs increased. Other reasons given for this road are that 'Highway 1 sometimes washes out' [true, but bypasses around those few places would be cheap and easy to build] and there are 'military reasons' for the road. If anyone has asked the Army if they would prefer the road or more military hardware, it has not come to the author's attention.
32 The Son La dam project northwest of Hanoi is the dam referred to. The flooding issue was raised by an expert Vietnamese in a private conversation. The project was approved in early 2004.
33 The Central Institute of Economic Management's annual survey of the Vietnamese economy, *Vietnam's Economy in 2002* (p. 97), gives a 15 to 30 per cent margin of excess on public construction.
34 Both conversations were with the author in 2003 in Hanoi.
35 Policies towards services or import-substituting investments are more restrictive.
36 The 2003 trade data were cited in a subscription-based website, www.intellasia.com. The actual trade deficit was $5 billion for 2003 and GDP for 2003 is estimated at about 600 trillion dong, or under US$40 billion.
37 The US imposed high (roughly 50 per cent) 'antidumping' tariffs on catfish from Vietnam in a much publicized and economically unsound decision. In addition, they imposed quota on garment exports, even though these are scheduled to expire in 2005 for all WTO members. This strengthens the perception of Vietnamese conservatives that the U.S. is unfriendly and the global marketplace is dangerous and needs more 'control.' There are, of course, similar economic arguments in the US, mainly from the side of labor, though also from protected industries. In fact, the U.S. has become the largest single market for Vietnam's exports. See www.fedstats.gov, Bureau of the Census, International Trade. It shows imports from Vietnam through November 2003 were $4.25 billion or

about $4.5 billion for all of 2003 compared to $20 billion in all Vietnamese exports. Exports have quadrupled since 2001.

38 This argument has been made by JICA, a Japanese aid agency, evidently looking to repeat the practices of Japan a generation earlier. Japan then chose 'sunrise' industries and particular firms and helped them flourish with cheap credit, protection, and other assistance. Departing from Japan's growth strategy, they argue that FDI is now crucial. They also propose phasing out protection over several years. Protection is also supported by a number of state enterprises that expect they can be placed or kept in a protected category.

39 GDP data can be found in World Bank 2002, 36. Employment data in 2002 Labour Survey, Table 115.

40 The 2003 e-readiness rankings is a white paper from the Economist Intelligence Unit prepared with IBM. The paper is available online at www-1.ibm.com/services/files/ibv_eiu2003.pdf. The table is on pages 4–5.

41 There are surcharges as well as the top 'standard' 50 per cent rate.

42 A good summary of many of these problems is found in the National Centre for Social Sciences and Humanities, *National Human Development Report 2001* (Hanoi: Political Publishing House, 2001), 61.

43 These schools have been criticized for very narrow preparation of bright children for math olympics or science competitions, with little training in other fields.

44 The Pew study was cited in the *International Herald Tribune*, 5 December 2002.

45 2003 *WDI*, Table 4.2

46 The United States is not the only actor that has shunned the Castro government; the Inter-American Development Bank and Organization of American States have used Cuba's non-democratic governance as cause to exclude Cuba from the organizations. Indeed, the EU and many nations in the western hemisphere have distanced themselves from the Castro government and its recent hardline tactics. Venezuela is a notable exception, but its support for Castro depends on the endurance of the Chavez administration, which is increasingly unpopular and unstable.

47 This argument is familiar to readers of Mancur Olson, *The Rise and Decline of Nations* (New Haven: Yale University Press, 1982) and ibid., *Power and Prosperity: Outgrowing Communist and Capitalist Dictatorships* (New York: Basic Books, 2000).

8

Can Cuba Bridge the Gap?: IMF and World Bank Membership for Socialist Countries

Daniel P. Erikson

Over the last two decades, a range of socialist and post-communist countries have become successfully integrated into the international financial system. This has occurred as the globalization of the world economy has increased the relevance of the international financial institutions (IFIs) in their intended role as key arbiters of economic policy, guardians of macroeconomic stability, and leading resources for knowledge and technical advice on development issues. In particular, the International Monetary Fund (IMF) and the World Bank have attempted to stem financial crisis and assist in the economic transition of the post-communist countries of Eastern Europe and the former Soviet Union. Of course, the effectiveness of these efforts has been hotly debated, and the institutions have been criticized in recent years for failing to prevent, and perhaps exacerbating, financial breakdown in Asia, Latin America, and Russia. The decision to join the IMF and World Bank clearly is not an economic panacea for the challenges facing developing countries, yet this has not diluted the appeal of membership for most of the world's nations. With 184 members and counting, the international financial institutions are among the most universal organizations in the world. Most socialist countries have already joined the IFIs, and it is likely that Cuba will follow their lead in the future.

While there are a range of other institutions that play a role in the international economic system – including regional development banks, the World Trade Organization, and various United Nations agencies – the IMF and the World Bank have been at the centre of the major economic developments and the key institutional gatekeepers for countries that desire full participation in the global economy. Aside from granting access to financial resources, a country's membership in the IMF and the World Bank facilitates access to funds from regional development organizations and provides an important signal to foreign investors that seek a stable economic climate. Although the free-market economic policies promoted by the IMF and World Bank often come under fire, and the development strategies they promote remain a work in progress, the international financial institutions are undeniably vital actors in managing the global economy and advancing economic development. Countries as diverse as China, Vietnam, and the Russian Federation have recognized this and sought out membership in the IFIs.

At first glance, socialist countries with centrally planned economies may seem to have little common ground with market-based institutions such as the IMF and World Bank. Indeed, many socialist and communist countries remained outside the international financial system for many years, and some, such as Cuba and North Korea, remain non-members today. However, the Soviet Union was an active participant in the original Bretton Woods conference in 1944, and the challenge of including socialist economies was an important consideration during the initial development of these institutions. As a result, there is little doubt that participants at the Bretton Woods conference were willing to accept socialist countries as members. The resulting Articles of Agreement contain no formal obstacle that would prevent a communist or socialist country from joining the IMF and the institutions of the World Bank Group.[1]

The international financial system was conceived at the end of the Second World War to promote financial and monetary stability, aid in reconstruction, and broaden the reach of the market system by offering trade and market access to all countries. Initially consisting only of the IMF and the World Bank, this system expanded to include the General Agreement on Tariffs and Trade in 1948 (which became the World Trade Organization in 1995). The IMF and the World Bank are often referred to as the 'Bretton Woods twins', and they share the same basic rules of governance (including weighted voting power), annual meetings, and a common development committee that advises their governors. The IMF was to provide exchange rate stability while the mission of the World Bank focused on long-term development, acting as an intermediary between the financial markets and developing countries, and providing favourable financing for development projects. In addition to their financial activities, the IMF and World Bank are engaged in establishing conditions for lending, providing surveillance of the monetary system, and generating intellectual contributions to understanding the processes of development and how policies can be improved.[2]

While the IMF is a single institution, the World Bank consists of a group of organizations in addition to its core component, the International Bank for Reconstruction and Development (IBRD). The IMF is the gatekeeper to the Bretton Woods twins. All countries must join the IMF before becoming a member of the World Bank and its affiliates; and no country has joined the IMF and declined membership in the World Bank. Furthermore, membership in the IBRD is required before a country can join the World Bank's four other affiliates: the International Development Association (IDA), International

Finance Corporation (IFC), the Multilateral Investment Guarantee Agency (MIGA), and the International Centre for the Settlement of Investment Disputes (ICSID). Each of these organizations was created in the decades following the Bretton Woods convention to address needs beyond the original mandate of the IBRD. In addition to the IMF and World Bank group, other important economic actors include the regional development banks for Africa, the Americas and Asia, which supplement the main IFIs by providing loans and grants to aid development at the regional level.

In this universe of economic organizations, there are unique challenges facing the relationship between the IMF and the World Bank and centrally planned economies. The first question is purely economic. Countries with socialist economic systems may lack any meaningful relationship between the price of their exports and the domestic costs of production or, conversely, between the internal price of imports and foreign export prices. Under such a scenario, exchange rates are meaningless as instruments to allocate resources effectively, although some authors have argued that the Articles of Agreement have been written in such a way to bypass this problem in socialist countries.[3] While the IMF may allow economic practices that are inconsistent with the Articles to persist for extensive periods, economic reform of a centrally planned economy will emerge as a continuous point of dialogue. In consultations, IFI officials can be expected to urge the benefits of eliminating multiple exchange rates and other practices inconsistent with the charter of the IMF.

Aside from the exchange rate and price dilemmas, the issue of transparency and information sharing can present a problem for countries accustomed to keeping their economic data secret. Article VIII of the IMF lists 'furnishing of information' as one of the general obligations of members, and specifies several types of economic information including national income, price indices, buying and selling rates for foreign currencies, exchange controls, and international balance of payments and investment positions.[4] Many centrally planned economies prefer not to share that information for security reasons, fear of demonstrating economic weakness, insufficient capacity to collect data, corruption, or bureaucratic competition. This was especially true during the Cold War period, but even today centrally planned economies often closely protect their economic data or use methods of dubious international validity.

Despite the potential economic and policy hurdles that can complicate IMF and World Bank membership for socialist and communist countries, the historical record shows that the primary obstacles to accession have been political. In particular, the Cold War created an environment where the Washington-based IMF and World Bank were political instruments of the West, with the United States as the most important shareholder. By contrast, most socialist and communist countries were bound together by their own trade and security arrangements, such as the Council for Mutual Economic

Assistance (CMEA). This geopolitical division resulted in several important disincentives with regard to socialist members in the IFIs. On the side of communist countries, an ideological commitment to socialism precluded membership in institutions representing the 'neoliberal international system', especially when there was little interest in market reform. Furthermore, there was trepidation about the political ramifications of joining an institution where the United States is both the largest shareholder and the leading proponent of the 'international will' expressed through these organizations. Of course, from the perspective of the West, there was little interest in integrating and providing development finance for avowed enemies of the democratic world, especially with regard to the Soviet Union.

Nevertheless, the IMF has in practice admitted applicants with state-controlled economies, including Romania in 1972, Hungary in 1982, and Poland in 1986. There were several rationales for socialist countries to join the IMF, and while the desire to incorporate more market mechanisms may not have been the primary motivation, this decision often led to some level of economic opening. Aside from the ability to borrow from the IMF to ease balance-of-payments bottlenecks, countries that join also improve the perception of their creditworthiness among foreign investors, leading to an increase in foreign direct investment. Access to research and technical expertise is also an incentive, as well as the political desire to stake a claim in some of the world's key financial institutions. In the case of the People's Republic of China, for example, the chance to evict the Taiwanese government from China's seat at the IMF and World Bank was undoubtedly an additional motivation.

Furthermore, many countries regard IMF membership as a necessary step in order to gain access to the World Bank's development loans. The World Bank's focus on development – along with that of its corollary institutions like the International Development Association, which provides concessionary lending for projects and programmes in poor countries – often makes this the more attractive of the Bretton Woods twins. Socialist countries that are wary of the IMF requirements and conditionalities may nonetheless join to gain access to World Bank resources. In fact, no country has joined the IMF and subsequently declined membership in the World Bank. Accession to the IFIs is an important stepping stone for countries to begin the process of opening to the world economy, but it requires political and economic reconciliation with the United States, a global economic power and key backer of these institutions.

The membership process

Despite the complexity of political and economic variables involved, the mechanics of accession to the International Monetary Fund and the World Bank are quite straightforward. Since the IMF is the gatekeeper for membership in the Bretton Woods institutions, the process for joining the IMF is both the most rigorous and requires the most information. Once a country is admitted to the IMF, membership to the World Bank only requires approval of the Board of Governors and payment of the determined subscription. In order to become a member of the IMF, an applicant must meet three basic eligibility requirements: it must be a country; it must be in control of its foreign affairs; and it must be capable and willing to assume the responsibilities of membership. Occasionally the IFIs will make exceptions to engage with regions outside their membership, as in the case of the Palestinian Authority, which receives support though it is not a country and thus not a member. Normally, however, an applicant must meet these three conditions. Then upon submitting an application for membership to the Fund, the country must receive a mission of IMF staff that collects the necessary data to prepare a background paper that describes the economy in detail and recommends a share consistent with the relative positions of other countries. While the admission process requires a separate vote by the governors of the two organizations, after acceptance by the IMF a country only needs to accept responsibility for the World Bank's own obligations up to the amount of its subscription and pay a small proportion of that amount to the Bank.

Once this first stage is completed, then the Executive Board of the IMF will establish an ad hoc committee of 6 to 8 Executive Directors that is constituted on the recommendation of the Managing Director. This committee will consider the applicant's initial quota in the Fund as well as other standard terms and conditions of membership. Once the committee agrees to an initial quota, the chairman – typically one of the Fund's major shareholders – will discuss its findings with the government concerned. Once the applicant agrees, the chairman of the committee sets forth a report of recommendations for approval by the Executive Board. If approved, the proposed quota and related terms of membership are submitted to the Board of Governor's for a vote in the form of a membership resolution. A vote on membership requires a majority of governors holding at least 85 per cent of the votes in the Fund, and must be approved by a majority of votes cast. In practice, however, all membership decisions are made by consensus, and the vote is a pro forma decision, not an opportunity for open debate on the potential new member. After membership has been approved, applicants typically have six months to complete the required legal paperwork; once the documents are approved by the Fund, then a signing ceremony is arranged whereby the country becomes a formal member of the IMF. New members must appoint a governor and alternate governor to the IMF's Board of Governors, posts typically held by the country's minister of finance or president of the Central Bank.

For communist countries, it is the juxtaposition of two central tenets of the membership process that can create frustration for those interested in IMF and World Bank accession. First, there is no inherent formal obstacle for membership by a socialist country – even one that has not undergone systemic reform. In theory, this means that the door should be open for application at any time. Second, although the rules allow for a member to join with only 85 per cent vote of the shareholders, in practice all membership decisions are made by broad consensus. During the Cold War, and even today, it can be difficult to achieve consensus among the 184 member countries of the IMF and World Bank. However, in practice, it has typically been the United States – backed by the 18 per cent voting share that effectively constitutes veto power over major policy decisions – that has helped to determine what consensus is in many key matters facing the international financial system.

In this context, the experiences of China, Russia, and Vietnam illustrate important lessons for Cuba and remaining socialist countries that may, at some point, contemplate accession to the IMF and the World Bank. The People's Republic of China joined the Fund and the Bank as a communist country in 1980, while the Republic of Vietnam initially joined in 1956 but was replaced by its socialist successor in 1976 after reunification. Russia was an initial participant in the Bretton Woods conference but did not join the international financial institutions until 1992, after its communist political and economic system had already unraveled. While the following case studies demonstrate that each of these socialist countries experienced an idiosyncratic process of accession to the IMF and the World Bank, there are several main themes that run through their experiences. First, in all cases, membership in the IFIs has been accompanied by significant economic reforms; in no instance did a country become more heavily dependent on central-planning or more resistant to market mechanisms after joining the IFIs. Secondly, the pace of reform varied widely; Russia engaged in a rapid transition to a market-based economy, while China and Vietnam opened their economies but remained essentially socialist states. Thirdly, the timetable for mending the bilateral relationship with the United States greatly affected both the pace of accession as well as the trajectory of the subsequent relationship with the IFIs. Although each process of insertion into the international financial system was beset by its own unique circumstances, the experiences of China, Russia, and Vietnam all hold important lessons for Cuba.

China's robust partnership

China was both an initial signatory at the Bretton Woods conference in 1944 and a founding member of the IMF when the Article of Agreements entered into force on 27 December 1945. However, when the Chinese revolution led to communist control of mainland China in 1949, nationalist leader Chiang Kai-Shek withdrew to the island province of Taiwan, which had only recently been released from half a century of Japanese rule. Taiwan occupied China's seat at the IMF and World Bank from the 1950s to the 1970s, as the island was seen as an important bulwark against communist expansionism. This arrangement resulted in occasional tension within the IFIs, as some countries rejected the legitimacy of the Taiwanese government to represent the seat of China. For example, at each annual meeting of the IMF's Board of Governors between 1950 and 1954, Czechoslovakia raised a challenge to the credentials of the governor from the Republic of China, as Taiwan was officially known, on the grounds that the country lacked authority to appoint a governor. The socialist People's Republic of China (PRC) registered its displeasure with the arrangement from the very beginning. In 1950, the foreign minister of the PRC sent a cable to the IMF's managing director, stating that the mainland government was the sole legal authority and that no other delegate was qualified to represent China in the Fund.[5] While the situation nevertheless endured for nearly thirty years, Taiwan eventually ceased borrowing from the international financial institutions, sensing the increasing precariousness of its position within the system.

In the late 1960s, Washington and Beijing began to develop closer ties to counter perceived Soviet expansionism, and in 1971, China's seat on the United Nations Security Council was taken over by the mainland government, thus removing Taiwan from the UN. The historic visit of President Richard Nixon to Beijing in 1972 set the stage for closer relations between the US and China, and rekindled the communist country's interest in assuming Taiwan's position at the IMF and World Bank. The People's Republic of China subsequently expressed concern about IMF and World Bank membership in 1973, when IMF officials received a cable at the annual meeting in Nairobi demanding the immediate expulsion of the 'Chang Kai-Shek clique'.[6] However, when Bretton Woods officials asked if China would be interested in replacing Taiwan, the country did not follow through with an application. In 1976, China issued another protest during the annual meeting in Manila, but again did not apply for membership.

However, the restoration of diplomatic relations between the United States and China in 1979 essentially removed the key political obstacle to China's accession to the IMF. In the run-up to membership, the United States transformed into a strong supporter of China's effort to join the international financial institutions. Nonetheless, there were significant doubts at the IMF as to whether the country would be capable of producing acceptable economic statistics, especially given the near-absence of information after the late 1950s, owing in part to the upheaval of the Cultural Revolution. In order to address this concern, China began publishing a large amount of economic data in mid-1979 to build its case for membership. In April 1980, China joined the IMF in a decision that ended Taiwan's 31 years of representation in the IFIs. Taiwan had represented China in the IMF since 1949, as one of 140 members.[7] The executive directors of the IMF voted to accept the People's Republic of China as a member, with a quota of 550 million special drawing rights, or SDRs, valued at about US$700 million at the time.[8] According to the late Thomas Leddy, then-assistant secretary of the Treasury, the United States backed the decision: 'The United States position was to welcome and support the People's Republic of China's entry into the Fund'.[9]

China had to accept a number of conditions that the IMF requires of its members, including a complete survey of its economy and annual consultations with the IMF under Article IV of the institutional charter. China's decision to join the IMF was thought to reflect its desire to enhance its international political position and guarantee access to large amounts of relatively inexpensive development credit. According to one observer, 'The prime reason why China is keen to join is straightforward. China needs to achieve the Four Modernizations and understandably wants to obtain those funds on the most advantageous terms'.[10] Membership benefited China in several concrete ways, including the ability to use various 'special facilities' of the IMF; gaining access to IMF assistance in the case of difficulties in balance-of-payments; sharing in the profits of the IMF's gold auction; and facilitating the flow of resources from export credit agencies.[11]

China's new membership also had two favourable side-effects: enhancing the country's creditworthiness in the eyes of the private banking sector and increasing the diplomatic isolation of Taiwan. China's entry into the IMF hinged on a compromise forged between China and Taiwan about the return of Taiwan's subscription to the Fund and the subsequent restitution of the subscription in gold.[12] Taiwanese officials, anticipating the possible expulsion, had already eliminated any clauses from loan agreements that required IMF membership and boosted international reserves to nearly US$7 billion.[13] While establishing the quota can often be the most contentious element of negotiating new membership, in China's case this was avoided by merely overtaking Taiwan's financial position. However, China did request a significant increase from the SDR of 550 million that it inherited from Taiwan – a very small fraction of the total quota.

China's economic decision to join had important political implications, and it was widely interpreted as a move towards a more active role in the international community. IMF membership was closely followed by accession to the World Bank and some time later in the Asian Development Bank (ADB). At the time of its acceptance, China became the largest communist country to be a member of the IMF.[14] Other communist countries included Vietnam, Cambodia, Laos, Romania, and Yugoslavia. In addition, China's entry occurred when there was growing global demand for IMF and World Bank resources, and China's large claim on these resources meant less for other countries. However, in practice, China only used the IMF's financial resources once, in the mid-1980s. It was a first tranche-drawing, with limited conditionality, that was repaid on time a few years later. Indeed, China's lack of dependence on IMF resources allowed it much greater freedom in charting economic policy than existed for major debtor countries in the developing world, particularly in Latin America.

Although China joined both the IMF and the World Bank, its relationship with the latter institution has proved to be the more robust partnership over the last twenty years. According to the written history of the World Bank, 'in the first few years the Bank's role was primarily a didactic one of educating a cadre of senior Chinese officials in new economic ideas and technical systems'.[15] In the process of moving from a centrally planned economy to a socialist market economy, China has intensively engaged with several development agencies, including the World Bank, and maintained active relations with the IMF, Asian Development Bank, and the Bank for International Settlements. However, the World Bank has emerged as China's pre-eminent development partner, with China as the largest client of the Bank during the 1990s. In this period, the Bank was the biggest single source of long-term foreign capital, with loans averaging between US$2.5 and US$3 billion per year.[16] The World Bank's programmes in China were allocated about half for transportation and energy, a quarter for agriculture, a sixth for industry and finance and 10 per cent for education.[17] The portfolio is considered to be very high quality; with projects that are well implemented and a correspondingly low failure rate. In fact, China's creditworthiness has increased to the point that the country is no longer eligible for IDA loans, the concessional source of financing that is an attractive element of World Bank membership for lower-income countries.

Chinese authorities have set clear parameters on policy conditions from the very beginning of the relationship with the international financial institutions. In one memorandum from a 1984 meeting with the Chinese delegation, a World Bank official noted that Minister of Finance Wang Bingjian 'explained China's view that assistance to developing countries should be unconditional ... [T]his did not mean that the Bank could not offer advice and ideas. The World Bank could put these forward and they would be considered if they were useful. But the Bank should not impose its views'.[18] China also set a policy of linking its IBRD borrowing to its IDA allocation that lasted until the late 1990s.

Taiwan remained a constant source of friction between China and the World Bank, due to the long-standing sensitivities regarding what China sees as its renegade province. China, for example, demanded that references to Taiwan be deleted from Bank documents or be rephrased as 'Taiwan Province, China'.[19] Evidently, the Bank felt that it had little option but to accommodate China on this point, lest the entire relationship be soured. Friction also arose regarding the relationship of China and India;

boundary disputes between the two countries resurfaced in discussions on how the countries were geographically represented in Bank documents. Furthermore, China's accession and subsequent use of IDA grants meant that less was available for India, especially during periods when the IDA coffers were declining.

After normalization of China's relations with the United States in the late 1970s, politics occasionally re-emerged to influence IFI decisions relating to the country. Most notably, the Tiananmen Square massacre in 1989 prompted the United States to strongly pressure the World Bank to condition its lending arrangement on the respect for political liberties and human rights. The World Bank and other multilateral agencies temporarily froze dealings with China as a result. Shielding World Bank programmes from the political fallout was a major priority for the organization's staff at this time. The IFIs resisted these entreaties more successfully than in many other cases; perhaps because China's sheer size produces a form of pragmatism not necessary in dealing with smaller countries such as Vietnam or, certainly, Cuba. Nevertheless, the crackdown in China did provoke limited repercussions, and some World Bank affiliates, such as the International Finance Corporation, did not resume investment in China until 1991.

The partnership between the World Bank and China has been recognized as highly successful, as measured by the effectiveness of Bank projects in China and the fulfillment of the country's fiscal responsibilities. This success is ironic when one considers the fact that US economic aid to Asian countries in the 1950s was geared to prevent 'another China' by alleviating the poverty of the rural peasantry thought to be at high risk for communist mobilization.[20] A review of China's accession and subsequent relationship with the IMF and the World Bank reveals both the advantages and the continuing challenges of having such a large, communist country take part in the international financial system. In 1980, China still had a great deal to learn about how the IFIs worked, especially with regard to substitution accounts, gold equivalents, SDR allocations, and the specifics of conditionality. In addition, there was considerable concern about China's ability to generate economic statistics that met IMF standards, as well as its willingness to share this information. (Some communist countries, such as Romania, had worked out confidentiality agreements with the IMF that restricted access to sensitive economic information.)

By joining the IMF and the World Bank and working through these issues, China both engaged in targeted economic reform at home and claimed an active role in the international economic community. In 2001, China finally became a member of the World Trade Organization. In retrospect, China's accession to the IMF and the World Bank marked an important step towards substantial market-oriented reform, greater integration into the global economy, and increased influence in the larger international political arena. However, the relative absence of dysfunction in China's relations with these organizations was by no means assured, as demonstrated by the problems faced by Russia and Vietnam in their efforts to integrate into the international financial system.

Russia's post-communist plight

The Soviet Union – like China and Cuba – was a participant in the Bretton Woods meetings in 1944 that led to the creation of the IMF and World Bank. However, the Soviet Union was the only country represented at the conference that did not become a member of the IFIs for nearly 50 years. Most participating countries were either original members or joined shortly thereafter; the second longest holdout from the original conference, Liberia, became a member in 1962. Although the Soviet Union ultimately declined to join, there is no doubt that the existence of such a large and influential communist state was taken into account by the leading architects of these international institutions. In April 1942, an early draft of the White Plan, which outlined the purpose of the proposed institutions, discussed the possible membership of USSR in detail:

> No restrictions as to membership should be imposed on grounds of the particular economic structure adopted by any country ... [T]o exclude a country such as Russia would be an egregious error. Russia, despite her socialist economy could both contribute and profit by participation ... If the Russian Government is willing to participate, her counsel in the preliminary negotiations should be as eagerly sought as that of any other country, and her membership in both Fund and Bank equally welcome.[21]

Similarly, an advanced draft of the Keynes Plan referred to the case of the USSR, stating that '[t]he position of Russia, which might be a third founder, if she can be party to so capitalist-looking an institution, would need special consideration'.[22]

While the final versions of the Bretton Woods proposals contained no statement pertaining to the membership of the USSR, Russia continued to play a role in the consultative process in 1943 and 1944. The head of the Russian delegation was one of four vice-chairmen of the Bretton Woods conference. Several historians have concluded that Russia's active participation undoubtedly influenced the decision to draw the charters of the Fund and the Bank sufficiently broadly to encompass communist and socialist countries. While the Soviet government never set forth a formal refusal to join the IMF, several factors may have led to this decision. These may have included dissatisfaction with the formula for voting power, reluctance to release economic data, concerns about the transparency of the IMF's governance, and resistance to its views on economic and monetary policy.[23]

Despite these concerns, there is no question that the Bretton Woods agreements were designed so that socialist countries could become members, and that this was primarily guided by the desire to accommodate the Soviet Union. As one analyst has noted, some of the Fund's Article of Agreements 'contain certain clauses that are completely unexplainable but from the angle of some Soviet idiosyncrasy'.[24]

Between the 1940s and the 1980s, there was no formal contact and little informal communication between the Soviet Union and the IMF and the World Bank. The heightened tensions of the Cold War prevented any type of policy dialogue and contributed to an atmosphere of mutual suspicion. This remained true even while the international financial institutions incorporated a growing number of communist members, including China, Vietnam, and several of the republics of Eastern Europe. However, in 1990, the economy of the Soviet Union began to unravel at the same time as the body politic lurched towards democracy. As a result, Soviet membership in the IMF and World Bank re-emerged as a possibility.

Three interlocking narratives dominated the run-up to Russia's accession to the international financial institutions. First, as the once superpower teetered both politically and economically on the edge of dissolution, the relationship of Russia's 15 republics presented a major legal and technical obstacle to membership in the IMF and the World Bank. Finalizing the structure of the Soviet Union's successor – the Russian Federation – was essential to the decision of incorporating it into membership. Secondly, the question of economic reform in Russia assumed paramount importance. The United States clearly supported Russia's entry into the international financial system, but some US policy makers also called for the country to abandon communism prior to membership. Conservative elements in the United States feared that quick action to help the Russian economy might inadvertently prolong communist control. Politically, it was difficult to argue that stabilizing the government of Mikhail Gorbachev was more important than ensuring the collapse of the Soviet system. Thirdly, the United States was considering a major quota increase to the IMF at the time that Russia's membership emerged as a possibility. The convergence of these two sensitive issues complicated Russia's path to membership due to resistance by congressional conservatives who equated IFI support for Russia with extravagant foreign aid. This was a hot button issue in early 1992, and something that then President George H. W. Bush was reluctant to confront directly in a presidential election year unfolding amidst a recession.

The approach phase between the Soviet Union and the international financial institutions originated with the Houston Economic Summit of July 1990. At this gathering, the leaders of the G-7 countries – with the support of President Gorbachev – asked the IMF, World Bank, Organization for Economic Cooperation and Development (OECD), and the European

Bank for Reconstruction and Development (EBRD) to initiate a collaborative study of the Soviet economy. This initiative was expressly intended to provide recommendations for reform, guide external aid efforts, and prepare the Soviet Union for membership in the IFIs.[25] However, this apparent consensus masked the lingering concerns of some shareholders. Japan, for example, worried that locking itself into a single aid strategy with western countries would reduce its leverage to negotiate the return of the northern territories from Russia.[26] The United States was similarly cautious about embracing its old enemy, while West Germany and France were keen to extend substantial immediate aid to Gorbachev. As a result, the IMF-led study of the Russian economy represented a compromise that allowed some nations to proceed with bilateral aid while opening an economic policy dialogue between the Soviet Union and the IFIs and – by proxy – the United States.

Steps towards formal membership in the IMF and the World Bank followed in mid-1991. On 19 August, a coup by Kremlin hardliners led to the end of Soviet communism when Russian President Boris Yeltsin opposed the power grab and marshalled broad support for a decree banning Communist party activities on Russian soil. Gorbachev resigned from the Communist Party shortly thereafter, thereby ending its control and setting in motion the dissolution of the Soviet Union. As a result, that month the World Bank approved the concept of 'associate' membership for the Soviet Union, which entitled the country to technical assistance. This was quickly followed by a recommendation to approve US$30 million in World Bank funds to support a programme including research on the Soviet economy, and training of Russian personnel.[27] In September 1991, US Treasury Secretary Nicholas Brady openly criticized the slow pace of the IMF in granting special membership status to the Soviet Union. Later that month, IMF officials proposed reductions in USSR arms expenditures to apply to economic needs; Soviets applied for full membership in the IMF soon thereafter, and associate status followed at both the IMF and the World Bank.

Due to the rapid pace of events in the Soviet Union and the sensitive issues facing the IMF, the World Bank and the US government, there was a strong push from Washington to move ahead with ties to Russia, even though many principal issues of membership remained unresolved throughout 1991. In particular, the months between the 'Group of Seven' summit in London in July and the October meetings of the IMF and World Bank in Bangkok proved to be critical both to the fate of the Soviet Union and to the process of IFI accession. On 15 July, the Soviet Union applied for full membership in the IMF.[28] On 5 October 1991, the Managing Director of the IMF and President Gorbachev signed an agreement on the 'special association' between the USSR and the Fund. This agreement enabled the IMF to examine economic developments in the USSR in a manner consistent with

Article IV consultations.[29] It also paved the way for technical assistance, Soviet representation at Executive Board meetings that dealt with the USSR or the world economy as a whole, and Soviet participation in IMF annual meetings. In return, the Soviet Union was required to provide regular economic data consistent with other member countries, while allowing the IMF to establish a permanent office in Moscow with diplomatic immunity for its staff, and potentially contributing to the cost of Fund services. This special association status was intended to endure until the USSR became a full member or either party terminated the agreement.[30]

While the World Bank's Articles of Agreement do not allow for the type of 'special association' status granted by the IMF, the World Bank did sign a Technical Cooperation Agreement with Moscow on 15 November 1991. This accord, signed by Bank president Lewis Preston and Gorbachev, allowed for the World Bank to provide technical assistance to the Soviet Union or its republics prior to membership. This included exchanges on the progress of the assistance programme, and the establishment of a World Bank office in Moscow with the concomitant immunities and privileges for its staff. The technical assistance included advice on economic management and reforms, creation of a social security network and food aid assessment, advice in the fields of privatization, agriculture and energy, and personnel training. This agreement was underwritten by a $30 million trust fund established by the Bank's executive board, and financed by the institutions' net income.[31]

The associate membership and technical cooperation agreements set the stage for much more extensive consultations between staff at the IMF and World Bank and all fifteen republics of the Soviet Union. IMF missions began to travel frequently to the USSR, with five separate missions to Moscow alone in November and December of 1991.[32] The mission teams gathered economic data and negotiated technical assistance and stabilization and reform programmes, which would lead to analytical reports similar to regular Article IV consultations with other IMF members. In particular, the IMF was responsible for developing reliable assessments of the external financing requirements of Russia and the other republics.

During this time, a perception gap developed as senior USSR administrators focused on the material costs and benefits of IMF membership, particularly the concern that paying the necessary quota would deplete Russia's monetary reserves.[33] As a result, little weight was given to the non-material benefits of membership, such as an improved perception for foreign investment or access to research and technical expertise. In addition, there was considerable trepidation about several aspects of joining the Fund, including the use of the US veto, the impact of stabilization programmes on the Soviet economy, and the need to release economic data still regarded as sensitive.[34]

For the international financial institutions, the dissolution of the Soviet Union and subsequent accession of all 15 states was a watershed moment that fundamentally changed the way in which the IMF and the World Bank operated. The sheer size of the task, historic nature of the change, and complexity of the economic issues involved forced the IFIs to dramatically reorient their thinking towards the challenges facing transition economies. In December 1991, the IMF created a new area department called European II that exclusively targeted work with the Baltic States and former members of the USSR. Over the course of a few months, the IMF substantially reoriented its staff to this challenge, increasing from 2,000 to 2,200 employees and assigning 150 to work full-time on the former Soviet Union.[35] (In 2003, this department was eliminated and the 15 countries were absorbed into other departments.)

In January 1992, a major stumbling block to Russia's accession was cleared when the IMF determined that the former Soviet republics would have a quota at 4.5 per cent of the global total, leaving Britain and France in their joint fourth-place positions behind the United States, Japan, and Germany.[36] On 27 April 1992, the IMF formally offered membership to Russia, enabling the rich G-7 countries to release US$24 billion in aid unveiled by President Bush and German Chancellor Helmut Kohl on 1 April at the London summit.[37] The package included US$4.5 billion in aid from the IMF and World Bank in 1992, a US$6 billion fund to stabilize the ruble, US$2.5 billion in debt deferral and US$11 billion in direct bilateral aid from wealthy countries.[38] The IMF accord was required both for the multilateral aid and for most of the other components of the aid package. Of the 15 Soviet republics, all but Azerbaijan were offered membership in the IMF at the 1992 Spring meetings, and the World Bank followed suit with all but Azerbaijan and Turkmenistan. (In both cases the delays were attributed to incomplete paperwork, and they joined subsequently.) The Russian Federation joined the IMF on 1 June 1992; its accession to the World Bank followed on 16 June. The IMF and the World Bank made US$1.6 billion available to Russia in mid-1992 with virtually no conditions, as authorized by their practice.[39] The aid effort to the former Soviet republics represented by far the most ambitious undertaking in the history of the IMF.

The IMF also needed a capital increase of US$60 billion, which had been provisionally approved by the membership in 1990 but had failed to fully materialize when the US Congress balked at the US$12 billion share due from the United States. President Bush favoured the increase, but did not want to go on record asking Congress to support it, due to the political sensitivity surrounding foreign aid prior to the 1992 presidential election. However, many Congressional Democrats required a specific request by the White House in order to support an increase; otherwise, they feared, they were being asked to take responsibility for effectively voting for aid for Russia, and face the political fallout alone. This unresolved issue shadowed most of Russia's membership negotiations, until President

Bush finally conceded the point and took a public stand in favour of the capital increase for the IMF. While this stance was not a significant factor in President Bush's loss in the 1992 election, it was consistent with the broader charge that his administration was overly focused on foreign policy and inattentive to domestic economic concerns.

In retrospect, Russia's courtship with the international financial institutions was a shotgun marriage characterized by an abbreviated period of non-lending assistance, from the fall of 1991 to the summer of 1992, followed by massive disbursements of aid through the country's 1998 financial crisis and even beyond. The role of the IMF in the Russian transition continues to be highly controversial. Some authors, such as Nobel laureate Joseph Stiglitz, have argued that IMF-backed policy prescriptions regarding capital market liberalization and privatization actually exacerbated the country's woes, while others posit that international advice actually prevented even worse economic performance. The IMF and World Bank may not have been responsible for the depth of Russia's decline, but they certainly proved unable to guide the country to economic success.

After reviewing the years 1991 to 2001, the World Bank's Country Assistance Evaluation report concluded that Russia would have benefited from a strategy oriented around analytical and advisory services with only limited financial support during the period from 1992 to 1998, instead of the large volumes of adjustment lending that were actually released.[40] World Bank assistance to Russia was rated unsatisfactory from 1992 to 1998. To facilitate Russia's transition, the Bank focused on helping to build the institutions of a market economy, develop the private sector, and alleviate the social costs of transition. The Bank committed 55 loans for US$12.6 billion through 2001; at that time US$7.8 billion had been disbursed and US$2.4 billion cancelled. However, as described in the evaluation report,

> at the behest of the international community, the Bank rushed the processing of many projects, both for investment and general budget support, even though the prospects for their success were highly uncertain. These high-risk/high-payoff operations did not succeed ... Bank advice and lending played a positive but marginal role in the design of policies and in their implementation until 1998.[41]

However, the report notes that some members of the World Bank group – such as the IFC and MIGA – were resistant to external pressure, selected their interventions carefully, and accrued an impressive record of technical assistance and service.

The former Soviet Union, like China, only joined the international financial institutions once it had reconciled its relationship with the West and its membership application gained the support of the United States.

However, the Russian experience also demonstrates the dangers inherent in a rapid transition to a market economy and in particular how the political imperative to quickly provide financing can overtake the need for well-thought-out institutional reforms. In particular, the IMF emerged as the preferred channel for the United States to give aid to Russia, and this pattern remained in place for most of the 1990s. In retrospect, Russia's accession to the IFIs may have benefited from a more extended period of technical assistance and economic policy dialogue. Russia's volatile transition phase created a chaotic policy environment that enabled the country to consume vast international resources with little to show in the way of progress.

Vietnam: the long wait for reunification

While both China and Russia joined the IMF and the World Bank and sustained active participation after accession, Vietnam illustrates another model of membership 'in name only' that did not consolidate into a normal working relationship for nearly four decades. This state of limbo was driven by the difficult bilateral relationship with the United States, which initiated with the Vietnam War but persisted until the early 1990s. Vietnam was established as a single state under the Geneva Agreements of July 1954, and free general elections were to be held under international supervision in July 1956. Vietnam entered its original application for IMF membership on 21 December 1955, and it was considered from March to May 1956. However, the government representing the 'Republic of Vietnam' that submitted the application only controlled the southern half of the country. Membership was granted to the Republic of Vietnam, although one Executive Director at the IMF abstained from the decision on the basis that the country lacked full sovereignty and instead consisted of two provisional governments.[42]

In 1959, a World Bank mission decided that Vietnam's high level of dependence on foreign aid made it unable to qualify for an IBRD loan. Several years later, on 7 May 1964, the United States notified the IMF that it had placed restrictions on payments and transfers to North Vietnam as of two days earlier, but the Fund took no subsequent action under the principle that North Vietnam was a non-member country.[43] Following the unification of Vietnam in 1976, the Socialist Republic of Vietnam assumed the membership previously held by the Republic of Vietnam that had occupied the South. In 1978, IDA approved its first credit to Vietnam for rehabilitation of irrigation systems in the Mekong Delta. However, throughout most of the 1980s the World Bank's interactions with Vietnam were limited to technical missions, as the United States objected to a closer relationship. The policy that prohibited high level missions and extending further credits lasted until 1993, when Vietnam reduced its spending on military activities in Cambodia and cleared its arrears with the IMF.[44]

Perhaps more than any other country, Vietnam's relations with the IMF and the World Bank were defined by its complex and difficult bilateral relationship with the United States. From the early 1960s to the mid-1970s, the United States and North Vietnam were locked in a long and bloody war intended to contain the spread of communism. On 30 April 1975, the United States withdrew its last batch of troops as the Viet Cong army successfully captured Saigon and unified the country under a socialist government. As a result, the US trade embargo that had been in effect against North Vietnam since 1964 was extended to the whole country. The broad US sanctions included a prohibition on commercial, financial, and investment transactions. As a pivotal shareholder in the IMF, World Bank, and Asian Development Bank, the US also blocked multilateral lending to Vietnam.

In 1977, the administration of US President Jimmy Carter took steps to improve the bilateral relationship, agreeing to unconditional establishment of diplomatic relations to be followed by the lifting of the embargo, renewed IFI support to Vietnam, and consideration of 'Most Favoured Nation' trading status.[45] Vietnam refused this offer pending inclusion of US$3.25 billion in economic assistance that President Richard Nixon had promised as part of the 1973 Paris Accords. Washington rejected the claim to reparations, and the US Congress passed legislation prohibiting aid to the North Vietnamese government that now controlled the country. Vietnam withdrew the demand in September 1978, but by that time the Carter administration was less inclined to opening with Hanoi because the attention had shifted to normalized relations with China.[46] Politically speaking, the moment had passed.

The closing months of 1978 delivered the coup de grâce to any détente between the United States and Vietnam. In October, the Soviet Union and Vietnam signed a mutual security treaty, and in December the government of Hanoi invaded neighbouring Cambodia and breathed further life into the US embargo. In 1979, the World Bank under Robert McNamara succumbed to pressure from congressional hardliners and placed a one-year moratorium on loans to Vietnam during the 1980 fiscal year.[47] Vietnam's incursion into Cambodia in the 1980s produced the political rationale that strengthened the technical reasons that Vietnam was blocked from borrowing from the IMF, namely its failure to pay arrears. The United States viewed the Vietnamese invasion of Cambodia as both an act of aggression and part of a proxy war between China and the Soviet Union. This situation persisted throughout the 1980s, freezing Vietnam's relations with the IFIs even while the country began a programme of significant economic reform beginning in 1986 known as '*doi-moi*'.

In February 1989, Vietnam received a bridge loan from France to pay off arrears of about US$130 million.[48] However, in September 1989, the United States and Japan blocked Vietnam's re-entry into the international financial institutions, despite a serious effort by Vietnam to achieve structural adjustment and economic stabilization. The international community decided that Vietnam's withdrawal of troops from Cambodia was insufficient without a political settlement of the Cambodian crisis. Tensions emerged between IMF and World Bank technocrats who wanted to base their lending decisions on Vietnam's economic reform programme and were opposed to the continuing political estrangement of Vietnam favoured by major shareholders. In March 1989, Vietnam began implementing an economic reform programme after extensive consultations with the IMF, and the country was relying on a favourable consensus from the IMF board to receive a bridge loan from commercial banks to pay off arrears and clear the way for an official IMF programme. In the meeting with the Executive Directors, Managing Director Michel Camdessus elicited a positive response from most board members, including Britain, West Germany, and France – the second, third, and fourth largest quota holders.[49] Only the United States and Japan were opposed to moving ahead with a formal IMF programme, putatively on the grounds that the economic reforms process lacked sufficient duration and the country remained burdened by 'low-priority expenditures' – shorthand for military expenses.[50]

In 1989, Vietnam withdrew troops from Cambodia only to discover that the goalposts had moved, with US responding that it was unacceptable to leave Cambodia in a state of civil war.[51] Furthermore, the United States demanded progress on the full accounting of soldiers missing in action from the Vietnam conflict. At the time, the block on lending to Vietnam caused significant consternation within the IMF and the World Bank, as summarized by one official quoted as saying that 'the US and Japan can do what they want with their bilateral aid, but they should not bring in their poorly disguised political agenda into multilateral institutions dedicated to solving economic problems'.[52] In April 1991, the US administration laid out a road map for the normalization of relations with Vietnam, predicated on two main conditions: the satisfactory resolution of the Cambodian conflict and an attempt to account for missing American servicemen in Vietnam. That October, four warring Cambodian factions signed a peace agreement in Paris, thereby ending the 12-year civil war. France, Sweden and Australia began lobbying for resources to help the country repay its unpaid debt of US$140 million to the IMF, which had been in default since 1985.

However, the issue of American prisoners of war in Vietnam was not yet resolved. In April 1993, an unconfirmed report revealed that Vietnam had more POWs than it claimed publicly and had failed to release 614 American POWs at the time of the 1973 Paris accords. This prompted the United States to delay granting Vietnam access to IFI loans that had been proposed at the annual meetings of the World Bank and IMF. That June, a Congressional delegation returned from Vietnam with a message of reconciliation that broke the deadlock in Washington.[53]

On 2 July 1993, Clinton signalled that the United States would no longer block multilateral lending to Vietnam.[54] This change in US policy paved the way for the countries known as the 'Friends of Vietnam' to arrange for the clearance of Vietnam's arrears to the IMF and open the way for lending from the World Bank and the Asian Development Bank. In the 1993 annual meeting, France and Japan were key players in clearing the arrears of both Vietnam and Cambodia – respectively US$140 million and US$51 million.[55] By October 1993, the arrears were cleared. Shortly thereafter, the World Bank and Asian Development Bank pledged loans valued at US$800 million for infrastructure development, while the IMF provided an additional US$223 million credit.[56] In November 1993, the first World Bank-chaired donors conference for Vietnam netted aid commitments of US$1.86 billion in additional multilateral and bilateral aid.[57]

With the multilateral funds released but the trade embargo maintained, the United States faced mounting pressure between two competing political constituencies: American business interests that wanted to invest and bid on IFI-financed projects, and veterans groups that resisted normalization without a full accounting of POWs and MIAs. However, by the end of 1993, the political momentum had shifted decisively towards lifting the embargo. US President Bill Clinton announced the repeal of the trade ban on Vietnam on 3 February 1994, several days after the Senate voted 62–38 to approve the move in a non-binding resolution. The support of Sen. John McCain (R-AZ), a former POW, and Sen. Bob Kerrey (D-NE), who lost part of his leg in the Vietnam War, was crucial to the bill's passing. On 11 July 1995, President Bill Clinton announced his intention to re-establish full diplomatic relations with Vietnam which was completed by 5 August of that year.

Vietnam's relationship with the IMF and World Bank since 1993 has garnered positive reviews, and the country's economic reform process has incorporated more market mechanisms. In retrospect, however, the period from 1989 to 1993 proved to be crucial for relations between Vietnam and the international financial institutions. Vietnam was forced to confront adjustment problems at a moment when political differences with major shareholders precluded any direct support from the IMF and the World Bank. In the absence of lending, officials from the two institutions remained engaged in an economic policy dialogue with Vietnam's key policy makers, and also managed some of the technical assistance provided by the United Nations Development Programme. For example, in 1991, the World Bank and the UNDP jointly organized a conference in Kuala Lumpur where top Vietnamese economic officials met with ministers from Indonesia, South Korea, and Malaysia to discuss comparative reform processes.[58] This type of information sharing was complemented by the World Bank's provision of training courses and policy workshops with Vietnam. Due to the political obstacles to lending, this economic policy dialogue emerged as a key avenue to explore different ideas and reform mechanisms in the absence of conditionality. As a result, during the critical period from 1989 to 1993, the focus of Vietnam-IFI relations was on ideas instead of lending arrangements. While there is no way to value precisely the effect of this policy dialogue on Vietnam's economic reform process, some argue that the intensive time spent by World Bank and IMF staff made an important contribution to Vietnam's subsequent economic development.[59]

Cuba's membership: a tale interrupted

China, Russia, and Vietnam have experienced firsthand the benefits and pitfalls for socialist countries that wish to pursue accession to the IMF and the World Bank at various stages of their economic transition. Despite the unique circumstances of each country, their membership processes share several features: the importance of normalizing relations with the United States and the West, the will to embrace at least limited market reform, and the importance of IFI membership as a step to opening up to the wider global economy. This insight will be important to the economic future of Cuba should the country choose to join the international financial institutions.

In fact, Cuba – and, more specifically, the Castro government – is no stranger to the multilateral banks. Indeed, the island was among the founding signatories of the Bretton Woods Institutions in 1944. During the administration of President Fulgencio Batista, Cuba criticized the 'Wall Street' approach of the IFIs at the 11th annual IMF–World Bank joint meetings in 1956. Joaquin A. Meyer, the alternate governor for Cuba, was quoted as saying 'my government believes that the pressing needs of the less developed countries are so numerous and urgent that the bank ought to revise some of its present policies in order to make available its resources to its members on a much larger scale than it has done in the past or is doing now'.[60] While the Cuban representative strongly criticized the policy of not granting loans to member countries in debt arrears, Meyer also noted that he was not speaking on behalf of Cuba, as the country had never tried to borrow from the Bank.

Beginning with Fidel Castro's ascension to power on 1 January 1959, relations between Cuba and the Washington-based institutions became increasingly strained. Initially, however, communication and exchange between Cuba and the IFIs actually represented an improvement over the end of Batista's term. Prior to Castro, the last IMF staff visit to Cuba occurred in March of 1957. By contrast, in the first few months of 1959, IMF staff travelled to Cuba twice – including a two-week mission to Havana – and three officers from the Cuban National Bank visited Washington. The initial IMF mission concluded that the new government inherited a seriously weakened financial situation, with 13 per cent unemployment at the end of 1958.[61] However, by 1960, communication between the IFIs and

Cuba had almost completely broken down, with multiple IMF correspondences left unanswered. To further complicate matters, President Castro announced on several occasions that Cuba had withdrawn from the institutions, sparking confusion among IMF and World Bank officials who had received no such notice through formal channels. On 18 October 1960, Cuba withdrew from the World Bank following a presidential decree stating that 'the economic policy of that institution is far from being effective in regard to the development and expansion of the Cuban economy, which the Revolutionary Government is carrying out according to a definite plan'.[62] The withdrawal became official on 14 November 1960, when the World Bank received written notification of the government's decision.[63] At the time of withdrawal, Cuba's capital subscription to the Bank was equivalent to $70,000,000 – with $700,000 paid in dollars, $6,700,000 available in pesos, and the remainder subject to call.[64]

Cuba's relationship with the IMF lasted for three more years, until the country withdrew in 1964 and settled its remaining accounts over a five-year period ending in 1969. However, the voluntary withdrawal occurred merely days before an executive board meeting was held to consider Cuba's failures to fulfill its obligations under the Articles of Agreement, including repurchasing IMF shares obtained by the previous government. Cuba purchased $25 million from the Fund in 1958 and negotiated a repurchasing agreement that was payable by 12 September 1963; thus five years had passed without the repurchase completed by Cuba. In addition, Cuba agreed to an increase of its quota from $50 million to $100 million, but it had not paid the subscription due in the fall of 1959. Cuba also lapsed in furnishing the necessary financial information to the Fund that was required for the calculation of repurchase obligations. Monetary, banking and balance of payments data had not been forthcoming since July 1961, and information on monetary reserves had not been furnished since the fiscal year ending in April 1960.[65]

As a result of these and other lapses, the Managing Director sent a notice to Cuba on 11 October 1963 detailing the concerns of the Executive Directors. However, no reply was received from Cuba, prompting the directors to arrange a meeting on 15 April 1964 to determine whether Cuba should be declared ineligible. However, once Cuba learned of these complaints and the plan for the forthcoming meeting, it responded by notifying the Fund of its withdrawal from membership, effective 2 April 1964. On 1 May, the Executive Directors approved a letter to Cuba that broadly accepted a previous Cuban proposal for the settlement of accounts. The proposal contained the following elements: Cuba's redemption of the Fund's holding of Cuban pesos valued at $12.5 million; payments were to be made in gold or convertible currency in five annual installments; and the Fund would return 50 million pesos to Cuba and pay the balance in gold to an account with the National Bank of Cuba.[66] Cuba formally accepted the terms of settlement on 29 May 1964, and completed the agreement accordingly, after receiving a six-month extension on the last payment installment, which was made in January 1969.

Although Cuba remains outside the international financial system, it is worth noting that the collapse of the Soviet Union in the early 1990s prompted the Cuban government to undertake a number of structural reforms that roughly correlated with IMF policy prescriptions. By 1993, Cuba faced a severe financial crisis due to the cut in foreign financing. Meanwhile, the United States had moved to strengthen the embargo through the 1992 Cuba Democracy Act and international lenders were prohibited in engaging with the island. Nevertheless, the Cuban government embraced a self-imposed structural adjustment programme, including stabilizing inflation, cutting subsidies and military expenditures, and balancing the budget. Cuba also moved to develop alternative productive sectors – including tourism, biotechnology, and energy – in the absence of external advice. During this period, social expenditures remained a high priority, and Cuba continued to emphasize health care, education, and other aspects of social policy. The Cuban economy still has not recovered from the collapse of the Soviet Union, but the island has experienced fairly sustained growth since the mid-1990s, with the exception of a slight dip following the post-9/11 global slowdown. In 2004, forty years after Cuba's initial withdrawal from the international financial system, the Cuban government remains committed to maintaining the socialist revolution and the centrally planned economic system that this implies.

Cuba's potential membership in the IMF and the World Bank remains fraught with political obstacles. Tensions between the United States and Cuba are high under the respective administrations of President George W. Bush and Fidel Castro. Relations are likely to remain frosty until 2008 at least if Bush wins a second term. If Senator John Kerry (D-MA) wins the 2004 US presidential election, the rhetoric may become less heated but major changes in US policy towards Cuba are unlikely while Castro stays in power. The Cuban government, for its part, remains one of the fiercest critics of the IMF and the World Bank and is unlikely to embrace these organizations in any manner that compromises the Communist Party's control over economic policy. In the view of many Cuban officials, the experience of Russia demonstrates the flaws of overreliance on outside 'expert advice' from IMF and World Bank staff who are not adequately schooled in the customs, institutional history, and cultural mentality of a country in the midst of rapid transformation. On an economic level, the governments of China and Vietnam have been much better custodians of their relationships with the IMF and World Bank, although neither has witnessed the dramatic expansion of political freedoms that occurred in the former Soviet Union.

Thus, the United States and Cuba remain a long way from the period of rapprochement that presaged IMF and World Bank membership for China,

Russia, and Vietnam. Nevertheless, the country's need for external financing for development projects remains critical, and the IMF and the World Bank may potentially be much better positioned to address the challenges of post-communist transition than they were during the collapse of the Soviet Union in the early 1990s. Given the importance of economic policy dialogue in shaping successful reforms in China and Vietnam, the international financial institutions would be well advised to initiate a formal policy discussion with Cuba prior to lending – regardless of whether the membership process begins while Fidel Castro is in power or under a successor government.

The recent experience of socialist countries demonstrates that the IMF and the World Bank, with the support of the United States, have pursued two distinct strategies towards centrally planned economies. The first model, illustrated by the Russian experience, favours the collapse of the communist system and rapid transition towards free-market democracy. This entailed massive financial flows to Russia, in the midst of severe economic decline, considerable corruption and wasted resources, accompanied by a parallel process of democratic reform. The second model, used with China and Vietnam, encouraged more limited financial flows, an expanded private sector and some market reform. This formula has achieved considerable economic success and rising living standards, but has also consolidated the strength of the communist governments at the expense of democratic reform.

These considerations will be central in shaping the potential relationship between the post-Castro regime and the international financial institutions. The potential for economic change in Cuba is significant, and if US–Cuba relations improve dramatically, then membership may in fact become the easy part. The international institutions can indeed help Cuba to obtain positive economic results and improved social welfare, but such an outcome is not necessarily preordained. The tougher challenge for the IMF and World Bank will be to constructively manage the competing political whims of their major shareholders in what is sure to be a highly politicized transition process in Cuba. If the past is any guide, then US policy will be the single most important factor to shape future relations between Cuba and the international financial institutions.

Notes

1 Joseph Gold, *Membership and Non-Membership in the International Monetary Fund* (Washington, DC: International Monetary Fund, 1974), 141.
2 Timothy King, 'Requirements for Participation in the International Monetary Fund and the World Bank', in Economic Reforms in Centrally Planned Economies and Their Impact on the Global Economy, ed. Josef M. Van Brabant, *Journal of Development Planning*, vol. 20 (1990): 286.
3 Gold, *Membership and Non-Membership in the International Monetary Fund*, 142.
4 *IMF Articles of Agreement*, Article VIII, Section 5.

5 Gold, *Membership and Non-Membership in the International Monetary Fund*, 67.
6 Larry Gurwin and Stanley Wilson, 'How Big a Splash Will China Make?', *IMF/World Bank IV* (September 1980).
7 'China Admitted to IMF', *New York Times*, 18 April 1980.
8 Oscar E. Naumann, 'China Joins International Monetary Fund', *Journal of Commerce*, 18 April 1980.
9 'China Admitted to IMF', *New York Times*, 18 April 1980.
10 Gurwin and Wilson, 'How Big a Splash Will China Make?'
11 Ibid.
12 Anthony Rowley, 'Compromising on a Gold Cache', *Far Eastern Economic Review*, vol. 108 (April 1980): 85.
13 Gurwin and Wilson, 'How Big a Splash Will China Make?', 176.
14 'Changing the Power Balance', *Far Eastern Economic Review*, vol. 108, (April 1980): 85.
15 Devesh Kapur, John P. Lewis, and Richard Webb, *The World Bank: Its First Half Century* (Washington, DC: the Brookings Institution, 1997), 24.
16 'Memorandum of the President of the International Bank for Reconstruction and Development and the International Finance Corporation to the Executive Directors on a Country Assistance Strategy of the World Bank Group for the People's Republic of China', Report No. 2541, 22 January 2003.
17 Kapur et al., *World Bank*, 24.
18 Ibid.
19 Ibid., 25.
20 Ibid., 112.
21 Gold, *Membership and Non-Membership in the International Monetary Fund*, 129.
22 Ibid., 129.
23 Ibid., 134.
24 Ibid., 142.
25 World Bank, *Assisting Russia's Transition: an Unprecedented Challenge* (Washington, DC: The World Bank, 2002), 6.
26 Kenji Kitahara, 'Japan Uneasy Over Economic Aid to Moscow', *The Daily Yomiuri*, 2 July 1990.
27 'A Bank Role for the Soviets', *The Journal of Commerce*, 26 August 1991.
28 Karl-Heinz Kleine and Ernst Thien, 'The Role of the IMF and the World Bank in the former Eastern Bloc Countries', *Intereconomics*, (January/February 1992): 23.
29 Article IV consultations.
30 Kleine and Thien, 'The role of the IMF', 23.
31 Ibid., 26.
32 Richard D. Erb, Deputy Managing Director of the International Monetary Fund, Remarks at the Conference on European Security and Regional Stability, Institute for Foreign Policy Analysis, Washington, DC, 24 January 1992.
33 Goergy Matyukhin, 'The Union of Soviet Socialist Republics and Other Socialist Countries in the International Monetary and Financial System', in Economic Reforms in Centrally Planned Economies and Their Impact on the Global Economy, ed. Josef M. Van Brabant, *Journal of Development Planning*, vol. 20 (1990): 273.
34 Ibid.
35 Steven Greenhouse, 'Point Man for the Rescue of the Century', *The New York Times*, 26 April 1992.
36 Ben Laurence, 'IMF Clears the way for ex-Soviet States', *The Guardian*, 24 January 1992, 24.

37 Steven H. Hanke, 'IMF Money Will Buy Trouble for Russia', *The Wall Street Journal*, 29 April 1992.
38 Steven Greenhouse, 'World's Lenders Offer Membership to Ex-Soviet Lands', *The New York Times,* 28 April 1992.
39 World Bank, *Assisting Russia's Transition: an Unprecedented Challenge*, 59.
40 Ibid., ix.
41 Ibid., xii.
42 Gold, *Membership and Non-Membership in the International Monetary Fund*, 50–51.
43 Ibid., 51.
44 *Vietnam: Country Assistance Evaluation*, Operations Evaluation Department (Washington, DC: World Bank, 2001), 46.
45 Frederick Z. Brown, 'U.S.-Vietnam Normalization: Past, Present, Future', in James W. Morley and Masashi Nishihara (eds), *Vietnam Joins the World*,(Armonk, NY: M.E. Sharpe, 1997), 204.
46 Ibid., 204.
47 James Srodes, 'An Enigma at the World Bank', *Far Eastern Economic Review*, vol. 106 (November 1979): 82.
48 Nayan Chanda, 'Rewards of Retreat', *Far Eastern Economic Review* (July 1989).
49 Susumu Awanohara, 'Fiscal Interdiction', *Far Eastern Economic Review* (September 1989): 22.
50 Ibid.
51 Charles P. Wallace, '15 Years After War's End, the U.S. Fights to Keep Vietnam Isolated', *Los Angeles Times*, 29 April 1990.
52 Awanohara, 'Fiscal interdiction', 23.
53 Brown, 'U.S.–Vietnam Normalization', 210.
54 John Rogers, 'Vietnam Getting Ready to Seek Infusion of Foreign Aid, Investment', *Journal of Commerce*, 26 July 1993, 5a.
55 Susumu Awanohara, 'Open the Floodgates', *Far Eastern Economic Review* (October 1993): 92.
56 Julie Marie Bunck, 'Marxism and the Market: Vietnam and Cuba in Transition', *Cuba In Transition,* vol. 6 (1996): 237.
57 'Vietnam's Economic Options: Coping With Mounting Resources', *Transition*, vol. 5, no. 1 (January 1994): 14.
58 World Bank and UNDP, *Assessing Aid: What Works, What Doesn't and Why* (New York: Oxford University Press, 1998), 106.
59 Ibid., 108.
60 Charles E. Egan, 'Cuba and Jordan Charge Creditor Countries Run World Bank', *New York Times*, 26 September 1956.
61 *Review of Cuba's Financial Position and Problems*, International Monetary Fund Archives, 6 April 1959.
62 'Cuba Withdraws from World Bank', *The New York Times*, 19 October 1960.
63 'Cuba Withdraws from Membership', Joint Press Release by International Finance Corporation and World Bank, 15 November 1960.
64 'Cuba Withdraws from World Bank'.
65 Gold, *Membership and Non-Membership in the International Monetary Fund*, 343–4.
66 Ibid., 380–1.

Part IV
Conclusion

9
Cuba's Economic Future: a Dozen Comparative Lessons

Jorge I. Domínguez and Daniel P. Erikson

In January 2004, the regime that President Fidel Castro founded in Cuba marked its 45 anniversary. As the only surviving communist regime outside East Asia, the Cuban system has withstood the collapse of the Soviet Union and resisted the sweeping transition from socialism experienced by the countries of Eastern Europe. In the future, however, Cuba will continue to grapple with the challenges posed by market-oriented reform. The essays in this book have reviewed the various paths to economic reform undertaken by a range of socialist and post-communist countries. The aim has been to develop lessons about economic organization and policy that may be useful for countries in transition generally, and for Cuba in particular. Although there is much debate about Cuba's potential democratic transformation, we have deliberately avoided prescribing what form Cuba's *political* system should take in the years to come. This conclusion serves to draw broad lessons on economic policy that will serve any future Cuban political regime.

Of course, the shape of Cuba's post-Castro politics will have an important impact on the nature of economic policy and the willingness to embrace market reform. Cuba today exhibits a commitment to Marxist economics that rivals North Korea's, despite initial steps towards liberalization implemented in the mid-1990s. It is certainly possible that a dramatically different Cuban political regime will attempt a comprehensive transition away from communism, as occurred in the Czech Republic and many other countries in Eastern Europe, but such an outcome is not inevitable. In that sense, our findings are intended to set a sensible baseline for reform, with the understanding that circumstances may warrant a more decisive break with central planning than is currently anticipated.

Equally important, the country studies underline that economic policy decisions have important political consequences, and that, in this sense, there is a political foundation to all economic activity. Government officials are the ones to make and implement economic decisions. Political careers will be determined by their success or failure, and the relative importance of state agencies will shift depending on the results. If Cuba achieves economic growth that is perceived as equitable, this will contribute to the political support for any government in power; and conversely, economic stagnation or deterioration will undermine any future political regime, irrespective of how it is organized. With this in mind, the lessons below apply to a wide variety of political structures, ranging from socialist regimes to political and economic systems that are vastly more open.

All of the countries in this study are or have been communist regimes. Russia had substantial ties to Cuba for the three decades prior to the collapse of the Soviet Union, and this partnership profoundly shaped how Cubans understand the meaning and operation of socialism. The collapse of Soviet communism dealt a deep economic and psychological blow to Cuba from which the island still has not fully recovered. The Central Asian Republics similarly suffered in the wake of the Soviet Union's demise, and none has yet achieved full market liberalization, although Kazakhstan and Kyrgyzstan have taken significant steps in that direction. In other cases in the region, however, the collapse into civil war or the rise of a personalistic dictatorship has thwarted more far-reaching economic ambitions and ensured continuing poverty. While the countries profiled in Eastern Europe (the Czech Republic, Slovakia, and Bulgaria) have broken fundamentally with their communist past, the reform process came in fits and starts. In East Asia, China and Vietnam remain communist countries, although they have significantly opened their economies and incorporated market forces. The role of the Washington-based international financial institutions, particularly the International Monetary Fund and the World Bank, has also shaped the trajectory of policy reform in several instances, and one chapter examines in greater depth how and why communist and post-communist countries have joined these market-oriented institutions. The analysis below reflects on this great variety of experience and traces out broad lessons for Cuba's future.

Baseline diagnosis

Cuba's regime has managed to endure despite tremendous economic difficulties. While its adversaries surely think otherwise and many of its supporters desire more substantial changes, a fair-minded analysis must begin with the premise that Fidel Castro's government has defied the odds against it. The government started the twenty-first century with a well-earned sense of success. It survived the collapse in 1991 of its premier ally and economic supporter, the Soviet Union, and it has withstood increased political and economic pressure from the United States since the early 1990s. Cuba's economy touched bottom in 1993, and began a recovery in the mid-1990s that continues today, despite a slight dip during the global economic slowdown in the wake of September 11, 2001. Cuba is still far from regaining its per capita income level of 1985 – when sustained economic growth there hit its peak – but the current recovery is a noteworthy accomplishment nevertheless. In order to achieve such a recovery, the Cuban government felt compelled to adopt significant changes in its economic policies, in particular welcoming foreign direct investment, tourism, and remittances from the Cuban diaspora.

This brief account highlights two important traits that Cuba shares with the more successful cases that we examine:

1. The central government must remain competent and powerful to design and implement economic policy. This was as true for the Czech Republic as it is for the People's Republic of China. Russia's experience is a noteworthy counterfactual to these cases; the temporary withering away of its state during much of the 1990s contributed significantly to its poor economic performance. At the other extreme, severe political unrest or even state failure can have a devastating impact on the economic welfare of a society. Tajikistan's civil war in the 1990s is the most tragic illustration of how state collapse undermines economic well-being.

2. Some significant market-oriented reforms are required to enable centrally planned economies to recover and grow. This is a clear lesson from China and Vietnam. They remain communist states, but they also have had rates of economic growth that range from good to excellent. These growth rates did not take off until each country adopted significant market-oriented economic reforms. Even in Russia and Eastern Europe, the initial precipitous decline was followed by stabilization and a more recent return to growth, which would have been impossible under central planning. By contrast, Turkmenistan's poor performance illustrates the opposite end of the range, where resistance to market-oriented reform has kept the country's economy constrained by Soviet-era policies and practices.

The utility of 'unorthodox' policies – and some cautions

In the late 1980s and early 1990s, the conventional wisdom promoted by many economists, as well as the leading international financial institutions, emphasized the virtues of instant economic orthodoxy and its speedy application as the path toward economic stability and growth. Immortalized as 'the Washington Consensus', the proposed measures included complete price and trade liberalization, privatization of state-owned assets, and the overhaul of the financial and banking system. Yet, in 2004, China boasts the fastest-growing economy of all current or former communist countries, despite the fact that market liberalization there is much less extensive than in Russia and Eastern Europe. Vietnam, too, has performed well, and its embrace of market reform lags even China's. Among the Central Asian Republics, Uzbekistan stands out as another relatively good economic performer, yet its political and economic system, albeit no longer communist, has changed little since the Soviet era. Cuba has been particularly reluctant to embrace the market, and its economic performance lags behind China, Vietnam, and Uzbekistan, although its official, preliminary 2.6 per cent growth rate in 2003 compares favourably with many countries in Latin America. A survey of the landscape of economic transition yields a number of lessons relevant to Cuba's economic future, as well as the long-term development strategies of other countries emerging from communism.

3. Gradualist and sequentialist economic strategies can succeed. 'Shock' strategies that generate fast change and implementation have worked well in the Czech Republic and the Baltic states, among others, but gradualist and sequentialist strategies have worked well in China, Vietnam, and Uzbekistan. In the early 1990s, the 'big bang' approach promoted the rapid embrace of market-oriented reforms, but the results were decidedly mixed for many of the countries that rushed into privatization before the appropriate legal and economic mechanisms were in place. The 'window of opportunity' for reforms may not remain open for long before disaster strikes, but the window does not shut instantly. History demonstrates that there is substantial room for gradual reform during the period when the 'window of opportunity' is open.

For example, China, Cuba, and Uzbekistan – three countries where agriculture matters greatly – delayed enacting fundamental changes in their foreign exchange regimes but China and Uzbekistan used their 'windows of opportunities' more effectively than has Cuba. China began with a decisive change – the privatization of agricultural production – and went on to adopt other important changes in the organization of production. Uzbekistan endeavoured to maintain a diversified production economy, sustaining its agricultural output and exports. Cuba, in contrast, adopted only very modest and insufficient agricultural reforms and still has yet to authorize significant changes in non-agricultural enterprises outside the state sector. Cuba has been marginally successful but that need not compel it to jettison economic gradualism – it does suggest that Cuba should enact reforms that other similarly situated countries have adopted to their benefit.

4. Gradualism excessively prolonged can bring about substantial harm. In the early 1990s, the people of Bulgaria, Slovakia, and Russia generally supported state socialism and a gradual approach to economic reforms, remaining sceptical of the free market. In Bulgaria and Slovakia, gradualist approaches to reform worked well enough at various times, and Russia's version of 'shock therapy' was clearly found wanting in several areas. The experiences of Eastern Europe and Russia have also illustrated a costly preference, implicit or explicit, for insider privatization of state enterprises while delaying needed price liberalization and banking reform. This was the Bulgarian experience of the early 1990s and the Slovakian experience of the mid-1990s, and the consequences for both countries proved to be severe. Bulgaria embarked on the path towards 'crony capitalism' and postponed restructuring its banking system, which contributed to its financial crash in 1997 and the subsequent bout with hyperinflation. In Slovakia, inadequate enterprise reform, a return to price controls, and a heavy dependence on borrowing resulted in an explosion in debt that rendered the country highly vulnerable to external pressures. The Russian case exemplifies most starkly the perils of insider privatization. In the future, Cuban policy makers will want to guard against the dangers of gradualism that wreaked havoc upon the economies of Eastern Europe, while avoiding the kind of insider privatization that crippled the reform process both there and in Russia.

5. Political decentralization short of full market liberalization can help socialist and near-socialist countries accelerate the rate of growth. China has had a very successful experience with town and village enterprises. Based on the system of communes, these enterprises were authorized in the 1980s and developed a non-agricultural economy parallel to the state economy. Organized as collectives with many different forms of ownership, they were not obliged to follow the state's complex planning and regulatory directives. However, they were required to employ a given workforce regardless of demand, and provide workers with health, recreational and day care facilities, transportation to work, and pensions. In Uzbekistan, traditional *mahallas* also illustrate the benefit of decentralization even without full market liberalization. These neighbourhood committees were re-created from pre-Soviet Uzbek traditions and served to replace the system of social protection that died with the Soviet Union, providing targeted social assistance and child allowances to low-income groups. By contrast, Cuba has yet to delegate any comparable authority to its municipalities or neighbourhood institutions, nor has it authorized small non-agricultural businesses beyond self-employment.

6. A country's principal long-term economic resource is its people. Investing in the health and education of citizens is not just a good general idea; it is also good economics in the long term. The quality of China's workforce is one of its assets, and the Cuban population has similar potential due to the significant state resources devoted to education and health care. The Czech Republic has become one of the most celebrated examples of post-communist economic orthodoxy, but the advanced education of the Czech people is also an important factor that has contributed to the country's good economic performance. Even Russia has managed to maintain a significant commitment to its educational system, and Vietnam's level of educational attainment has risen dramatically in the period since *Doi Moi* was introduced. By contrast, the collapse in the educational and health system in the Central Asian Republics has severely undermined the economic potential of this region, and facilitated an overreliance on natural resources in place of human capital. Access to education and physical well-being are important determinants in development throughout the world, and their role can be especially crucial for centrally planned economies that are opening up to market forces and attempting to compete in the global economy.

Broad lessons of economic reform

Even if one concedes that unorthodox policies can play an important role in the reform process, there is no question that market liberalization is the crucial element for future economic success in all cases. The following observations are particularly relevant to Cuba's future.

7. **Liberalization of agriculture, particularly reliance on market prices and low levels of state regulation, can produce excellent results.** China is, of course, the best example of this, but Vietnam has also gained from policies of agricultural liberalization. By allowing decentralization of agricultural production and allowing farmers' markets, governments can boost productivity and income levels for workers in rural areas, and contribute to their enhanced well-being. In the industrialized countries of Eastern Europe and Russia, agricultural liberalization was less crucial than in the rural, peasant societies of East Asia, but it still played a role in the overall trajectory of reform. Cuba's own experience shows that its more liberalized non-sugar agricultural subsectors have made important gains.

8. **Full price liberalization even beyond agriculture is most likely to improve compliance with law, create productive trading markets, and generate tax revenues for the state.** The difficult experience with partial reforms from Russia to Bulgaria and Kyrgyzstan strongly points in this direction. Partial reforms empower and entrench insiders and block further change, instead rewarding corruption. In contrast, price liberalization is likely to lead as well to improvements in the quality of products and the efficiency of services. Bulgaria's experience with price controls in 1995 is an important cautionary tale: it repressed prices and helped to spark hyperinflation. Yet full price liberalization should be attractive to any government because it makes two outcomes more likely. First, state revenues are likely to increase in a growing market economy with transparent price accounts open to tax collectors. Second, full price liberalization removes the incentives that foster illegal or 'black' markets. In Cuba, the Interior Ministry – not just the Ministry of the Economy – should back full price liberalization.

9. **Fiscal stabilization is ultimately indispensable, yet it can be timed to accommodate political circumstances.** Fiscal stabilization may not be politically feasible early in a crisis, when rulers over-spend and under-tax to purchase political support. However, fiscal stabilization is ultimately necessary if protracted economic and political crises are to be avoided. Throughout the 1990s, Russia illustrated the perils of poor fiscal policies and so did

Bulgaria in the late 1990s. Both countries demonstrate that poor performers can learn from their mistakes and improve their results substantially. Cuba has performed well on fiscal stabilization, but it must do better. Its overspending in the early 1990s garnered social and political peace; the fiscal and budgetary adjustment that followed in the mid-1990s was also impressively successful. But Cuba still excessively subsidizes loss-generating enterprises and it must address the de facto insolvency of many of its state enterprises that cannot and do not pay their bills. Unless fiscal stabilization is seriously addressed in the medium and long term, any short-term flexibility may ultimately exact a high price on economic performance.

10. Institutional reforms must set clear foundations for property rights. In this realm, too, partial reforms are a recipe for trouble. Partial privatization of state enterprises opens the window to state capture and very high levels of corruption. Instead, the rules for privatization must be clear and transparent to avoid crony capitalism and rent-seeking. On the positive side, the Chinese agricultural reforms and subsequent enterprise reforms provided a web of rights to motivate peasants and small town producers to launch the country's economic revolution via the market. At a minimum, as in Uzbekistan, the walls that protect the state from private enterprise capture must remain in place. Russia sadly illustrates the negative example of a privatization process rife with corruption. Cuba has no strong bases for property rights in its 1992 Constitution, and it has left its state open to capture by quasi-private enterprises and their foreign partners. Cuba's prevailing policies already close off inter-enterprise competition, and the eventual unlawful privatization of public assets represents one of the major dangers that the Cuban economy may face in the future.

11. Communist countries can join and benefit from the international financial institutions (IFIs). The participation of the Soviet Union in the 1944 Bretton Woods conference ensured that the communist countries could enjoy full membership in the market-oriented international financial institutions of the International Monetary Fund and the World Bank. Although Russia only joined these organizations as a post-communist country in 1992, during the Cold War countries as diverse as China, Hungary, Poland, and Romania all became members. A member since the mid-1950s, socialist Vietnam normalized its relationship with the IFIs in the early 1990s, following the resumption of diplomatic relations with the United States. As a practical matter, such membership requires improving relations with the US government. Short of that, the information and analyses generated by these institutions and the knowledge of their staff can be resources that facilitate Cuba's eventual membership. Even before lending becomes politically feasible, Cuba could benefit from technical exchanges, training and development, and an economic policy dialogue on the challenges facing Cuba's integration into the global economy.

12. Failure to learn from the experiences of other countries is costly. This conclusion is the driving force behind the elaboration of lessons for Cuba, and it has proven true in many of the other countries in this study. The case of Slovakia encapsulates the costs of ignoring the experiences of others. Slovakia attempted to undertake its transition employing only domestic managers, and its record is not without merit. Yet the restructuring of Slovakia's economy was much delayed because political cronies took advantage of this domestic favouritism, benefited early on from initial reforms, and stopped the progress of further reforms. A policy that welcomes foreign direct investment in a context of enterprise competition is one very effective way to learn from others. But much can be learned simply from a careful study of the experiences of other countries, as China and Vietnam have demonstrated. Cuba's future solutions have the potential to benefit from the wisdom of hindsight, but only if Cuban policy makers are careful students of reform in other transition countries.

Conclusions

Cuba's economic future remains difficult to predict, but there are certainties amid the unknowns. No matter what the name of its president or the form of its political regime, every government of Cuba will wish to complete the economic recovery from the early 1990s and generate sufficient resources to improve the standard of living of its people. Cuba could accomplish this goal under different forms of political organization, but there is little question that the dozen lessons sketched in this chapter are essential regardless of whether the country remains governed by communists or moves more aggressively towards greater political and economic liberalization.

Despite its apparent durability, Cuba's current economic framework is unlikely to generate sustained economic growth. Continued reliance on tourism and remittances, at the expense of developing the country's productive capacity, cannot substitute for a sustainable long-term development strategy. Moreover, Cuba remains at high risk for insider privatization and crony capitalism in the future, even if the organization of the political system remains formally socialist. Cuba's internal and external financial imbalances are extremely serious and can be the detonator of severe economic distortions and eventually crises.

That need not happen. Countries as diverse as China, Vietnam and Uzbekistan, with political systems not too dissimilar from Cuba's, have adopted a mix of market-oriented policies that have yielded superior economic performance within the context of the ongoing political regime. At the other end of the spectrum, the Czech Republic and other examples in Eastern Europe have succeeded in liberalizing their economies while changing their political structures. Even Russia has made great strides in escaping from the Soviet shadows. Without predetermining Cuba's political future, this essay has highlighted economic policies that are both sound and essential to creating economic growth and improving the well-being of the Cuban people. Throughout the developing world, economic growth is a critical element in ensuring political health, and Cuba is no exception. Cuba's economic future will be vastly better if the island's leaders move further along the path of substantial economic reform.

Index